The Africa House

ALSO BY CHRISTINA LAMB

The Sewing Circles of Herat: A Personal Voyage Through Afghanistan

Waiting for Allah

The Africa House

The True Story of an English Gentleman and His African Dream

CHRISTINA LAMB

HarperCollins*Publishers*

HarperCollins books may be purchased for educational, business, or sales promotional use. For information, please write: Special Markets Department, HarperCollins Publishers Inc., 10 East 53rd Street, New York, NY 10022.

First published in Great Britain in 1999 by Viking. Reissued in Great Britain in 2004 with new material by Penguin Books Ltd.

FIRST U.S. EDITION 2004

Printed on acid-free paper

Library of Congress Cataloging-in-Publication Data
Lamb, Christina.
The Africa house : the true story of an English gentleman and his African dream / Christina Lamb.—1st U.S. ed.
p. cm.
ISBN 0-06-073587-2
1. Gore-Browne, Stewart, Sir, 1883-1967. 2. Colonial administrators—Zambia—Biography. 3. Zambia—History. I. Title
DT3106.G78L36 2004
968.94'02'092—dc22
[B] 2004042370

04 05 06 07 08 RRD 10 9 8 7 6 5 4 3 2 1

To Paulo

'Até ao fim do mundo'

Ille Terrarum Mihi Super Omnes Angulus Ridet
(This corner of the earth smiles on me more than
any other)

– Inscription on the library mantelpiece at Shiwa House,
Northern Rhodesia (Stewart Gore-Browne's rewording of
Horace)

Umushi wamukali upya kumbali (The village of a
powerful man is destroyed when he is gone)

– Bemba proverb

Contents

List of Illustrations

Maps

Section One

Section Two

All the photographs unless otherwise credited have come from the Gore-Browne family collection.

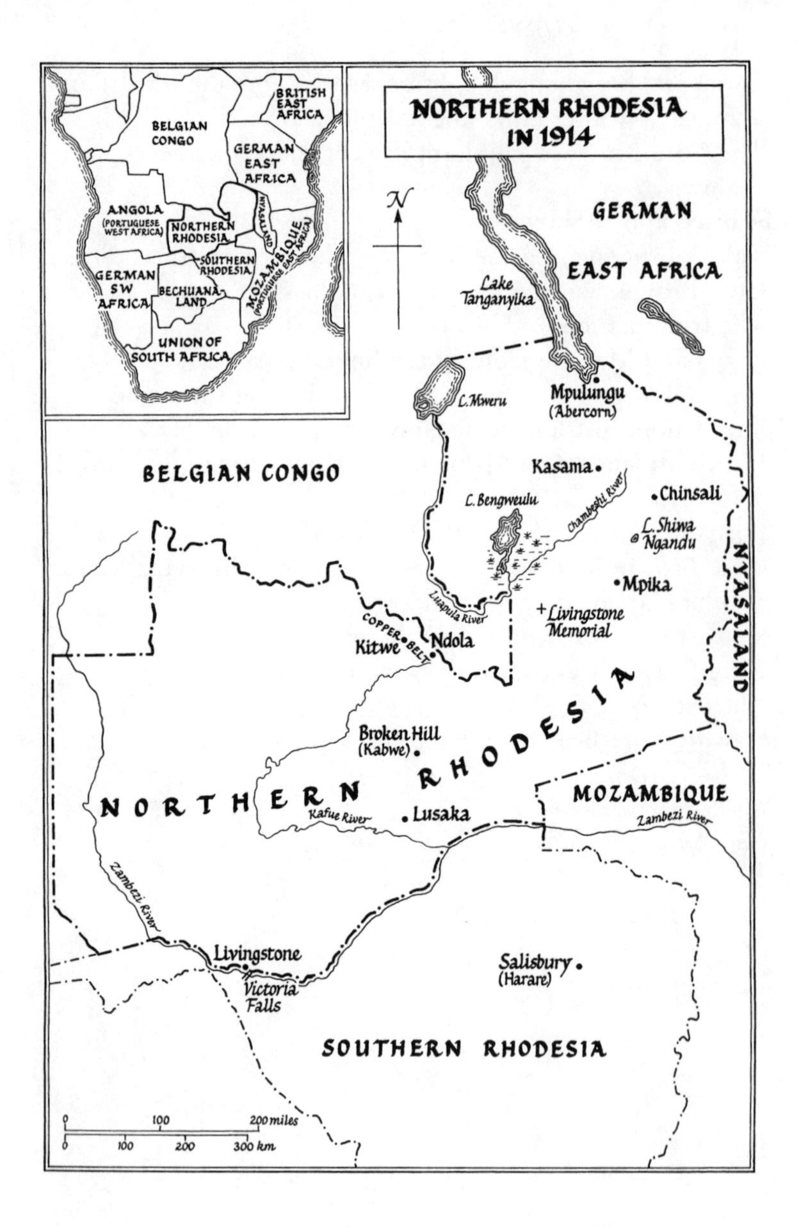
NORTHERN RHODESIA IN 1914
BRITISH EAST AFRICA
BELGIAN CONGO
GERMAN EAST AFRICA
ANGOLA (PORTUGUESE WEST AFRICA)
NORTHERN RHODESIA
NYASALAND
MOZAMBIQUE (PORTUGUESE EAST AFRICA)
SOUTHERN RHODESIA
GERMAN SW AFRICA
BECHUANA-LAND
UNION OF SOUTH AFRICA
N
GERMAN
EAST AFRICA
Lake Tanganyika
L. Mweru
Mpulungu (Abercorn)
BELGIAN CONGO
Kasama
Chinsali
C. Bengweulu
Chambeshi River
L. Shiwa Ngandu
Mpika
Luapula River
Livingstone Memorial
COPPER BELT
Kitwe
Ndola
NYASALAND
NORTHERN RHODESIA
Broken Hill (Kabwe)
MOZAMBIQUE
Kafue River
Lusaka
Zambezi River
Zambezi River
Livingstone
Victoria Falls
Salisbury (Harare)
SOUTHERN RHODESIA
0 100 200 miles
0 100 200 300 km

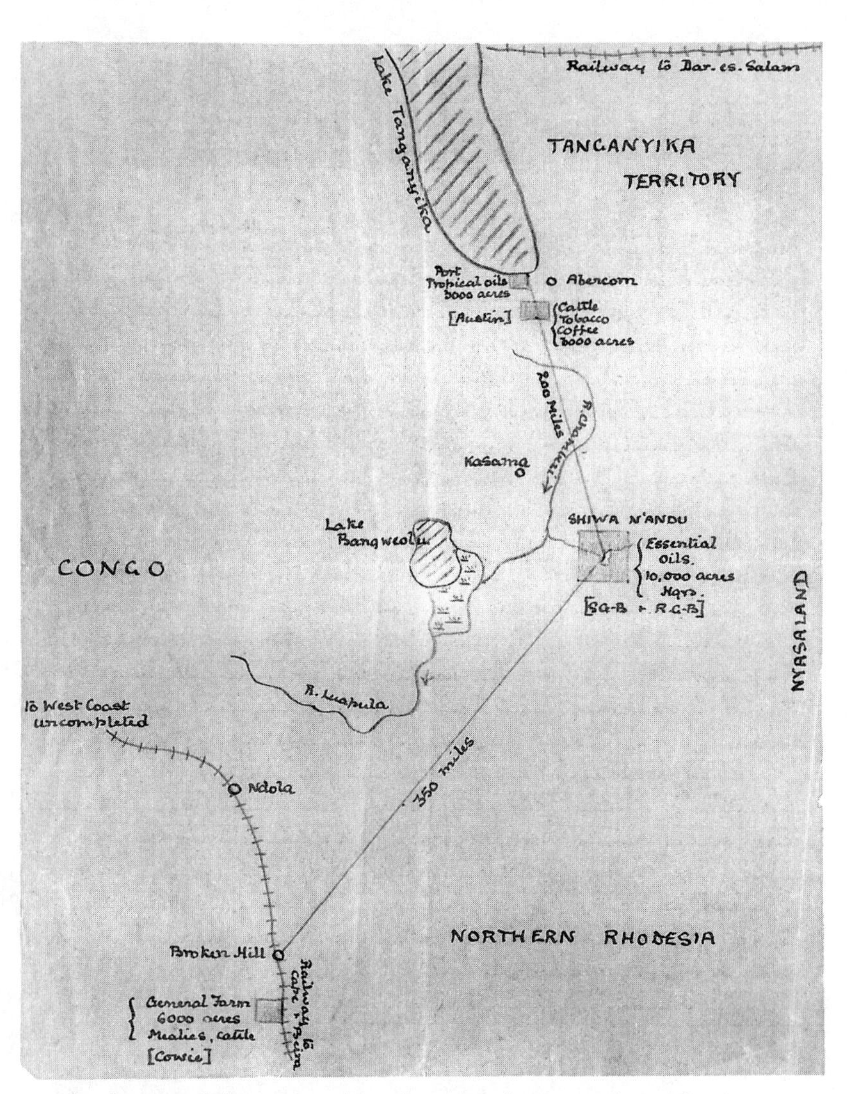

Sketch map of Shiwa Ngandu and surrounding area, drawn by Stewart Gore-Browne.

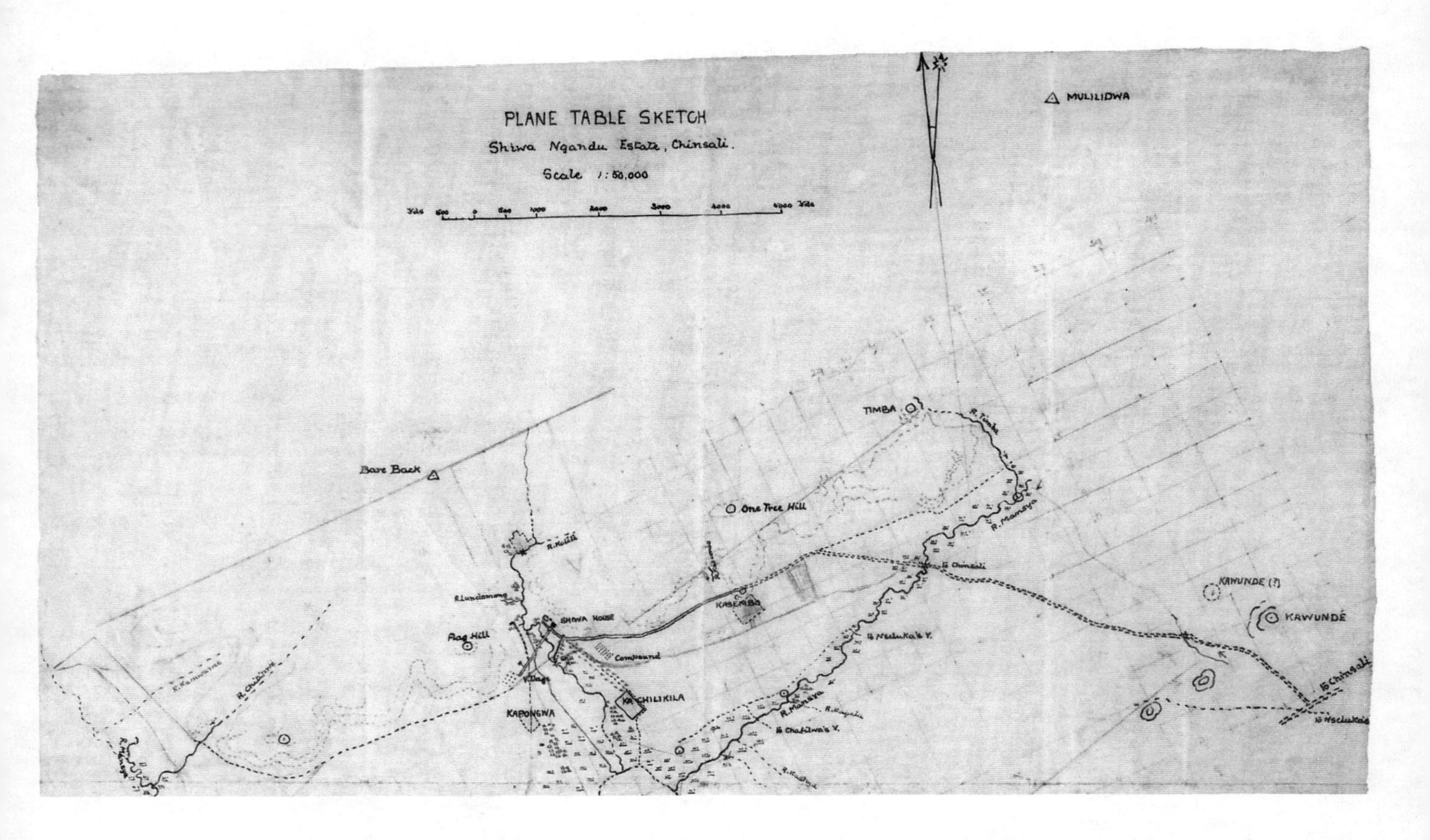
PLANE TABLE SKETCH
Shiwa Ngandu Estate, Chinsali.
Scale 1:50,000
Yds 500 0 500 1000 2000 3000 4000 5000 Yds
MULILIDWA
Bare Back
TIMBA
R. Timba
One Tree Hill
R. Mansya
Chinsali
KAWUNDE (?)
KAWUNDÉ
R. Lundamong
SHIWA HOUSE
Flag Hill
KASEMBO
Compound
Nseluka's V.
KA-CHILIKILA
KAPONGWA
Chabilwa's V.
to Chinsali
to Nseluka

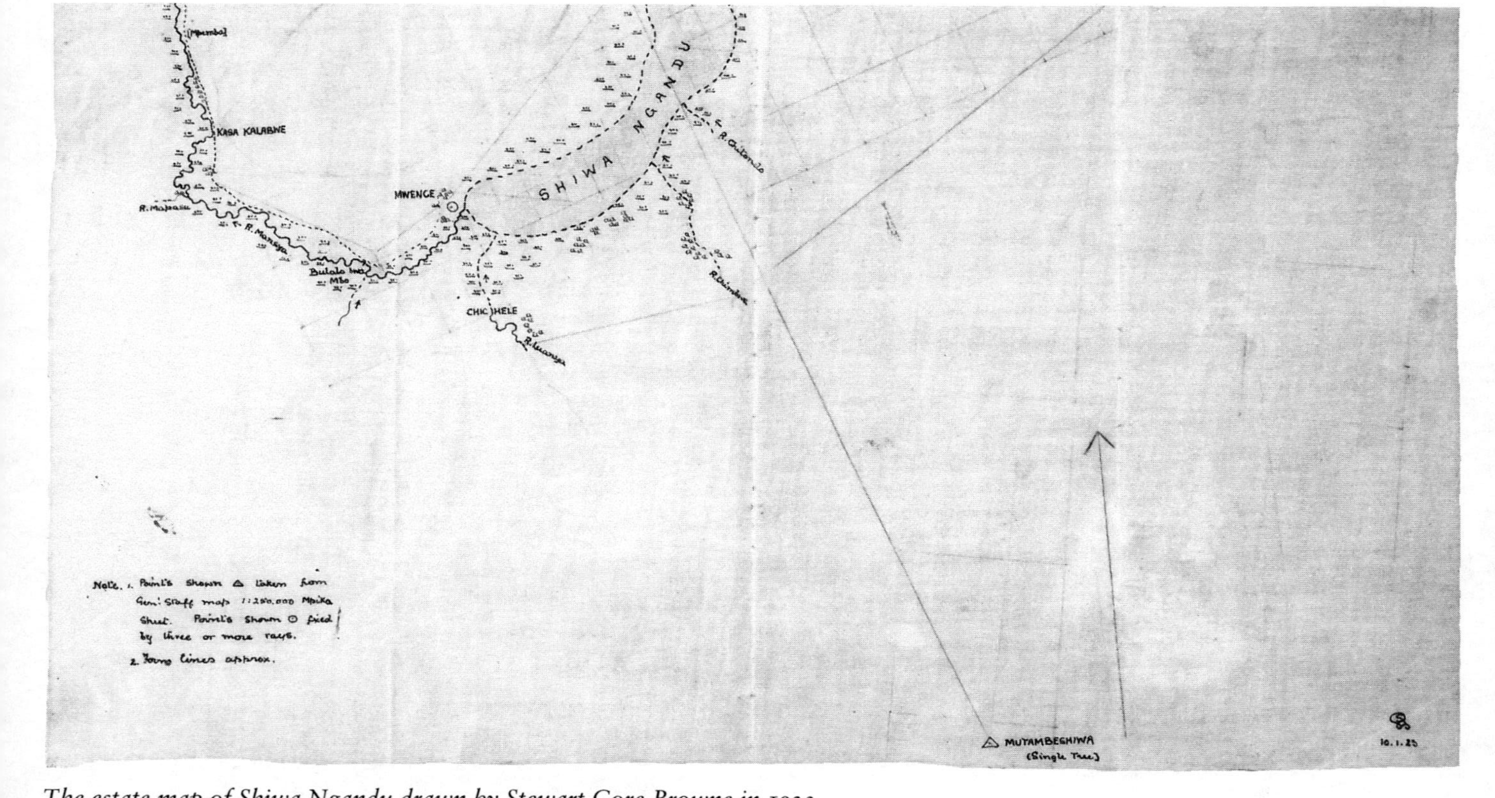

The estate map of Shiwa Ngandu drawn by Stewart Gore-Browne in 1923.

Acknowledgements

This book would not have been possible without the help of the grandchildren of Sir Stewart Gore-Browne, who allowed me complete access to their grandfather's house and vast collection of letters (a few of which have appeared previously in Robert Rotberg's *Black Heart*), estate books, photographs and diaries, as well as letting me pick their minds for sometimes painful memories. *The Africa House* is based on these papers and recollections, as well as on interviews with Gore-Browne's contemporaries and former servants.

In particular I would like to thank Dai and Carol Harvey for their friendship and hospitality at their house at Shiwa Ngandu – for Carol's delicious muffins conjured up in a brick woodfire oven, and Dai's unforgettable green eggs, and not least for providing me with a live chicken as a suitable gift for a Bemba chief.

Mark Harvey deserves a special note for first taking me to Shiwa, paving the way for this book, for somehow serving up amazing gin and tonics in the bush, and for patiently answering endless inquiries about the Bemba. I'm also very grateful to Penelope Daly (née Harvey) for all her reminiscences and to Charles and Jo Harvey for theirs.

I cannot say a big enough thank you to Stewart Gore-Browne's only surviving daughter, Angela Sutton, for all her encouragement and e-mails, for her warm welcome to myself and my fiancé Paulo at her house in Kenya, with its

Shiwa-inspired arches and magical bird table, and for taking me to meet her mother, the late Lady Gore-Browne.

Nor will I forget the two days spent with Monica Fisher at her stunning home, Greystone, on the Kafue river, listening to her tales of working as a young doctor at Shiwa. I am very grateful to her for the memoirs of her mother, Sapphire, Stewart Gore-Browne's sister.

At Shiwa, I received tremendous help from several of Gore-Browne's old servants. In particular from Kalaka, his hunter, famed throughout northern Zambia for once slaying eight buffalo with one axe, and brother of the late Henry Mulenga, Gore-Browne's batman and companion. Also from John Parafin, Joe and Lloyd 'Gift' Nbupe. Many thanks to Paramount Chief Chitimukulu, head of the whole Bemba tribe, and to senior chief Nkula for granting me audiences.

A special mention of thanks to Kenneth Kaunda for spending so much time with me, recalling the man of whom he says 'his vision saved us from bloodshed', and to John Pulford, curator of Brooklands Museum, for his friendly help and encouragement. Thanks also to Dick Hobson of the Zambia Society, John and Greta Hudson in Lusaka, the late Sir Douglas Hall who spent almost 30 years in the colonial service in northern Rhodesia, Professor Andrew Roberts of the London School of Oriental and African Studies, the librarians of Rhodes House, Oxford, the staff at the National Archive of Zambia, and Rajiv Kaul, manager of the Mena House Hotel.

Thanks to John Witherow and Mark Lambert for sparing time from their hectic schedules for reading the manuscript and making valuable suggestions. To my agent, David Godwin, for his endless enthusiasm and for talking me out of Brazilian samba and into colonial Africa. And last, but not least, to my computer-literate mother for being on the end of the phone to deal with endless word-processing emergencies, and for scouring the library to answer questions on everything, from the route of Imperial Airways mailplanes to Africa to how to produce eau-de-Cologne from orange blossom.

Christina Lamb
Estoril

Introduction

The date etched on the heavy oak front door was 1923, but the house looked much older, its sloping tiled roof and arched terraces battered by the African sun and rains. A magnificent three-storey pink-bricked mansion, with a tower in the centre, a red tiled roof, and a line of elegant arches supporting a first-floor terrace from which a Union Jack fluttered limply. Rising behind it, a granite hill provided a dramatic backdrop. Part Tuscan manor house, part grand English ancestral home, and all completely unexpected and out of place in this remote corner of the African bush. Surely, only a madman or a megalomaniac could have built such a place.

The only obvious concessions to Africa were two carved wooden rhinoceroses acting as supports for a jutting side window, and the wooden crocodile over the top of the front door frame. The name was African too – Shiwa House, called after the lake which we could just see glimmering blue in the distance. Those details aside, the house looked like something one might find in Surrey or Hampshire, belonging to a duke or a lord.

As we moved closer, I could see gaping holes in the roof where tiles had fallen, and some of the window-panes were cracked or spider-webbed over. The main gardens were quite neat, the air perfumed by the honeysuckle and bougainvillaea winding round a tall cypress tree, in and out of which flitted bee-eaters, tiny flashes of colour and sound. But to the side, what had once been a walled rose garden was a tangled mess, and a broken pathway led to an empty swimming-pool with a cracked concrete floor. The tennis court was long overgrown, and steps down to the village through a series of arches were choked with tropical creepers, casting a strange green light. It looked as if the African bush was wilfully trying to take back the house.

Peculiar things can happen over a gin and tonic in McGinty's Pub at the Lusaka Holiday Inn, the Friday night watering-hole for the local expat community. On such a Friday in August 1996 I had been sitting on the hotel terrace overlooking the crocodile pool, entranced by the yellow male weaver-birds with beaks full of grass, engaged in their courtship ritual – a sort of ongoing Ideal Nest Exhibition to try to lure the female of the species by threading circular nests which dangled basket-like from the branches. As the sun cocked a final red-eyed snook at the African dusk, setting off the electric hum of cicadas, I found myself in conversation with a safari guide with a shaven head. His name was Mark Harvey, he had shaved off his hair as a Zambian mark of respect for the death of a friend, and he told me the strangest tale of an abandoned house deep in the Central African bush.

The house, he said, had been built by his grandfather, an English soldier and aristocrat, in the early part of the century when Zambia was still Northern Rhodesia and the sun never set on the British Empire. It was in a remote part of north-eastern Zambia called Shiwa Ngandu, which means Lake of the Royal Crocodiles, and one of these very crocodiles had devoured Livingstone's little dog Chitane as the explorer passed through on his ill-fated last journey in search of the source of the Nile.

buildings and an abandoned sawmill. Further on were more red-brick cottages, clearly inhabited judging by the smoke from the chimneys and the runny-nosed African children watching silent and wide-eyed from the doorsteps.

The clocktower stood over an archway, decorated with a carved black rhino and the date 1920. We drove through and up a long steep drive bordered by Italian cypress trees, of all things to find in Africa, passing terraced gardens ablaze with colours – blue morning glory, deep pink bougainvillaea, violet jacaranda. A great stillness seemed to hang on the air. *And then there it was*. The House. I drew in my breath. n all my travels in ten years as a foreign correspondent in Africa, Asia and South America, I had never seen anything ike it.

Ve entered through the double front door, which creaked esentfully as Mark pushed, and somewhere deep inside nother door banged. There was something terribly silent bout the place and we kept our voices hushed as we stepped nto an entrance hall hung with Shiraz carpets, leading on a grand wooden staircase guarded by two spear-bearing arriors. Off to the right was a dining-room the size of a nall banqueting-hall, a heavy chandelier bearing hundreds crystal droplets hanging over a long table. I ran my index nger across its surface and drew lines in the dust. Gilt-framed l-paintings of various stiff-necked Victorian gentlemen and ce-ruffled women stared down with the disapproving eyes ancestors. Three sets of enormous horns protruded from wall above the vast fireplace, and there were animal oppings on the flagstone floor.

The main sitting-room was large and cold, with a dark wardian feel, missing a fire to crackle in the grate to give ome warmth and purge the dank smell. Leather armchairs

Explorers, crocodiles, mysterious lakes, aristocrats building dreams in the bush . . . adventure beckoned. Livingstone is one of my heroes, and, whenever possible, I try to visit places where the great man trod. Besides, I had completed the work that had brought me to Zambia – an interview with Kenneth Kaunda for the *Sunday Times*, conducted over tea which he does not drink but insisted on pouring himself, holding the teapot high to form a great arc of brown liquid, his trademark white handkerchief fluttering from the other hand. A long weekend prolonged by a National Farmers' Day holiday stretched ahead before I could get a plane out.

So it was that at dawn the next morning, while my head was still addled from gin, Mark and his friend Paul came knocking on my hotel-room door and I found myself following them down to a battered Land Rover, heading out of Lusaka. Over the bridge, past the sprawling market where giggling hair-plaiters Beauty and Precious had earlier in the week tried unsuccessfully to teach me to dance 'like an African Mama'; along Cairo Road, past the man selling 'Knowledge is Life' exercise books spread over the pavement; past the stock exchange, which behind the modern black glass consisted of a few school-desks around a small blackboard; and past the post office where ancient post buses were setting off in all directions, crammed with Africans, goats and chickens, mounds of corn sacks and enormous bundles of finger bananas tied precariously on to the roof.

Abruptly, the city clutter ended and we were out in wide open veld, bumping between crater-sized potholes on the Great North Road, a red ribbon of a highway, unfurling and uncurling until eventually it would reach Nairobi. Above us the Equatorial sun beat down from an endless blue sky, and on either side stretched mile upon mile of flat savannah, pockmarked with scrubby olive-coloured bush, dreary to look upon. Everything was parched and waiting for the rains, and a film of red dust covered the road, the leaves, the bushes, Mark's Land Rover, and soon us too.

For much of the journey there was little sign of human habitation – just occasional glimpses of smoke columns rising from a cluster of beehive huts, probably no different from what Livingstone had seen more than a century earlier, though to my disappointment there were no wild animals, just a few goats. At a checkpoint police waved us down with Uzi guns, and asked for sweets. A little further we were stopped by a bespectacled man brandishing a butterfly net. He dangled his net along the side of the jeep and across the tyres like a character from a *Monty Python* sketch, and I giggled at Mark's explanation that he was looking for tsetse flies which had cadged a lift on our wheels.

The sun climbed higher, and we headed towards the Equator. Through Kabwe, where Broken Hill Man was discovered back in 1921 – the first clue that man's origins lay in Africa; past Kapiri Mposhi, one of Africa's rail and lorry hubs, crowded with motels where locals joke wryly that Aids comes free with the room charge. Beyond Kapiri, the potholes became so large it was hard to spot any road at all. Some had been partly filled with mud and grass by enterprising children who stretched brown hands out for almost worthless *kwacha* notes as we passed. Others were so deep that a car wheel could be lost in them and driving required all the skill of one of those video-games where virtual obstacles keep coming faster and furiouser until the virtual car is driven off the virtual road.

Eventually we emerged on to the Muchinga escarpment, a harsher land of ravines and grey boulders in strange moon-like piles. Small children appeared from nowhere to sell us wild honeycomb. I tasted it gingerly, unaccustomed to sucking

from the wax, but found it so much like a liquefie
of my favourite Crunchie bars that I could not ge
and it was soon dripping down my face.

The sun was lighting the undersides of leaves b
we started climbing Danger Hill, into a far greer
scheme. A pastoral valley unfolded to our left, bey
rose the soft blur of blue mountains, hiding wha
Mobutu's Zaïre. We turned off the road into the bu
ing a mud track through a grove of blue gum tr
said Mark, stopping the jeep. Rousing myself fron
of thirteen bone-shaking hours of travel, I follov
across row upon row of trees in every shade of gr
to see, far below, a lake shining blue-silver,
purple-smudged hills. Through the open windov
the wind in the leaves of the gum trees was surpr
like waves crashing on an invisible shore. We car
the track through the trees, bumping over ridg
and eventually came to a clearing.

In the undergrowth to the left, a black-painted
lay on its side like a sleeping donkey, jungle cr
round its body, and a brass 'Fowler of Leeds'
in the fading sun. To the right, a road-sign m
and 'Hospital' pointed towards another trac
us the trail widened into a clearing dotted
buildings. I gasped. Were it not for the fiery b
flamboyant trees and that strange African sm
and woodsmoke, we could have been in an E

The first building on the left had a sign h
door, painted 'Post Office'. Next to that w
Store', and after that the 'Estate Office', all s
red bricks and tiled roofs. Beyond these wa
gatehouse with a clocktower, the hands app
ever at ten to four. Across the road were

stood around moth-eaten baize card-tables, and heavy velvet drapes hung at the windows, but the room was dominated by a life-sized portrait of a beautiful strawberry-haired lady holding an ostrich feather fan, the apricot tones of her long satin gown bringing out the amused blue of her watching eyes.

Around the back, the kitchen was primitive and cavernous, with store-rooms, meat-holds and stairs down to a wine cellar, and it was easy to picture an army of servants at work to feed lavish house-parties. Cracked pots of dead hydrangeas decorated an inner courtyard from which more rooms led off, including a store-room crammed with dust-covered gold-rimmed crystal glasses, Meissen plates and a pink and gold Spode china tea service inside which an enormous spider had made its home, and I realized that the house was even bigger than it looked from the outside. Mark was vague but thought there were more than forty rooms. Far along the corridor to the right, with a direct entrance from outside, was a chapel, with wooden pews set into a flagstone floor, walls lined with blue and white Portuguese tiles, and a large leather-bound family bible open on the pulpit, the pages eaten away in gorgonzola pattern by white ants.

Upstairs, an embroidered panel hung over the door of the study. Inside stood a carved Zanzibari chest, the lid partly ajar and crammed with thousands of letters in neat black copperplate, most of which were addressed 'Dearest' and signed SGB with a flourish. Behind a Queen Anne desk, shelves were filled with estate books going back to 1922, and bound leather journals. Feeling half snooper, half detective, I opened one to read the inscription, *Stewart Gore-Browne, Harrow, July–September 1899*. The same writing as the letters filled the pages, meticulously recording every detail of the owner's life, some pasted with newspaper cuttings of *l'affaire*

Dreyfus. I smiled as I read the first page: *First day of the Lord's Exeant. Great excitement because my tailcoat has not arrived from home.*

On the bottom shelf, a pile of cellar-books listed arrivals of fine wine, champagne, brandy, sherry and port from faraway France and Portugal via ship to Angola, rail and then road. Opening randomly on 1 July 1960, I was intrigued to read: *Kaunda – 2 Port Red 2 Port White 2 red wine 29 beer 3 sherry.* Quite a dinner! Many entries were typical of 13 March 1965: *Hippo shot – 1 champagne, 1 port white.*

Mark called me over to an Oriental lacquer cabinet, inlaid with mother-of-pearl, and inside which shelves sagged with photograph albums. Black and white photographs, neatly labelled in the same handwriting as the diaries, showed the building of the house, successful hunting expeditions, visits of chieftains in flowing robes, naked African men washing each other in a river, house-parties of women in fur stoles and pearls and men in dinner-jackets, an old woman in a ludicrous hat who had clearly once been a beauty, a young girl with bobbed hair and a faraway look, and a middle-aged black man looking cold and uncomfortable in smart overcoat, gloves and trilby in front of the Houses of Parliament.

'That's the old man,' said Mark suddenly, pointing at a fierce-looking character with a large hooked nose, bristly moustache, stiff military bearing, monocle in his right eye and black bowler hat. I studied the photograph. This then was Stewart Gore-Browne, the man who had built this incredible place in the middle of nowhere, and clearly enjoyed the finer things in life.

I would have liked to tarry over the photographs, the battered pith-helmet hung on a peg, and the boxes of records by an old Decca wind-up gramophone, but there was little daylight left and much to see. We hurried along a corridor

Explorers, crocodiles, mysterious lakes, aristocrats building dreams in the bush . . . adventure beckoned. Livingstone is one of my heroes, and, whenever possible, I try to visit places where the great man trod. Besides, I had completed the work that had brought me to Zambia – an interview with Kenneth Kaunda for the *Sunday Times*, conducted over tea which he does not drink but insisted on pouring himself, holding the teapot high to form a great arc of brown liquid, his trademark white handkerchief fluttering from the other hand. A long weekend prolonged by a National Farmers' Day holiday stretched ahead before I could get a plane out.

So it was that at dawn the next morning, while my head was still addled from gin, Mark and his friend Paul came knocking on my hotel-room door and I found myself following them down to a battered Land Rover, heading out of Lusaka. Over the bridge, past the sprawling market where giggling hair-plaiters Beauty and Precious had earlier in the week tried unsuccessfully to teach me to dance 'like an African Mama'; along Cairo Road, past the man selling 'Knowledge is Life' exercise books spread over the pavement; past the stock exchange, which behind the modern black glass consisted of a few school-desks around a small blackboard; and past the post office where ancient post buses were setting off in all directions, crammed with Africans, goats and chickens, mounds of corn sacks and enormous bundles of finger bananas tied precariously on to the roof.

Abruptly, the city clutter ended and we were out in wide open veld, bumping between crater-sized potholes on the Great North Road, a red ribbon of a highway, unfurling and uncurling until eventually it would reach Nairobi. Above us the Equatorial sun beat down from an endless blue sky, and on either side stretched mile upon mile of flat savannah, pockmarked with scrubby olive-coloured bush, dreary to look upon. Everything was parched and waiting for the rains, and a film of red dust covered the road, the leaves, the bushes, Mark's Land Rover, and soon us too.

For much of the journey there was little sign of human habitation – just occasional glimpses of smoke columns rising from a cluster of beehive huts, probably no different from what Livingstone had seen more than a century earlier, though to my disappointment there were no wild animals, just a few goats. At a checkpoint police waved us down with Uzi guns, and asked for sweets. A little further we were stopped by a bespectacled man brandishing a butterfly net. He dangled his net along the side of the jeep and across the tyres like a character from a *Monty Python* sketch, and I giggled at Mark's explanation that he was looking for tsetse flies which had cadged a lift on our wheels.

The sun climbed higher, and we headed towards the Equator. Through Kabwe, where Broken Hill Man was discovered back in 1921 – the first clue that man's origins lay in Africa; past Kapiri Mposhi, one of Africa's rail and lorry hubs, crowded with motels where locals joke wryly that Aids comes free with the room charge. Beyond Kapiri, the potholes became so large it was hard to spot any road at all. Some had been partly filled with mud and grass by enterprising children who stretched brown hands out for almost worthless *kwacha* notes as we passed. Others were so deep that a car wheel could be lost in them and driving required all the skill of one of those video-games where virtual obstacles keep coming faster and furiouser until the virtual car is driven off the virtual road.

Eventually we emerged on to the Muchinga escarpment, a harsher land of ravines and grey boulders in strange moon-like piles. Small children appeared from nowhere to sell us wild honeycomb. I tasted it gingerly, unaccustomed to sucking from the wax, but found it so much like a liquefied version of my favourite Crunchie bars that I could not get enough, and it was soon dripping down my face.

The sun was lighting the undersides of leaves by the time we started climbing Danger Hill, into a far greener colour-scheme. A pastoral valley unfolded to our left, beyond which rose the soft blur of blue mountains, hiding what was then Mobutu's Zaïre. We turned off the road into the bush, following a mud track through a grove of blue gum trees. 'Look,' said Mark, stopping the jeep. Rousing myself from the stupor of thirteen bone-shaking hours of travel, I followed his gaze across row upon row of trees in every shade of green and red, to see, far below, a lake shining blue-silver, encircled by purple-smudged hills. Through the open window the rush of the wind in the leaves of the gum trees was surprisingly loud, like waves crashing on an invisible shore. We carried on along the track through the trees, bumping over ridges and roots, and eventually came to a clearing.

In the undergrowth to the left, a black-painted steam-engine lay on its side like a sleeping donkey, jungle creepers wound round its body, and a brass 'Fowler of Leeds' plate gleaming in the fading sun. To the right, a road-sign marked 'School' and 'Hospital' pointed towards another track. In front of us the trail widened into a clearing dotted with red-brick buildings. I gasped. Were it not for the fiery blossoms of the flamboyant trees and that strange African smell of hot dust and woodsmoke, we could have been in an English village.

The first building on the left had a sign hanging over the door, painted 'Post Office'. Next to that was the 'Village Store', and after that the 'Estate Office', all solidly built with red bricks and tiled roofs. Beyond these was an impressive gatehouse with a clocktower, the hands apparently stuck for ever at ten to four. Across the road were a series of farm buildings and an abandoned sawmill. Further on were more red-brick cottages, clearly inhabited judging by the smoke from the chimneys and the runny-nosed African children watching silent and wide-eyed from the doorsteps.

The clocktower stood over an archway, decorated with a carved black rhino and the date 1920. We drove through and up a long steep drive bordered by Italian cypress trees, of all things to find in Africa, passing terraced gardens ablaze with colours – blue morning glory, deep pink bougainvillaea, violet jacaranda. A great stillness seemed to hang on the air. *And then there it was*. The House. I drew in my breath. In all my travels in ten years as a foreign correspondent in Africa, Asia and South America, I had never seen anything like it.

We entered through the double front door, which creaked resentfully as Mark pushed, and somewhere deep inside another door banged. There was something terribly silent about the place and we kept our voices hushed as we stepped into an entrance hall hung with Shiraz carpets, leading on to a grand wooden staircase guarded by two spear-bearing warriors. Off to the right was a dining-room the size of a small banqueting-hall, a heavy chandelier bearing hundreds of crystal droplets hanging over a long table. I ran my index finger across its surface and drew lines in the dust. Gilt-framed oil-paintings of various stiff-necked Victorian gentlemen and lace-ruffled women stared down with the disapproving eyes of ancestors. Three sets of enormous horns protruded from the wall above the vast fireplace, and there were animal droppings on the flagstone floor.

The main sitting-room was large and cold, with a dark Edwardian feel, missing a fire to crackle in the grate to give it some warmth and purge the dank smell. Leather armchairs stood around moth-eaten baize card-tables, and heavy velvet drapes hung at the windows, but the room was dominated by a life-sized portrait of a beautiful strawberry-haired lady holding an ostrich feather fan, the apricot tones of her long satin gown bringing out the amused blue of her watching eyes.

Around the back, the kitchen was primitive and cavernous, with store-rooms, meat-holds and stairs down to a wine cellar, and it was easy to picture an army of servants at work to feed lavish house-parties. Cracked pots of dead hydrangeas decorated an inner courtyard from which more rooms led off, including a store-room crammed with dust-covered gold-rimmed crystal glasses, Meissen plates and a pink and gold Spode china tea service inside which an enormous spider had made its home, and I realized that the house was even bigger than it looked from the outside. Mark was vague but thought there were more than forty rooms. Far along the corridor to the right, with a direct entrance from outside, was a chapel, with wooden pews set into a flagstone floor, walls lined with blue and white Portuguese tiles, and a large leather-bound family bible open on the pulpit, the pages eaten away in gorgonzola pattern by white ants.

Upstairs, an embroidered panel hung over the door of the study. Inside stood a carved Zanzibari chest, the lid partly ajar and crammed with thousands of letters in neat black copperplate, most of which were addressed 'Dearest' and signed SGB with a flourish. Behind a Queen Anne desk, shelves were filled with estate books going back to 1922, and bound leather journals. Feeling half snooper, half detective, I opened one to read the inscription, *Stewart Gore-Browne, Harrow, July–September 1899*. The same writing as the letters filled the pages, meticulously recording every detail of the owner's life, some pasted with newspaper cuttings of *l'affaire*

Dreyfus. I smiled as I read the first page: *First day of the Lord's Exeant. Great excitement because my tailcoat has not arrived from home.*

On the bottom shelf, a pile of cellar-books listed arrivals of fine wine, champagne, brandy, sherry and port from faraway France and Portugal via ship to Angola, rail and then road. Opening randomly on 1 July 1960, I was intrigued to read: *Kaunda – 2 Port Red 2 Port White 2 red wine 29 beer 3 sherry*. Quite a dinner! Many entries were typical of 13 March 1965: *Hippo shot – 1 champagne, 1 port white*.

Mark called me over to an Oriental lacquer cabinet, inlaid with mother-of-pearl, and inside which shelves sagged with photograph albums. Black and white photographs, neatly labelled in the same handwriting as the diaries, showed the building of the house, successful hunting expeditions, visits of chieftains in flowing robes, naked African men washing each other in a river, house-parties of women in fur stoles and pearls and men in dinner-jackets, an old woman in a ludicrous hat who had clearly once been a beauty, a young girl with bobbed hair and a faraway look, and a middle-aged black man looking cold and uncomfortable in smart overcoat, gloves and trilby in front of the Houses of Parliament.

'That's the old man,' said Mark suddenly, pointing at a fierce-looking character with a large hooked nose, bristly moustache, stiff military bearing, monocle in his right eye and black bowler hat. I studied the photograph. This then was Stewart Gore-Browne, the man who had built this incredible place in the middle of nowhere, and clearly enjoyed the finer things in life.

I would have liked to tarry over the photographs, the battered pith-helmet hung on a peg, and the boxes of records by an old Decca wind-up gramophone, but there was little daylight left and much to see. We hurried along a corridor lined with prints of uniformed men from different military regiments and framed certificates. Some of the floorboards were rotting and had to be skipped over. We passed numerous bedrooms, each with its own dressing-room and bathroom equipped with a flush toilet mounted on a wooden box. I tried to ignore some of the fattest-bodied spiders I had ever seen, presiding over the white ceramic bathtubs. All the rooms had high ceilings and sweeping views over the bush, but many of the rafters had been eaten away by termites and there were piles of dust and plaster everywhere. In one room an oil-painting of St Mark's Square in Venice, done in the style of Canaletto, lay on the floor, one corner of the canvas completely rotten and its gilt frame peeling. Grandest of all was the master bedroom with its canopied four-poster bed, a rhino head carved on the top of each post. Further along a covered bridge style walkway, steps led up to the tower-room where a brass telescope was set up to watch the heavens by night. Our movements disturbed some bats which flew out of a cupboard squeaking, their velvety wings brushing our faces as they flapped blindly around, and I wasn't sorry when Mark suggested we move on.

The best surprise of all was left till last. The central part of the first floor was taken up by a splendid library that was clearly the owner's pride and joy, a bright airy place with big french windows leading out to a terrace. Apart from a fireplace at one end and the windows on one side, every wall was lined with shelves from floor to ceiling, packed with a tempting selection of leather-bound books including the best collection of Africana I had ever seen. A coat of arms was embossed over the door with the motto 'Spero Meliora' (I hope for better things) and a Latin inscription over the mantelpiece read 'Ille Terrarum Mihi Super Omnes Angulus Ridet' in golden letters – a misquotation of Horace's 'Ille Terrarum

Mihi *Praeter* Omnes Angulus Ridet' – 'This corner of the earth smiles on me more than any other'.

A thick film of dust covered everything and there was a lingering smell of mildew from where the rains had evidently got in. I tried to ignore my arachnoid friends and concentrate on the books. There were biographies of every famous leader one could think of, from Alexander the Great and Genghis Khan, to Churchill and Napoleon. There were works of philosophy and all the classics such as Plutarch's *Moralia* and Thomas More's *Utopia*, many of the books in precious first editions with beautifully engraved frontispieces, their pages sadly spotted with damp. The owner liked to travel, judging from the number of books on other countries, many of which were illustrated in the fashion of the time by delicate watercolours. But his biggest passion was clearly military history – three whole cases filled with volumes on subjects such as the Relief of Chitral and the Crimean War, *The History of the British Army in 10 volumes* by the Hon. J. W. Fortescue, as well as a much thumbed and annotated *History of the 5th Division in the Great War*.

Two padded-leather visitors' books stood on a circular table by the windows. I blew off the dust and flicked through, recognizing names such as Nancy Astor, Denys Finch Hatton, Kenneth Kaunda, the Montagus of Beaulieu, and the Duke and Duchess of Montrose. Shiwa Ngandu had clearly been a glittering place once, attracting more visitors each year than there were days. Now the only inhabitants seemed to be bats and spiders.

Mark opened the french windows and we walked out on to the terrace overlooking the lake, which was turning mauve and gold in the incipient sunset. Down below in the gardens, I could almost fancy hearing the clink of cocktails being served by a uniformed waiter to people wearing tennis whites, and crisp English accents, Mozart's Horn Concerto playing on the gramophone. It all seemed so serene that it was hard to believe that the lake was full of twelve-foot long crocodiles, descendants of those which had devoured Livingstone's dog, and that only the previous week had eaten the wife of one of the villagers, Mark recounted with some relish.

As always in the bush, night came quickly, a curtain visibly falling. A strange, near human cry came from somewhere not far off, a hyena perhaps, and we wandered back inside. The house had no electric light, we had brought no candles, and it was dark, full of chasing shadows. Suddenly, I wanted to leave. I thought back to the photograph and imagined what sort of man had created a place like this in the middle of nowhere. More than anywhere I had ever seen, Shiwa Ngandu seemed to symbolize the arrogance, paternalism, vision, and sheer bloody-mindedness of British colonials in Africa.

Outside, I looked back at the house, silent and secretive, mercury moonlight reflected in the windows. Above one of the doors, catching the light, I noticed the initials L and S carved in white. Shivering a little in the unexpected evening chill, I wondered what had happened to cause such a spectacular place, so lovingly built, to be abandoned.

Over the following year, the Harvey family kindly let me loose in Shiwa House to read the diaries, thousands of letters and papers, study the photos, and talk to those who had known, worked for, or hunted with their grandfather. The story I pieced together turned out to be a remarkable tale of passion, far stranger than anything I had imagined as I sipped my gin and watched the male weaver-birds spin their nests that balmy night in Lusaka.

This then is the true account of one man's African dream . . .

Part One

1914–1927

I

Shiwa Ngandu, Northern Rhodesia,
Good Friday 1914

It began as it would end, in the place he had always known he would find one day. In front of him, under an endless sky, stretched the lake, shining like a Queen's sapphire in the morning sunlight. Shiwa Ngandu, the local Bemba people called it, the Lake of the Royal Crocodiles. 'Shiwa N-ganndu.' The young British Army lieutenant tested the name on his tongue, emphasizing the penultimate syllable as he had heard the Bemba do, and enjoyed its sound.

The lake was quite small, about five miles long and one and a half broad, and lay cupped in a circle of hills, garbed with lush grass and trees. Here and there a sensual burst of colour broke up the green – the scarlet of a bubu tree, bursting with African tulips, a pair of tiny flame-breasted sunbirds singing, and a patch of yellow diamonds on the ground which rose up and became a cloud of butterflies. There was a flat meadow-like area between the hills and the far shore, and through his field-glasses the officer could make out a herd of zebra, skittishly parading their finely painted stripes and black manes. Everything seemed to be revelling in life. Removing his pith-helmet, Stewart Gore-Browne lay back against his pack and sighed up at the clear sky with satisfaction. *It was all so magical that I felt I had entered a fairy kingdom*, he later wrote. The rainy season over, the air tasted so crisp and pure that he fancied himself the first to breathe it. It had been a long, hazardous journey. But at last he had arrived at the place where he could build his manor and be lord of all he surveyed.

His thoughts were interrupted by Bulaya, the young orphan he had been trying to train as his cook, proffering a Spode china cup and saucer. Like all his servants, Bulaya was clad in white calico shirt and shorts and black and yellow waistcoat, which Gore-Browne had had sent out from the Army & Navy store in London. *I fancy the colours will set off their coppery skins*, he had written in one of his thrice-weekly letters to his beloved aunt Ethel, adding, *Just because one is in Africa, is no reason not to do things properly.* He took the teacup and smiled at Bulaya's big white-toothed grin. The forty porters he had brought with him were all Bemba people who had worked for him over the last three years on the Border Commission marking out the frontier between Northern Rhodesia and the Belgian Congo, and they were overjoyed to be back in their homeland.

He was about to ask Bulaya to knock up some celebratory breakfast from their dwindling supplies, when a rustling down by the shore caught his attention. Instinctively, he reached for his rifle, the .318 Richards given to him by his uncle Goff, the naval commander who had taught him to shoot, and edged forward. Three small reedbuck were cavorting at the edge of the water, their pelts *quivering with alertness*, their arched bodies and legs reminding him of young ballerinas.

He held the sight against the monocle he wore on his right eye and selected his prey. It was a clear shot and he squeezed the trigger quickly. 'Pow.' The single retort echoed round the silent hills and sent a flock of dark geese shrieking into the distance, low over the shining water. Two of the bucks fled and the other fell, right on target. There would be meat for lunch. He made a thumbs-up sign to his headman, Chikwanda, who set off with Kakumbi, the hunter, to collect and skin the body. Watching them go, Gore-Browne sat on the canvas chair outside his tent and took his pen from his pack along with a small black leather-bound book. Opening the page at 10 April, noting with surprise that it was Good Friday, he recounted the event in his diary, followed by the single word *Happy*.

Summoning a small boy who came running with a fan woven of banana leaves to keep him cool, he looked around the place contentedly, thinking about where he would build his grand estate and imagining himself on the terrace, commanding his servants, or striding about the grounds, a rifle under his arm and a Great Dane by his side. For as long as he could remember, he had dreamed of owning an imposing house, something like Brooklands, the Surrey estate of his father's favourite sister Ethel and her husband Hugh Locke King, which always seemed to be full of interesting people, the table replete with fine food and wine. The couple had no children of their own, and he and his younger brother Robert and sister Sapphire had often spent school holidays there, preferring it to their parents' place, Oakley, near Abingdon, where their mother, the beautiful Helenor Shaw-Stewart, who claimed descendancy from Robert III of Scotland, was always occupied in socializing and organizing London balls and their father, Francis Gore-Browne, a brilliant barrister, was either off at his chambers or buried in his books. *Father, I think of as always away or busy*, he once wrote. *Mother, I never managed to get on with*.

Young Stewart had become unusually close to his aunt, and he would cry when his mother came to collect him at the end of the holidays. From an early age it was Ethel he had gone to when he was unhappy, when he was sent away to Wixenford prep school at the age of nine, then to Harrow where he was bullied as a 'worm', being painfully shy, and neither clever like his father, nor athletic like his father's three brothers, Harold, Wilfred and Godfrey, all of whom had studied there.

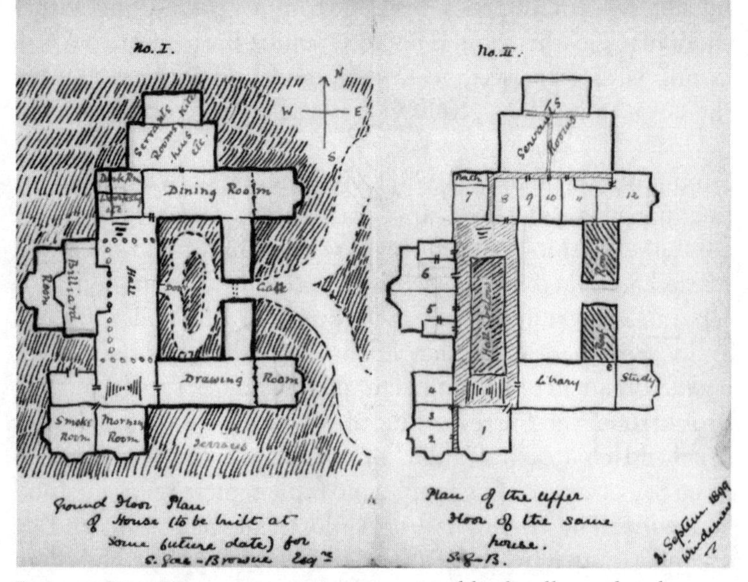

Stewart Gore-Browne was a sixteen-year-old schoolboy when he drew these plans of his dream house in 1899.

It was Ethel to whom he admitted *crossing the road to avoid being kicked by a crowd of boys*, and who kept him going as he counted the quarter hours on the school clock. Brooklands was the one place where he could forget about Roman history, Greek declensions, and being 'ragged', and he had fond memories of summers of croquet, bicycle polo, feasting on cherries, and rowing on the Wey with his cousins, the two Muriels.

Gore-Browne confessed his dreams of becoming a country squire in his first diary, begun in the summer of 1899 when he was still a schoolboy, just sixteen and enjoying the cricket at Lord's and his first cigar (describing it as *a glorious taste . . . though I did not feel quite happy afterwards*). Towards the end of that vacation, he travelled by train with William

Falcon, a fellow Harrovian, to stay at Newton Manor, a large country estate near Gosforth in Cumbria, which Falcon was to inherit when he came of age. Seeing the tenants coming out to greet his classmate, Gore-Browne was intensely envious, writing: *Why didn't anybody ever leave me a place – I'm sure I would manage it well and it would be ripping to own a little land to take an interest in.*

During his stay, he penned in the back of the diary a detailed plan in black and red ink of a *House (to be built at some future date) for S. Gore-Browne Esquire.* Facing east, it was to be a two-storey building with a sweeping entrance, twelve bedrooms, a long hall cum ballroom, a library, billiard-room, morning-room, smoking-room and servants' quarters to the side. Over the following years as Gore-Browne travelled about, staying with his Campbell-Craigie cousins in castles in Scotland, going to house-parties at various English estates, and doing motor tours of the Loire valley, Switzerland and Tuscany, often accompanied by Ethel, he drew detailed architectural sketches of châteaux, villas and mansions that caught his eye. Now, at the age of thirty-one, he had a clear picture in his mind of his ideal house, though as a lowly officer with little prospect of promotion and only a few hundred pounds a year income, hardly the means to achieve it.

That was where Africa came in. With his income from his father and trust fund of around £500 a year and £1,000 savings, Gore-Browne thought he could *make little impact* in England, but in Northern Rhodesia it would enable him to *live like an Emperor.* Yet, ironically, he had landed up in Africa by accident. Not academic enough to follow his father's footsteps to Oxford and the Bar, or spiritually inspired to enter the Church, following his great-uncle Edward, Bishop of Winchester, and uncle Wilfred who had recently become first bishop of Kimberley in South Africa, Gore-Browne had hoped to enter either the Navy like his late uncle Godfrey, a Vice-Admiral, or the Indian Civil Service. He had been bitterly disappointed at his rejection. Then the Boer War had broken out, inspiring him to apply to the Royal Military Academy at Woolwich, or the Shop as it was known, using Ethel's influence as a friend of several generals to get his poor eyesight overlooked. He did quite well in his two years there, and in 1901 was commissioned into the Royal Field Artillery. Initially revelling in the life of a gentleman cadet, he had eventually tired of balls (at one of which he noted in his diary, *a man dropped dead while dancing*), hunting, dining and drinking champagne at the Criterion and Trocadero, opera parties and gambling. Having watched the girl he loved marry another, he became depressed. One fine spring morning, he was teeing up on Byfleet golf links when he bumped into the officer from the Royal Engineers who had run the Ordnance Survey course he had taken in Southampton, and asked if he would like to go to Northern Rhodesia to work on the Border Commission. 'Yes indeed,' he had replied, 'but where is it?' Recounting the story, many years on, Gore-Browne told the *New Yorker*, 'The chap at the War Office who offered me the post didn't know where it was either.'

Such geographical uncertainties merely added to the job's attraction, and a few months later, in August 1911, the twenty-eight-year-old gunner subaltern was stepping off the boat at Cape Town, remembering the adventure stories of Rider Haggard he had read as a schoolboy and feeling that his own King Solomon's Mines awaited. The previous half century had seen many of the big blanks on the map of Africa filled in by the likes of Burton, Speke, Livingstone and Stanley, but to Gore-Browne, like most of the British public, interior Africa was still a vast thrilling unknown, a place of wild beasts, cannibals, and untold riches. His first glimpse of the Victoria Falls had given him the pioneer feeling of treading where few had trod before. Though, as he confessed in a letter to Ethel, *I felt rather ashamed to be simply stepping down from the platform of a restaurant car instead of stumbling across the thundering waters as Livingstone had done half a century before me after a perilous journey, hundreds of miles from any white man.*

But Africa was not as he had expected, and it did not take him long to develop misgivings about the same British Rule that back in London had given him such pride. Northern Rhodesia had been acquired by the British – or rather by Cecil Rhodes's British South Africa Company – at the tail-end of the European powers' nineteenth-century scramble for Africa. Starting with King Lewanika's concession of Barotseland in 1890, a series of dubious treaties had been negotiated between chiefs and Rhodes's agents, ostensibly acting as representatives of Queen Victoria, eventually giving the company control of the whole of the territory, naming it Northern Rhodesia. Having never been conquered through force of arms, the people had always received white men warmly, and were surprised and hurt when British officials treated them with contempt.

Shortly after arriving at the Commission's base-camp in Ndola, a small settlement marking the furthest point of Rhodes's Cape to Cairo railway, which consisted of a *boma* office, a post office, houses for a magistrate, an Assistant Native Commissioner, doctor and railway manager, Gore-Browne wrote to Ethel:

I wish I could describe the country to you so you could picture it, but it is very difficult. I personally had not the slightest idea of it. The little round huts and black men and occasional palm tree are all here, but that is the only part that fits in with one's ideas. For the rest there are miles and miles of red and green leaved trees which look when you climb a tree and see them from above, for all the world like a great mass of gorgeously painted waves. The most remarkable thing of all is the sensation of British Rule and frankly it stirs you. When the magistrate sits up in the courthouse, trying men for murders, rapes, witchcraft and such like primitive things, absolute governor of 20,000 wild black men who he never set eyes on and then turns round to you and says 'You see it is all bluff, I have only one white native commissioner and 10 native policemen and there is not the slightest reason anyone should do what I tell him.' And yet the same magistrate is merely a very ordinary Scotchman, not by any means a gentleman but an enthusiast and real ruler of men. It's very odd. And how miserably ashamed one is of the doings of white men out here and what a ghastly example of all the beastly vices we set.

The Anglo-Belgian Boundary Commission had been something of a disappointment too, though he had revelled in the outdoor life and the hunting. It was just all *far too bureaucratic and tied up with the petty egos of other officers.* Within three months Captain Everett, the second-in-command, was eaten by a lion, *a most ill-omened start.* Major Gillam, who headed the Commission, spent most of his time in a haze of whisky and kept issuing and rescinding orders, the loneliness of the African bush finally driving him to a complete breakdown. At the end, his senior officer Major Steel had pocketed the finishing bonus for the natives, prompting Gore-Browne to send an angry letter of complaint to Lord Herbert Gladstone, the British High Commissioner in South Africa, though his opinion of colonial officials was such that he doubted anything would be done.

The work marking out the border had been *damnably slow.* The 1894 agreement between Britain and Belgium's King Leopold was vague, simply stating that the border was to run southwards from Lake Bangweulu to its junction with the watershed separating the Congo and Zambezi rivers, following this line for the 550 miles till it reached the Portuguese frontier. 'The King of Italy had drawn the boundaries some years before – he'd been chosen as an impartial arbiter,' Gore-Browne told the *New Yorker* years later, 'and I suspect he simply ran his thumb across a map.' He was dismayed by the lack of regard to tribal borders, writing in an unpublished memoir of his experiences, *It was, and still is, by no means unknown for half a tribe including the paramount chief to be on one side of an international border, with the rest of the tribe on the other side.**

They had no decent instruments and there was too much sitting around waiting for the clearance of rains and mists, or the smoke from Africans burning their fields for planting, so that they could take sightings to establish high points between the two great rivers and erect wooden beacons on the hills to mark the border. The beacons, which were thirty feet high, had to be visible from three other sites to give triangulations for mapmakers. The terrain was tough and mostly untrodden, so isolated that most of their supplies had to be carried with them by large numbers of porters or hunted, and he was eternally grateful for his late uncle Godfrey's lessons in shooting rabbits and woodpigeons at Brooklands that summer when he was sixteen. During the long periods of waiting they would organize races between the Africans, taking bets on who would win.

Eventually, on New Year's Day 1914, they had reached the end, meeting up with the Anglo-Portuguese Commission which had been marking out the border between Angola and Northern Rhodesia. They had toasted in champagne, standing triumphantly with one foot on Britain, and one on Portugal or Belgium, cigars in hand. *Another few parcels of Africa squared off on the map*, Gore-Browne wrote in his diary.

*'As I Look Back', unpublished article by Stewart Gore-Browne.

When he was born in 1883, less than a tenth of the continent had been colonized by Europe, but by 1914 more than ninety per cent of it was under European rule. Despite the frustrations with the work, doubts over the ways of colonial rule, and his dislike of the Belgians, the wide skies and intensity of Africa had got to him. *I never imagined that the sense of being surrounded by sun, behind, around and reflected in everything until one almost felt one could drink it, could feel so good*, he wrote to Ethel. He loved going off into the bush where perhaps no white man had ever trod, the feeling of being surrounded by unsuppressed nature, and travelling *like a king with 15 or 20 bearers just to carry my personal belongings* [and another 100 for supplies and equipment], *and villagers prostrating themselves at my feet.* He liked Africans, particularly the Bemba who were *so masculine, proud and loyal*, and enjoyed hunting, pleased to be good at something after his lack of prowess on the playing fields of Harrow. One day he realized with some surprise that he wanted to make his home in this place.

When he heard that the British South Africa Company was making land in Northern Rhodesia available cheaply to white settlers, he decided to apply. Once the work on the border was finished, he said a final, not altogether sorry, goodbye to the Commission's base-camp at Ndola. Accompanied by some of the best porters, he headed north-east, planning to cross Rhodesia and Tanganyika, looking for land, before finally getting the steamer back to England from Dar es Salaam. They travelled by foot and canoe, retracing Livingstone's last footsteps in the opposite direction, all the time searching for the ideal place to make his home.

Now at Shiwa Ngandu he thought he had found it, *the loveliest thing in all of Africa, my own personal paradise.* He listened to the competing birdsongs and the tinselly whisper of leaves, and took another deep breath of the delicious air, feeling that at last his real life was beginning. Rereading his diary entry, he decided it did not do justice to the momentous day. From the side pocket of his pack he pulled out a red pencil and sharpened it with his penknife. At the bottom of the page, he added in capitals: *FIRST SIGHT OF SHIWA NGANDU.*

Gore-Browne had heard about Shiwa Ngandu before. The local British District Commissioner, Robert 'Bobo' Young, had been there and written about it, and some people called it Lake Young, rather than its Bemba name. But he had never expected it to be so enchanted. It was after all the place which Livingstone had cursed on his last journey in 1867, when his faithful little yellow dog Chitane had been devoured by the lake's crocodiles, and in the ensuing fuss two of his porters had run off with his medicine chest. 'I felt as if I had now received the sentence of death,'* wrote the great explorer, whose supplies by that point were so short that they were reduced to roasting grain to make believe it was coffee. Already very weak and haemorrhaging, Livingstone had later suffered another malaria attack and had no quinine to treat it. He died not far off to the south in Chitambo's village.

The few settlements around Lake Shiwa Ngandu were Bemba, Northern Rhodesia's largest tribe, and many of the men had worked as porters on the Border Commission, carrying loads of 50 or 60lb on their head to earn five shillings a month, to pay their yearly tax of five shillings per hut (many Bemba were polygamous and had huts for each wife) to the British South Africa Company. Unlike his fellow British officers who denigrated the Bemba as 'lazy' and 'liars', Gore-Browne greatly admired the tribe, their noble warrior stock

*Livingstone's *Last Journals*, 15 and 20 January 1867.

appealing to him. He had done his best to learn their language and his porters had told him their story many times. Their ancestors had come from the Congo at the end of the seventeenth century, led by Chitimukulu, the Crocodile King, intent on conquering all Africa. But as they marched towards the fabled country of the great lakes, they clashed with one tribe after another, sustaining heavy losses, and were cheated by Arab traders who took their women for slaves in exchange for glass beads. Finally the bedraggled remainder, still clutching the mighty crocodile totem, arrived on the great north-eastern plateau and came across a dead crocodile near a lake, which they took as a good omen. Being told that the local name for crocodile was *Ngandu*, they settled in various villages around the shores of the lake (*Shiba*) which consequently became known as Shiwa Ngandu. The community flourished, spreading out and coming into contact with the first European traders and explorers, but those on the shores were continually harassed by crocodiles. One day near the beginning of this century, 200 men decided to go out on the lake in canoes to slaughter them. By dusk only two men remained, and one lake-shore village, Kacilikila, whose men had not joined the hunting party, and it was there that Gore-Browne had arrived.

The current Bemba king, or Paramount Chief as they called him, Chitimukulu the 32nd, ruled over his people from a village to the north-west, near the town of Kasama. Gore-Browne knew Africa well enough to realize that it was no good trying to set up home without the chief's blessing, and planned to visit him with some suitable gift – a fine jacket, penknife or field-glasses, and his last bottle of whisky. Thinking about this, he set off to explore the area more thoroughly, and was pleased with what he found. The soil was sandy, but the spoor around indicated that there was plenty of game. There were fish in the lake and no shortage of water from the river running into it. He thought that the small hill, overlooking the lake, sheltered by the other higher ones which Livingstone had described as 'beautiful white and pink dolomite, scantily covered by upland trees', would be a perfect site for his manor. Down below in the vale, he would build a village for his estate workers. He pictured something *English style – redbricked and tiled rooves – with workshops, farm buildings, schools, a village shop and a post office, where blacks and whites would live in harmony*. Of course it was remote – there was no road, and it was 400 miles of harsh terrain and crocodile-infested swamps from the nearest railway station at Ndola, which would make it hard bringing things in, but the isolation rather appealed to him.

The sun was already low in the sky, tinting the lake a kingly purple, when he returned to camp. Excited shouting greeted him, and he heard Kakumbi exclaim *'Ni Chipembele!'* – 'It's a rhinoceros!' Hurrying towards Kakumbi's cry, Gore-Browne looked through the field-glasses and to his astonishment saw a black sullen beast coming slowly along, the first he had ever seen in the wilds. It looked, he thought, like *something out of Wagner, a survivor of another age of giants and dwarves and valkyrie and dragons, not a twentieth century animal at all*. Following the hunters Kakumbi and Chakusami, he rushed down into the reeds and long grass towards it.

I had been in Africa long enough to know that the rhinoceros will charge as soon as they get wind of one, and that I had to take a decent shot as soon as I could, he wrote afterwards.

But I needed to hit a vital spot, if not the rhino would charge furiously toward me. Chakusami handed me the heavy double barrelled .470 and I fired at the flank where I thought the heart might be. It was the first time I'd used this rifle since Father sent it out from England, and it knocked the glass out of my eye as it went off with a deep moan. The rhino, which seemed of battleship proportions now we were nearer, spun round and went slowly off into the high reeds. I fired again, heart thudding. Everything seemed to go completely silent. There were no signs of the rhino. Was it wounded, waiting in the reeds? It was impossible to see, the greenery was so high. A hunter should never follow wounded dangerous game into thick cover, but I could see no option. The only alternative would have been to run away and I couldn't do that, as many of my men had shinned up the trees to watch. I edged forward gingerly through the long, sharp-edged grass, my heart hammering wildly against my chest. To my relief, there in front of me was a black lump, completely inert. The rhino had been killed stone dead with my first bullet which had gone straight through the heart.

Seeing the dead rhino, Kakumbi and Chakusami burst into song and began dancing, lifting Gore-Browne on to their shoulders to celebrate. The other carriers slithered down from the trees and flocked round to join in the jubilation. There would be meat for weeks. 'From now on we will call you Chipembele,'* Kakumbi said solemnly. 'Your *mupashi* [ancestral spirit] is a good one, it will watch over you and give you a long life.'

It took six men to drag the beast into camp, where they began hacking and chopping. Gore-Browne had no idea there was so much hide on a rhino. They would be at work long into the night. Some of the others began erecting wooden frames on which the meat would be grilled. He lay on the ground, watching the activity and feeling absurdly pleased with himself. He had killed his first rhino, it was Easter Day and he was *in paradise*.

*The Bemba word for rhinoceros is actually *chipembere* but as the 'r' sound is unknown in their language it is pronounced *chipembele*.

Solemnly, Chakusami presented him with the large white horn which they had removed and cleaned. It was, he wrote to Ethel, *an awful looking weapon and I shuddered to think of it ripping anyone.* Calling Bulaya for whisky, he placed the horn by his side and, with the fiery liquid warming his throat agreeably, turned his attention back to the sun going down over the lake.

Gore-Browne had always liked being near water, and he found something particularly soothing about that late afternoon light which cast a milky pink glow across the lake. The end of the rains had left the air fresh and sparkling like champagne, and it was *as exhilarating as being by the sea.* He closed his eyes and pictured himself standing on the terrace of his great house. A white-jacketed waiter would bring him a cocktail on a silver tray, and he would sit, enjoying the solitude and a thousand sunsets like this one. But he would have visitors too, organize grand hunts and swank parties full of interesting people. His house would become famous all over Africa.

There was only one very important thing missing. As so often on his travels, an image formed in his mind of a woman with lively grey-blue eyes, her strawberry-coloured hair pulled back into a soft knot behind her strong expressive face. He took out a pencil, tore some sheets from his exercise book and began to write to Ethel.

Oh my dear if only you were doing this trip with me it would be so perfect. Take my hand and step out of the tent with me now and look at the lake, a strip of blue silver with clumps of dark, deep-green, trees and behind purple hills coming down to the waterside. I'd like to stop here and set up our house it's so jolly . . . oh my dearest, why don't you come?

2

Charing Cross station.
Wednesday, 5 August 1914

It was raining when the boat-train pulled into Charing Cross, a sultry summer rain that sent dragon breaths of steam rising from the hot platform to mingle with the clouds puffing out of the locomotive. The pistons pumped for a last shuddering time and the engine spluttered to a halt. Gore-Browne opened the door of his first class compartment and squinted through his monocle along the platform as if searching for someone, then stepped down.

There were crowds of people on the concourse, far more than on an ordinary Wednesday evening. The usual clusters of city gents in bowler hats going home after a day at the office were outnumbered by young men in uniform, some with caps set jauntily, others with a more serious air, piling into special trains. Many were bidding farewell to their sweethearts. English girls with fresh complexions, shining eyes, bouncing curls and full red lips planting departure-emboldened kisses on the cheeks of the soldiers. After so long away, Gore-Browne admitted, *I found it hard not to stare.*

His attention was distracted by a group of rough male voices belting out Rule Britannia. Within minutes the whole station seemed to be singing, even the city gents joining in, the patriotic fervour surprising Gore-Browne. *There was a rush in the air*, he wrote, *like that of people going off to a spring race meeting*. A group of middle-aged women in head-scarves who he presumed were mothers, started tossing sweets and packets of cigarettes through the windows of the departing trains of soldiers to loud cheers.

He pushed his way through the noisy crowds impatiently, trying to spot Bulaya and Kakumbi walking up from third class. He had hoped Ethel would be there, but he supposed he couldn't have expected her to come up from Brooklands, not with the way life had suddenly been turned upside down. All his plans for Shiwa Ngandu had been thrown into confusion since the previous Tuesday on board the SS *Emir* from Dar es Salaam. He had come down late to breakfast as the steamer was entering the Suez Canal, to be informed by a doctor who had come on board to examine them that Archduke Franz Ferdinand had been assassinated and that war had broken out between Austria and Serbia.

Homecomings always took too long in his experience, but with such news the last week of the voyage had seemed *interminable*. Initially he hadn't realized the implications, simply noting the information in his diary, and going on to write of the *lovely colours* of Suez, and describing the various ships they passed. But after changing ship at Port Said to the P&O *Moldavia*, alarming Marconi-grams started arriving in the radio-room. Each day had brought news of other powers issuing ultimatums then mobilizing forces: Germany declaring war on Russia, then invading France through Belgium, and then France declaring war on Germany, which could only mean one thing. When he disembarked at Marseille and boarded the train to Paris, he found it full of reservists. By the time he had reached the Hotel Folkestone in Boulogne late the previous night, to find it crowded with soldiers, Britain had declared war on Germany and talk was of nothing else.

Even so, he had wired Ethel from France with the details of his arrival, and had somehow expected to find that distinctive figure waiting for him, auburn hair tumbling from under one of her elaborate hats and pigeon-blue eyes sparkling with gaiety. It was hard to imagine that the outbreak of war would deter his determined aunt and he wondered if there was some other reason, perhaps linked to her husband's cousin Peter, the heir to Brooklands, running off with a married woman – a scandal which she had written to him about as 'shocking all London'. The disappointment of her absence quashed all the thrill he had expected to feel returning home after three years in Africa.

Through the crowds he spotted Kakumbi struggling towards him with some of the luggage, two trunks balanced on his head and a leather Gladstone bag in either hand, while Bulaya stood stock still on the platform with the rest of the baggage in a pile, looking so petrified that Gore-Browne couldn't help smiling. The lad's eyes were white with wonder and streaming in the steam from the engine, which he had not got the sense to move away from. *Poor fellow*, he later wrote. *Until a month ago when we arrived at Dar es Salaam to board the SS Emir, he'd never seen a city before, or a motor car*. Until Bulaya had started working for him on the Border Commission two years earlier, the African had never even seen a white man. Now, *with so many white faces everywhere, it must be overwhelming*. In fact, after the vast silence and space of Africa, Gore-Browne himself was having some trouble adjusting to the rush and hum of London.

He patted Bulaya on the shoulder, reassuring the Boys that they would soon be with '*Mâ-ma*'. He used the Bemba word, meaning not exactly mother, but principal female relative. He didn't know quite what his servants made of his relationship with his aunt, to whom they had watched him writing letters almost every night by firelight. He assumed they imagined some kind of mother figure who would look after them all. Kakumbi had once asked him if his kinsfolk could come to

Shiwa when they lived there. Gore-Browne wrote to Ethel, *I said I was certain my Ba-mayo (closest female relative) would. He said 'we will all go down to Kabwe (that's Broken Hill) with machilas* and carry her oh so gently.'*

He had not consulted with Ethel about bringing the two Boys; it had been a last-minute decision. *The thing is the gap between their world and ours is so huge that it's often hard to explain things*, he had written to her, too late for any reply.

The more time one spends with these folk the more one realizes the gulf which separates our ordinary common things and thought from theirs. I just thought that if they came here and saw how things are, that it would help so much. I have an idea that it would be good for them to see my home, learn some English cooking and manners, how to set tables and that kind of thing, so that they can run my house properly in Africa.

He thought Ethel would like handsome Kakumbi, *a tall beautifully made swaggering fellow* with his noble bearing and coppery skin, *and a litheness which makes for pure beauty of line as one imagines the Greeks knew it*. Bulaya, he wasn't so sure. *He always seems eager enough to please, but has a streak of rebel in him and has turned out darker and uglier than I hoped when the lad first entered my service and attached himself to me, following me everywhere*, he wrote. Had he had any inkling that war was about to break out, he would never have brought them with him.

They made an exotic trio as they pushed their way out of the station. Gore-Browne striding forward, his face tanned against his tropical suit and panama hat, his lean frame making him look more than six feet tall and the monocle on his right

*Hammocks used to carry white men in early colonial years.

eye adding an air of distinction, and his black bearers behind with all the luggage, almost as if they were on safari in the centre of London. The station clock showed almost six, which didn't give him much time if he was to report to the War Office and make it down to Brooklands at a reasonable hour that evening.

Emerging on to the Strand to see lights across the road gave him an idea. Blinking a little in the rain and the forgotten clip-clop of carriages, he led the way over to Lyons Corner House. The two Boys followed reluctantly, jabbering away to each other in frightened Bemba at the sight of a tram rattling past and staring open-mouthed at the pigeons. Gore-Browne pushed open the glass door of the café. It was *like entering a bubble of light and sound* which froze with their entry. Ladies in large hats taking tea stopped to stare mid-conversation, cup and pastry fork suspended in mid-air, as he beckoned the heavily laden Boys to follow him to a table. Africans were a rare sight in London, particularly in the company of a white gentleman, but he had hoped everyone would be too engrossed in the news and preparations for war to bother. Praying the Boys would not disgrace him too much, and would remember what he had taught them about English manners the few times he had gone down to third class on the boat over, he frowned at Bulaya who was dipping his fingers in the sugar bowl, and told them he would be back soon. Ordering them some tea and toast, he left for the War Office.

Outside, Gore-Browne hailed an approaching cab. With war coming, who knew what might happen. The evening papers he had seen on the station stands were already talking of fuel rationing and requisition of vehicles. *I just hope they keep their hands off Donne Quixote*, he wrote in his diary, referring to his favourite motor at Brooklands, the sister car of his uncle's *Don Quixote*.

As they turned down into Whitehall, he reflected how strange it was that only a week earlier he had been planning to quit the Army for good. The rain which had been lashing the windscreen eased to a gentle patter. Gore-Browne stared out impatiently through the light grey mist, surprised that *the streets seemed so congested and the buildings so dingy.* After the wide sunlit skies of Africa, England suddenly felt much too small. On a wall, he noticed some posters advertising an exhibition at Madame Tussaud's Waxworks. 'The European Crisis,' he read. 'Lifesized Models of Their Majesties King George and Queen Mary, HM The Emperor of Austria, HM King Peter of Serbia, Tsar Nikolai of Russia.' He could take Bulaya and Kakumbi to that, he thought, wondering what they would make of it. He had explained to them several times about the King and Queen of England as being super Paramount Chiefs, but he wasn't sure they understood.

The War Office was packed, numerous men milling around in the street outside, waiting to enlist. There was an air of excitement, people muttering that they would 'soon show Fritz what we're made of' and that it would all be over by Christmas. Inside, a harassed-looking secretary informed Gore-Browne that mobilization orders had gone out to all regulars two days before and warships were already on standby. When he finally got to speak to a staff officer, *a crisp fellow with a thin moustache and an unfamiliar name*, he tried to explain that he was newly arrived from Africa. The officer cut off his explanations curtly, telling him that the Expeditionary Force was already full, but that he would be contacted with orders shortly as there might be other contingents going out later. The secretary made a note of his details and he was ushered out. *So much for glory in France*, he wrote in his diary that night.

In some ways he was relieved not to have an instant call-up, though surprised at how quickly those running the War Office seemed to think the Germans would be defeated. At least it gave him a chance to go down to Brooklands, see Ethel and settle in the Boys. Outside he could see a man lighting the gas-lamps, and he thought about Ethel's face as he used to watch it in the firelight at Brooklands, eyes bright as she talked about her latest passion for motor cars or aeroplanes or some new writer she had discovered.

3

Brooklands, Weybridge, Surrey.
That evening.

The sense of alienation Gore-Browne had felt in London shed as suddenly as if he had removed a heavy coat from his shoulders, as the cab from Weybridge station swung into the familiar drive. Passing along the dark soldierly lines of fir trees, he could just make out the shadowy forms of the banks of rhododendrons where he, his brother and sister used to play hide and seek as children, tears staining Sapphire's cheeks as she hunted for Aristides, her pet chameleon which was always getting lost. He got out and looked up fondly at the imposing red-brick mansion, square in shape and four storeys high, dominated by a clocktower and green copper turret. Lights burnt a welcome in the windows. *Brooklands.* So many happy days spent there.

Before he could ring the bell, the double oak doors swung open and there was the familiar welcoming figure of Annie in her neat grey and white uniform, all frothy white hair, and what as children they used to call her *currant-bun eyes*. Bounding out behind her, barking loudly, came his uncle Hugh's five white Austrian poodles, huge creatures with long plumed tails and bright intelligent eyes, and suddenly all was activity. The butler emerged to direct the removal of luggage from the car, and Lowrey, one of the footmen who served as Gore-Browne's valet whenever he was in residence, stepped forward to greet him.

In the warmth of the servants' welcome, Gore-Browne

forgot about Bulaya and Kakumbi, and turned round in surprise when Annie asked him, somewhat awkwardly, what to do about his 'two companions'. He looked back to see Bulaya cowering behind the open car door, terrified by the dogs. *Funny these fellows who are used to lions and buffalo should be scared of a pet dog or two*, he later wrote. Somewhere in the dark of the gardens a peacock screamed and Bulaya looked as if he was about to faint from fear. Kakumbi was staring with open interest at Jacqueline, the French ladies' maid, who had just come to the door.

He introduced the two Boys to Annie and asked her to arrange them a room in the stable block and some food, lowering his voice as he inquired whether they had been expected. The housekeeper reassured him that her mistress had warned her about 'Master Stewart's visitors from Africa', but added that she had not really known what to expect, not ever having seen an African before.

Finally the luggage was all unloaded, the driver paid and tipped, and the Boys led off round the back by one of the footmen. Gore-Browne followed the butler into the large hall, his eyes drawn as always to the vast gold-framed portrait of Ethel in white and amber silk jacket and long skirt, the train attached to her wrist. A door to the left opened, there was a swish of silks, and the tall strawberry-haired woman of the portrait bustled out, greeting him affectionately in her deep husky voice. 'Aunt Ethel, dearest . . .' He rushed forward to embrace her, *feeling like a young boy again*, inhaling her familiar perfume mixed with the spicy aroma of the Turkish cigarettes she loved, and admiring her long swan-like neck.

With a familiar cackle of laughter, Ethel linked her arm through his and led him into the drawing-room, where her husband, Hugh Fortescue Locke King, was seated in a leather armchair by the fire. Looking whiter-haired and more sunken-eyed than Gore-Browne remembered, his uncle, whom he addressed affectionately as Nunkie, was sucking at a pipe, occasionally breaking into a wheezing cough. The day's newspapers lay on a table by his side and Johnnie, his favourite poodle, was curled in a half-moon at his feet. Shaking his hand, and teasing him about 'the return of the Great African Explorer', his uncle ordered him a whisky. Ethel asked Annie to bring in a cold supper for her nephew as they had already dined, and to direct Lowrey to prepare a bath. As Gore-Browne left the room to change, she told him to hurry so that they could hear his news, calling after him, 'Come and tell us all about it!' just as she always had when as a youth he arrived for the holidays or back after a ball. *It's a rum thing*, he later wrote in his diary. *It seemed like only yesterday that I left, yet now I had come back to find the whole of Europe ablaze.*

He followed the valet up the grand staircase to his room in the east wing, noting with satisfaction that the rhino horn, his rhino horn which he had sent back ahead of him, had been placed above the library door. Not many of the great houses in England could boast one of those. A steaming bath was soon waiting, and one of his old lounge suits laid out on the bed. When he emerged from the bath, a tumbler of whisky had been placed on the dressing-table next to a vase of wild violets from the garden, just like the ones he used to pick for Ethel when he was a small boy. Taking a sip of Uncle Hugh's ten-year-old malt, he sat at the mirror and rubbed some pomade on his hair from the glass jar, picking up one of the silver-backed hairbrushes that had been a long-ago birthday present from Ethel. He professed to despise vanity, but he did wish that his face wasn't so long, that his hairline was less receding and what hair he had less reddish, and that his nose was not quite such a pronounced version of his father's.

When he re-entered the drawing-room, Ethel was lying on

the chaise-longue, her head wreathed in its usual cloud of Turkish smoke, her shoes kicked off on the floor and her elegant ankles visible below the hem of her green skirt. Her cigarette was in the twisted silver and ivory holder he had sent her from Africa, her expressive white fingers dominated by the large ruby ring which had been a wedding present from Hugh. She was, he thought, as beautiful as ever, her hair coppery in the firelight and swept back from high cheek-bones, which had once moved him to write to her, *I wish that there were dragons in the path I could slay for you.* Like him she had the distinctive Gore-Browne nose but the effect of hers was lessened by grey-blue eyes alive with adventure. She was wearing a vivid emerald and black suit, with a long embroidered jacket over an ankle-length skirt with nipped-in waist which accentuated her ample breast, and a jewelled comb in her hair.

The story of Hugh and Ethel was the stuff of legend in the family and among the Surrey Set. Ethel was just sixteen when they met in London, on a visit to the Lily Mission which her elder sister ran for the washer girls of Notting Hill. The youngest of six children, she was by all accounts rather wild, having been born and brought up in Tasmania, and later Bermuda, where her father (Stewart's grandfather), Sir Thomas Gore-Browne, was Governor, and had never been to school, though she had outspoken opinions and a passionate love of books which she had passed on to her nephew. Hugh was the son of Peter Locke King, the MP for East Surrey, nephew of the Earl of Lovelace and descendant of the philosopher John Locke. He was more than twice her age, and practically an invalid, suffering from consumption, but had been so captivated by her beauty that he had pursued her relentlessly and recklessly, once even getting drenched in pouring rain just to see her pass by. Hugh amused his friends by telling them he had proposed because he took Ethel into a conservatory at a dance shortly after they met, and she told him her favourite flowers were orange blossoms. 'The only way to continue the conversation was to ask her to wear them.' Flattered by the attention and the gifts he was always leaving with the butler at 7 Kensington Square, the Gore-Brownes' London house, Ethel had been won over by his shy manner, interesting character, detailed knowledge of how things worked, and madcap schemes.

Sir Thomas Gore-Browne had initially refused the alliance, worried by Hugh's poor health and the age difference (though he himself had been twenty-two years older than his wife Harriet when they married in 1851). But the Locke King fortune was hardly something to ignore, and on 27 December 1883 he and Peter Locke King signed an agreement under which he provided an allowance of £120 per annum to his youngest daughter, while Locke King would pay £1,000 per annum to his son, and the couple were married a week later. Gore-Browne couldn't remember the wedding as he was only eight months old at the time, but Ethel had shown him a scrapbook of cuttings about the day, her white satin dress, Brussels lace veil and crown of orange blossoms, the lavish presents of diamonds, pearls and silverware from duchesses, earls, African emperors and Indian princes, and their departure in a gilded carriage for a honeymoon in Morocco.

Hugh's weak chest meant that for the first years of their marriage they had wintered in Egypt, like many fashionable couples. As Ethel was unable to find a hotel luxurious enough for her tastes in which to stay four to six months each year, they acquired Mena House, a former royal hunting lodge of the Khedive Ismail at the foot of the Pyramids, and converted it into an English country house, keeping the oriental décor, but installing great log fireplaces in every room and filling it with antiques. Deciding it would be fun to turn it into a luxury hotel 'to end all hotels', no expense was spared in designing a dining-room like the interior of a mosque, beautiful Moorish lamps hanging from the domed ceiling, acquiring exquisite carved *mashrabia* furniture inlaid with ivory and mother-of-pearl and installing latticework balconies leading from french windows in every bedroom so that guests could breakfast out of doors, something unheard of in hotels at that time.

Set in forty acres of jasmine-filled gardens, with a magnificent view to the Pyramids, the Mena House Hotel was soon attracting a glittering clientele of their aristocratic friends, particularly after the train was extended from Cairo. The guest-list for Christmas 1890 reads: 'His Royal Highness Prince and the Princess of Sweden and Norway and suite, Comte and Comtesse de la Gardie, M. le Baron and Madame la Baronne de Liliencron, Lord Ribblesdale and the Honourable Miss Lister, Lady and the Misses Montague Pollok, Sir John Corry etc.' Thomas Cook started taking bookings for the hotel but, despite all the wealthy visitors, the Mena House was run at a loss because the Locke Kings were very extravagant and when it came to paying the bill tended to tell people they were their guests.

The Mena House Hotel was not their only architectural venture. Not long after their marriage, Hugh's father Peter Locke King died, bequeathing Brooklands to his only surviving son. Peter Locke King had built the house in the 1860s on land inherited from his father, the 7th Lord King of Ockham. Before moving in, Hugh and Ethel hired the fashionable architect Blomfield to make many alterations, adding the green copper turret and the billiard-room wing, and installing electric lights long before anyone else had them.

The estate, with its large grounds and many rooms, was a

paradise for children, and the Brooklands Easter Egg Hunts were soon famous throughout Surrey. Not having any children of their own, the Locke Kings surrounded themselves with other people's, mostly those of friends and Ethel's family, as Hugh's three sisters were all unmarried and his closest male relative was his cousin Peter King, the one who had recently returned from the Royal Engineers in India and absconded with the married woman. Most Easters, summers and Christmases the couple played host to the children of Ethel's favourite brother, Frank. While his wife Helenor remained in their house in Kensington or Abingdon, giving teas, musical evenings and organizing balls, Francis Gore-Browne would often take refuge at Brooklands, writing his Company Law books in a second-floor study while the children, Stewart, Robert and Sapphire, played in the gardens, or with one of Nunk's latest toys.

Hugh loved new-fangled things and his greatest love of all, apart from Ethel, was motor cars. He had been one of the first people in England to own a motor car, back in the 1890s – a green Austrian Daimler. Gore-Browne could still remember the first few family outings in the car with its beautiful walnut interior, when he was about fourteen. People would stop and stare as they drove past at what seemed like great speed but was probably less than the limit of twenty miles per hour, sending up great clouds of dust until they were brought to a halt by the chain dropping off and he would jump out to run and fetch it. Always keen to try out new things, Ethel was soon taking turns at the wheel, and claimed to be the first woman in Britain to drive.

Hugh's greatest dream was to own a racetrack, and a few years before his nephew's departure for Africa he had made a considerable dent in his fortune by building Brooklands racetrack, the first motor-racing course in Britain. A vast concrete bowl with a three-mile-long track so steeply banked that one could reach great speeds of 120 miles per hour, it had opened on a glorious July day in 1907, attracting a crowd of more than 13,000. More than forty cars had taken part in the procession. Ethel, resplendent in a wide turquoise flowered hat, had led, triumphant at the wheel of their car *Bamba* as the only woman driver, while Hugh sat alongside her, content to play passenger, wearing his habitual cloth cap and puffing his pipe.

Now in his late sixties, Hugh had survived longer than anyone had expected and was supposed to have got stronger in recent years, though looking at the papery texture of his skin and his thin silver moustache, Gore-Browne wondered. He hoped he had, anyway, because he planned to entice Ethel to Africa, and he feared that for all her spirit of adventure, her sense of duty was such that she would not come without her husband. Surely the warm pure air of Shiwa Ngandu would be good for Nunk. He knew Ethel would love it. English winters had always depressed them both and he had recently written to her, *People like us are not supposed to live in cold climates*. He intended that she should live in style in his African house, explaining, *We'd find it impossible to leave most of the things that make this life so priceless, you and I, the well-ordered decent comforts, the well-trained boys and the rather regal magnificence . . .*

Ethel had always been the most glamorous creature in Gore-Browne's world. He had never met another woman like her. Even his first real girlfriend, Lorna Bosworth Smith, whom he had courted all those years ago when he was twenty-one and she twenty-three, was a pale shadow of his exotic aunt. He often wondered how Lorna had changed. Losing her at such an early age meant that to him she would always be that golden young girl, her smiling face with its serious eyes all-knowing *like those of a Madonna in an Italian painting*, looking up at him from under her hat, a few wisps of hair escaping and turning gold in the morning sun. He would never forget first glimpsing her at Harrow when going for tea at her father's, old Boz the history beak. He must have been about fifteen then, and she a little older, but he could still picture her in that white pinafore over a long brown dress, disappearing shyly behind a door. It was like a snapshot that he always carried with him. Remembering Lorna meant remembering carefree days of youth, endless summers of cricket on the lawn, boating on the Wey, dancing parties, and taking her for rides in *Bird*, the capricious single-cylindered Renault which had been his first car, bought with his coming-of-age money. He had driven Lorna, accompanied by her sister Joan, to Cambridge, where their brother Neville was studying. He had brought Lorna to Brooklands and they had ridden on Tweedledum and Tweedledee and picked violets in the gardens, then played the piano together, their favourite 'Sonata Pathétique'. Afterwards, he had confessed to Ethel, *Lorna is all the spring of life to me*. His aunt had reminded him that he was only just of age and a young cadet with little to offer a wife, and that he should be looking for someone with money of their own, or at least concentrating on bettering his own prospects.

If he was honest, it was his fascination with Ethel that had stopped him asking Lorna for her hand that dreadful July day when they had sat on the hill overlooking Bingham's Melcombe, her family estate in Dorset, and she had told him that she had been proposed to by Edwin Goldman, a forty-five-year-old South African medical professor who had recently joined their circle. Perhaps she had been expecting Gore-Browne to object and offer his own suit, but remembering Ethel's advice he said nothing. They had said a sad farewell in the dark on the bowling-green by the old yew hedge, where they had first kissed, and with *a stone heart and silent lips*, he had watched Lorna set off for a life with another man, whom he was convinced she didn't love, to Mannheim in Germany where Goldman had a post teaching at the university. The last he had heard from her sister, Lady Grogan, was that the couple were out in Johannesburg and Goldman was working as a surgeon. After the wedding, Gore-Browne had fled to Europe in *Bird*, to Monte Carlo to play the tables and to the Riviera where he and his friend Cecil Kerr had wined and dined, bemoaning the fairer sex. As always, it was Ethel who had comforted him, travelling out to join him in accompanying Pope's record attempt from Monte Carlo to London, followed by a motor tour of the châteaux of the Loire, with Baedeker's guidebook at the ready. His diary of that trip is full of details of the performance of the car, miles covered and frequent breakdowns, *enormous teas of chocolate and cakes*, and nothing of the torrid emotional time it must have been, though in letters afterwards he referred to a special conversation in the Café de la Madeleine in Paris, *where you and I ate little strawberries.*

Looking at Ethel silhouetted in the firelight as he tucked into a supper of cold poached salmon washed down by champagne to celebrate his return, he found it hard to believe that his aunt was now fifty. But apart from a few grey hairs, age seemed to have done little more than add distinction to her features. Listening to her talking about the war, he marvelled at how, despite her lack of schooling, she was always so well-informed. He had never met a woman with such energy: few men could keep up with the way she threw herself into everything. She never cared what other people thought, had little time for other women and loved to shock by kicking off her shoes and smoking like a chimney even in front of duchesses and counts. She always knew the latest dance craze and shared her husband's passion for cars, often racing at Brooklands. Ever since the Wright brothers had kept a plane aloft for an hour, her ambition had been to be the first woman to fly, and in 1910 she had been up on a couple of trial flights with the French aviator M. Paulham before he flew from London to Manchester, and was almost strangled in mid-air when her long silk scarf got caught in the propeller, becoming the inspiration for the female lead in the film *Those Magnificent Men in Their Flying Machines*. She would be such a success in Africa, thought Gore-Browne.

He often wondered what had drawn her to Nunkie. Of course Hugh was wealthy, and indulged her every whim. And he always had interesting stories to tell, *though one never quite knows if they are true or not*. But a woman like Ethel needed more than that. *Yours is a fiery spirit and a romantic soul which need constant stoking*, he had once written to her. Hugh was a retiring sort of person, perhaps because of his poor health, and they had never had children, keeping instead a menagerie of pets.

Knowing their love for animals, Gore-Browne had shipped them a blue galago, a kind of bushbaby from Northern Rhodesia. He'd laughed out loud, reading Ethel's account of how the creature had caused havoc at one of their grand dinners with lords and cabinet ministers. 'I knew Mary Galago had got into the room', she wrote,

> because I suddenly heard a small chattering but I couldn't see her and didn't want to alarm the guests. They were all so stuffy, you know how these politicians are. Anyway, she must have climbed the drapes because all of a sudden she landed on X's shoulders in

the middle of dessert. You never heard anyone let out such a yell and as for the racket from the ladies, you would have thought it was a lion from all the screaming. It made me think of you out there in the bush with all those wild creatures. Still at least it got rid of them early!

His mother had been horrified when she had heard of his gift, and made her disapproval clear to her sister-in-law, telling her 'the thing must be full of diseases and fleas, the African kind, they're the worst!' and demanding she send it to London Zoo immediately. 'I said at least we'd give it a holiday here in Surrey first,' wrote Ethel.

He dreaded to think what his mother would say when she heard about the Boys. He would never have brought them if he had had any idea that war was about to break out. When he left Shiwa for England, he had thought he would be away just for a few months to sort out acquiring the land from the British South Africa Company and buy all the things he needed for Africa, as well as to persuade Ethel and his best friend Cecil Kerr to join him. The trip had seemed like an ideal chance for the Boys to learn English manners and for Bulaya to learn how to cook English food, as in the eight months he had been serving as his cook, he had only picked up odd things from the missions they had passed, and Gore-Browne could teach him only how to boil and fry eggs. If he got sent to France, he did not know what he would do with them.

To his relief, Ethel said they could stay at Brooklands in the stable block for the time being. One of her friends had an African they called Samba driving her carriage, and Ethel seemed rather to fancy having the handsome Kakumbi serving at table once he had had a few lessons. Gore-Browne was hoping Annie could teach Bulaya some basic cooking, and his aunt teased him about his own culinary abilities, saying that he knew only how to pick a good wine, remarking that she remembered 'some wickedly good picnics in France'. In her usual no-nonsense manner, she said that the Boys would have to get used to eating lamb stew, as they didn't have any of the mealies or wild animals which he wrote about in his letters, and he smiled when she told him that Annie had come in earlier, asking whether Africans used cutlery.

Gore-Browne was dreading having to go to Oakley, his parents' place near Abingdon. His father at least pretty much left him alone, being too wrapped up in his work or writing his books on Company Law (*beastly things*, as his son referred to them), though Francis Gore-Browne had never hidden his disappointment at Stewart's failure to follow him to Oxford. But his mother was a terrible snob, and as far as she was concerned he couldn't do a thing right, *all the time finding fault and criticizing*. Dreamy-looking Robert, his twenty-one-year-old brother, who had never worked a day in his life and fantasized about being a novelist,* was the apple of her eye. Although they had little to do with each other, he knew she was not happy about the idea of him settling down in Africa, and he had been deliberately vague about his plans. 'You've got a perfectly good career in the army and should stick at it', she had admonished him in one of her very rare letters.

Furious, Gore-Browne had immediately dashed off a letter to his aunt.

Perfectly good career, fiddlesticks! She must be mad. I'm 31 and still on the bottom rung of the official ladder. I seem to always be told what a good job I'm doing yet I never get promoted. Even if I work for years, I'm only ever going to be a junior officer, a major or

*Robert Gore-Browne went on to write *An Imperfect Lover*, about Darnley, the lover of Mary Queen of Scots who was murdered.

something, whereas in Africa the fact of my having a few hundred pounds a year will give me a chance over my fellow men . . . She's no right to say a word about my career as she's never raised a finger to help me.

Even with the war on, he couldn't see much hope of promotion. Matters hadn't been helped by his dismissal from the Border Commission for 'wilful disobedience', after he had complained about Major Steel, his superior, cheating the natives out of their final wages and refused to do the same. He had tried to reassure his father that it was all academic as the work had already finished, and he still felt he had done the right thing, though he had to admit it wouldn't look good on his records. *Father's always so obsessed with obedience to authority*, he had moaned to Ethel. *But what if those in authority are wrong? Surely we have a Christian duty to say so. I'm fed up with all these hierarchical institutions. Honestly, sometimes one feels one never left Harrow!*

He knew his parents worried too about his lack of inclination towards marriage. No doubt Mother would produce some 'suitable girls' for him to take tea with at Oakley. For a while Sapphire had taken the heat off him by marrying a missionary, a fellow by the name of Hugh Hanford, of far too humble means for their mother's liking. Much to her brother's amusement, she had met Hanford, who was working as a clergyman in Pretoria, when she was dispatched to stay with relatives in South Africa after a scandalous liaison with an Austrian count. Now she had gone there to live, and Gore-Browne was once more his mother's hope for a good match. Aware of her scheming, he wrote bitterly to Ethel, *where am I supposed to have found a blushing bride, riding an elephant under a jacaranda tree in the middle of the bush? Honestly I don't know what Mother would have me do.*

Marry a girl of her choice and live in the country on my £500 a year and perhaps the girl's £400 . . .

Only Ethel knew how close he had come to proposing to Lorna, and it was to her that he fled after that awful night when he danced in Lorna's arms for the last time, staying at Bingham's Melcombe on the eve of her wedding. After watching Lorna become Mrs Goldman, when he thought there was no more to look forward to in life, it was Ethel's company on their trip round France that made life worth living again. Her enthusiasm for everything was infectious, and they shared each other's concern for what they called *the big things in life*. She was the only one, he felt, who could see there was something special about him inside, even if he hadn't found a way to show the world at large, or the Army in particular. When they were apart, he and Ethel wrote to each other almost daily, addressing each other as *dearest*, or *my very dear*, telling each other everything, writing of books they had read and dreams they had had, and always expressing their great longing to be together again, though never discussing what it all meant. *You know what you've been to me all of my life*, he often wrote. But his upbringing had made him conscious of subjects one does not broach with a woman, and once when he had dared allude to their relationship during a motor trip to France, she had changed conversation most deliberately.

He often wondered what Hugh made of his closeness to Ethel, and as he got older felt increasingly awkward in his presence. *I used to fancy that Nunk didn't like me*, he wrote to Ethel. But his uncle had always been outwardly affable, and a few months earlier had even written to him saying that he would be happy to sponsor his application for land from the British South Africa Company, as well as help him financially, and put a word in with one of the fellows on the Board.

Even so, Gore-Browne was completely taken aback when,

later that week, Ethel told him they had decided to make him heir of Brooklands instead of Peter King, Hugh's cuckolding cousin. He knew Peter had been the object of much parlour gossip in London since absconding with a married woman called Doris. In one of Ethel's latest letters to him in Africa, she had written, 'He's still living with this Mrs Lewis in London and insisting that they love each other and that's all that matters, quite like something out of a twopenny romance. Your father went to the flat to try and reason with him. He said it was all quite sordid, the two of them there, doing nothing but playing patience all day.' Replying, Gore-Browne had commiserated, *It must be awful for you.* Ethel had mentioned then that Hugh was considering changing his will in his nephew's favour, and he had protested, *I would feel bad, profiting from Peter's disgrace*, confessing, *One never knows what one would do in a similar situation . . .*

It was still a shock to hear Ethel say the words, 'We want you to inherit Brooklands, Stewart.' The idea of being *lord of all this, the swank house, the terraced gardens with the fig trees and strawberries, the cherry orchards, the fountains, the bridge over the river, the Jersey cows on the fields, the fine horses in the stables* and the woods where he and Ethel – and one summer he and Lorna – used to ride. *It was*, he wrote afterwards, *too much to take in.*

Later Gore-Browne was to bless his good fortune, for the Brooklands wealth would play a key part in his future. But his first reaction was of a more personal nature. *Oh my dear*, he wrote to Ethel, *the thought of belonging to you really . . . or better, both of us belonging to the same place . . . if Nunk truly wants me above anyone else and if I'm not wronging Peter then that would be the most priceless thing that ever happened to me.*

*

Like families all over England, on Gore-Browne's first night back, they talked not of Peter nor of Brooklands, but of the war, Hugh asking him whether he shared the newspaper editors' opinion that it would be over quickly. He told his uncle how only a month ago, on the steamer crossing Lake Tanganyika, he had fallen into easy conversation with the only other first class passenger, a German officer. *He was an Ober Lieutenant from the famous 99th regiment*, Gore-Browne had written at the time, *a good chap, one of our sort really, and we decided if Britain and Germany got together we could rule the world.* How things changed. His uncle told him he had several times met General Lord Kitchener, who had been co-opted to Asquith's cabinet as War Minister, describing him as 'a sound enough fellow', and Gore-Browne would like to have heard more, but Ethel stepped in, refusing to hear any more war talk, saying she was scared that a wire would arrive 'in those dreadful capital letters' demanding 'Lieutenant Gore-Browne to report at once'.

To Gore-Browne's delight, she told him that his old friend Kerr was back from India and that she had invited him over for dinner the next evening. Not only did that give him an excuse to delay heading down to Oakley, but he was hoping Kerr would agree to become a partner on his Africa venture. Suddenly he found himself feeling sleepy and, spotting his drooping eyelids, Ethel called Lowrey to make him some bedtime cocoa. He did not protest. *I'm looking forward to sleeping in a proper bed again*, he had written in his diary during the Channel crossing, *not on a boat or train or French fleapit of a hotel, or camped in the bush with lions prowling around outside.*

Entering his room, he smiled as he saw that his aunt had left the latest *Punch* for him to read. Undressing, he climbed into the big bed and lay between the crisp white linen sheets.

He had almost forgotten the joy of fresh sheets, the blue smell of cleanness. On his bedside cabinet a younger Ethel stared out breezily from a silver frame. For a while the frame had held a photograph of Lorna with a far shyer expression. He had removed it when she'd told him of her engagement, and torn it into pieces. He looked quizzically at the woman in the yellowing photo for a moment, then snuggled down to read *Punch*. He was almost asleep when he heard a light tap on the door. Ethel came in, hair unpinned, to say goodnight with a soft brush of her lips on his forehead, just as she used to when he was a child. Outside, after she had gone, he could hear one of the dogs barking. Africa seemed a very long way away.

4

The Front Line, Arras,
Good Friday 1916

Dearest

I'm writing this when other folk are going to bed just as I used to in Africa; only then it was by a roaring fire out in the limitless silence and peace of the forest, with the great big starlit sky showing through the tree-tops. Here is a grubby little dugout with a smoky paraffin lamp and a tiny speck of warmth from a dreary iron stove, while outside there's rain and the ceaseless sniper fire in the infantry trenches, with about every half hour big guns going off. There, that very moment, four shells rumbled and echoed as they burst over the hill.

Alongside me there's a lad, a subaltern in the battery, reading over and over again the casualty list that's got his brother's name in it, killed, almost the first time that he was out here. I think that a quite certain death hangs over one here – shells have dropped all round this shanty, the ground is ploughed up with them, and any time the German batteries want to turn onto us they could, and yet one lives on and jokes and tells stories and we've just eaten a quite excellent pheasant (slain in the woods by a Frenchman).

We're not heroes, far from it, though I think the Infantry are, only very ordinary people trying all of us to do our best. Every night before I go to sleep, I say 'Lighten our darkness, o Lord (but not with bursting shells) and by Thy Great Mercy defend us from all perils and dangers of this night for the love of thine only son, our Saviour Jesus Christ', then I get quite comfortably off to sleep if there's no toothache or chilblains or rats, and when I wake up in the morning and see it's daylight and I am still alive, I say, 'that's another night gone, thank you Oh Lord, now there's the day to get through.' And so on . . .

Writing letters under shellfire was no easy task, and Gore-Browne's pencil was frequently forced to a halt, particularly on nights like this when the Boche was busy. Identifying the whine of a 17-inch – a ton of high explosive which he knew they would feel even if it landed three or four miles away – he sometimes wished that his ears were not so well trained to recognize all different kinds of firepower. Right on cue, a nearby explosion rocked the shelter, filling his nostrils with the acrid smell of cordite and sending a rain of splinters down. Next to him, Tremlett, the subaltern whose brother had been killed, looked ahead with blank windows for eyes, apparently oblivious to the dust falling on to his hair and eyelashes.

The 5th Division had been on the front line for almost seven weeks, moving there just after Gore-Browne joined the unit in January as Brigade-Major. He and the other staff officers were billeted in Arras, a seventeenth-century town much of which had been reduced to rubble, and whose population had almost all fled. His own work was away from the main fighting in divisional headquarters, and involved communication with GHQ and interpreting and relaying orders for his brigades. But he accompanied General Hussey every morning on his walk around the artillery batteries and trenches, and often stayed there much of the day, checking on morale and supplies, and helping cut through any red tape, something he quickly developed a reputation for being good at. The conditions in the trenches were far worse than he had imagined. *I have never seen such utter desolation*, he had written to Ethel. *Flies like you'd expect at a buzzing swamp in the tropics, stumps of trees, two or three feet of mud and maybe some wet straw to sleep on. Worst of all is the smell – a mixture of rotting bodies, cordite, and the lingering remnants of gas from attacks, a sort of sickly sweet smell like being suffocated by the hothouse flowers.* Afterwards the *vile taste* would remain on his tongue all night.

He wrote to Ethel every day when he could, and she to him. War had changed the tenure of their relationship, she now addressing him as 'dearest beloved' or 'dear who are more dear to me than I can ever show you', rather than 'dearest lad'. He tried not to include the most gruesome details in his letters though she pleaded, 'Spare me nothing.' But he thought it unfair to load too much on his aunt, who had enough to worry about at Brooklands, which, true to form, she had turned into a Red Cross hospital, and was busy tending wounded soldiers day and night.

But occasionally, as on this Easter night, he felt in morbid mood, needing to confide in someone, perhaps because of the increasing sense that the Big Push was finally coming, or maybe because of the time of year. He found it hard to believe that it was exactly two years since he had arrived at Shiwa Ngandu and seen the zebra and puku grazing by the shining lake. It seemed so far away now, *like a Promised Land one would never again see, or a dream of heaven.* Sometimes during the previous winter when they had been marching day after day through blizzards and mud, almost dropping with fatigue, the pain raging in his teeth from abscesses, he had thought he could see gates ahead of him leading to the gardens and orchards he had dreamt of creating. Better, he supposed, than his colleague Carruthers who told him that in the depths of his fatigue he saw war maps all over the sky. Mostly he tried not to think of it because it hurt to remember Africa and the sky and the light and above all the lake. It was the quiet of the place he most longed for, *a ceasing of this constant hateful noise of shells*. If he ever got back there, he vowed, he would never shoot game again but would hunt with spears and bows and arrows.

Earlier that day, realizing it was Good Friday, he had found himself drawn to the crypt of the shattered Arras Cathedral. Kneeling there, trying to pray amid the broken stone and rubble, his thoughts wandered to the previous Easter. He had been back in England after the horrors of Flanders, based in Swanage and engaged in what sometimes seemed a hopeless task of giving artillery training to the latest recruits to Kitchener's New Army – the 17th Division, which he described to Ethel as *a bunch of varsity lads, schoolmasters, businessmen, some fairy-heeled beyond belief*. He had had to instruct them most of the time without horses, harnesses, rifles or sights, yet they had shown such tremendous keenness that he felt humbled, and had become close to the Commander, General Purvis. On Easter Day, Ethel had escaped her Red Cross work and driven down from Brooklands, and they spent the day together, walking and talking as if they had never been apart. Later, they had gone to evensong at Winchester Cathedral, where his great-uncle Edward had been bishop and was now buried. One of the hymns was 'The Lord's My Shepherd' and he wrote to Ethel afterwards:

I remember that evening, I still think of it always particularly the psalm and the clear alto voice of one of the choirboys suddenly rising above the great body of sound to the high vaulted ceilings like a promise.
In Pastures Green
He Leadeth Me
The Quiet Waters By.

Even during the hardest times, like the previous May when his best friend Kerr had been killed at Ypres, shot through the head, he had clung to the thought that somewhere up there was a God. But sometimes with so much death, he asked himself whether there really could be. *Arras is far, far worse than Ypres*, he had written, shortly after arriving there from the 17th Division, sorry to leave his eager recruits, but glad to be back with regulars and in the thick of things.

And we all know that the real battle, the big one, is still to come. While Ypres was a skeleton, a place of dead bones, Arras seems like a corpse, a still beautiful corpse with terrible wounds that keep on bleeding.

Yet strangely, he found himself becoming fond of the place, partly because of his interest in architecture. *I've never been to Arras before*, he wrote,

but think it must have once been one of the nicest towns in all France, full of character. It gives the feeling of being full of people still – even though only a few hundred souls are left where once there used to be 30,000. Not ghosts, but real people who built and lived in the jolly old houses with their big gardens of grottos and ponds and orchards, and a sort of solid antiquity that makes it seem all the more sacrilegious to batter and destroy them.

Of course he knew that in war if a town held troops it had to be bombarded whether it was Arras or anywhere else, and if a building had a tower that would make an observation post then it had to be smashed whether it was a cathedral or a distillery. In Flanders he had seen modern Belgian villas blown to bits and thought the world *a richer place for the loss of such monstrosities*. But here, when he saw glorious old places, reminding him of Bingham's Melcombe, the Bosworths' rambling estate down in Dorset where he used to court Lorna, then he felt a kind of impotent rage.

Lorna. He closed his eyes and leant back against the cold mud wall. Eleven years had passed since that ball in Dorchester where they had first properly met and he had filled her dance-card, even though he never particularly liked dancing, awkward with his height and stiff-backed demeanour. *The prettiest girl there*, he had written in his diary. Afterwards they had gone back to Bingham's Melcombe and drunk hot chocolate in the kitchen. Yet after all this time, he still felt *a burning pain* when he remembered her. *Sometimes I think it would be better not to have loved at all than to have loved and lost*, he wrote in his diary. Not that he had realized at the time what he had. Often he watched the men in the trenches writing banalities to their sweethearts and wives – he knew the sort of things they wrote because one of his duties was to censor them, and wished he had someone that cared like that for him, who would write all about the doings of their children and the neighbours and have his photograph by their bed and pray for him every night. Of course he had Ethel, but she had still given him no clear commitment about coming to Africa.

So many times he had relived that scene with Lorna on the hill overlooking Bingham's Melcombe, that hot summer day when she had looked at him shyly from under the lashes of her big bluebell eyes in that way she had, then told him that Goldman had asked for her hand in marriage and she was planning to accept. Lost for words, he had muttered congratulations and then left, after saying goodbye to the Lorna he knew, under the dark shadow of the old yew hedge. On her wedding day, a bitter February morning in 1906, he had not been able to face going into the church but had stood at the end of the lane in the snow, watching her carriage pass, knowing she could never be his. He wondered if she had any idea how he felt. Recently she had written to him a few times from South Africa but he tried to dampen the flame of hope her letters kindled, supposing she was probably just doing her wartime duty, sending words of comfort to a lonely soldier. Perhaps she was lonely too – Goldman had died, supposedly as a result of doing experiments on himself, the man was so *damnably heroic*. But she never mentioned such feelings, instead jotting a few sentences about daily life in Johannesburg, and her young son and daughter. In her most recent letter, she had mentioned she had been coughing a lot again, and he had heard she was suffering from TB.

On his last leave almost a year ago, he had gone to Bingham's Melcombe, not thinking about where he was going until he had almost arrived at the honey-stone gateposts with the carved eagles perched as if ready for flight, guarding the estate which nestled so neatly at the side of a stream with the Dorset downs sweeping up on either side. He stopped by the gatehouse where he and Lorna had arranged books for the writer Thomas Hardy, who was a friend of her father and often stayed there, and remembered how Hardy had told them he'd written much of *Tess* 'unconsciously'. There were daffodils in the drive and honeysuckle creeping up the front wall and around the mullioned windows. *It was all so much what I think best of England, that it was like looking into that other world, the world before war*, he wrote. *It reminded one of the words of Rupert Brooke 'and laughter learnt of friends and gentleness of hearts at peace under an English heaven*'. Thinking of it, those sunlit days among the buttercup fields with Lorna picking flowers by the fishponds and the daisy chain she had made him after playing 'he loves me, he loves me not' with the petals, he could smell the jasmine scent she always wore, and see that small heart-shaped face looking up beguilingly from under its hat.

A scramble of arms and legs interrupted his reverie, and Hewson appeared through the hole, flashing his boyish grin. Greeting him as usual with 'Evening, Major GB', Hewson was quick to spot the half-written letter, and teased him as always about his 'secret love', refusing to believe that all the letters in black ink, and parcels of vests and apricot jam really came from an old aunt. 'You must have met some girl at all those balls and hunts and things you artillery cadets at the Shop used to get up to,' Hewson kept insisting. 'No offence meant, but after all you're no spring chicken.' Gore-Browne refused to be drawn. He liked Hewson, describing him to Ethel as *a gruff sort of fellow one wouldn't normally have met, a bank clerk from north London with a ready wit and boundless energy*, but even under fire did not find it easy to share confidences with his fellow man.

Hewson took out a flask from his inside jacket pocket and after gulping some back, offered it. Gore-Browne wiped the top and took a swig, wincing as the rough whisky scoured the back of his throat. Noticing Tremlett, Hewson pushed the flask into the subaltern's trembling hand and commiserated with him over his brother's death, telling him, 'It's up to us to make all these deaths count for something.' Tremlett ventured a grateful half-smile as Gore-Browne watched the easy rapport Hewson had with the men. For his part, he always felt he had to work so hard to win their trust, let alone their liking. The moment he opened his mouth, they looked at him with misgivings. Ethel kept him supplied with Woodbines to hand out, one of their only forms of solace from the cold and rumble of gunfire all about.

A few days earlier he had run into a fellow from New Zealand in the trenches who said he wouldn't swap this life if he was offered a thousand pounds. Gore-Browne wasn't so sure. He liked the companionship and feeling of doing something useful. He thought he did his job well; he always seemed to get encouraging comments from his superiors, and, although it had taken him a while to win their confidence, many of the men at the 17th Division and the 32nd Brigade had written to him after he left, saying they missed him, letters which he was to treasure for the rest of his life. It was all the death he didn't think he could ever get used to. And far from being the hero, leading his brigade valiantly into battle as he had pictured, following the example of his late grandfather Thomas Gore-Browne who had distinguished himself guarding the retreat to India during the Afghan war of 1842, he was still yet to really be in the thick of things. Prior to his present staff job, he had been in charge of an ammunition column, which usually stopped on high ridges half a mile or so behind the batteries, except during a battle when their horse-drawn wagons would be in the middle constantly resupplying. But in between battles it was just *ceaseless hammering away and killing and getting killed*, particularly that spring in Arras where a long war of attrition seemed to have set in.

Not that he would ever admit such doubts to Hewson. Although Hewson was doing staff work now, he longed to be in the middle of things and was out in the field at every opportunity. He had told Gore-Browne once that he had joined up as soon as he heard the news. 'Kissed the Missus and littl'un goodbye and jumped on the train.' Everyone in the regiment had heard the story of how during an attack he had got bound hand and foot in German wire in front of a German trench among dead bodies and a blazing rocket had come right at him. Somehow he had extricated himself and was sent home with blood poisoning, trench fever and nearly lost his foot. He was supposed to be off for six months, but after only half that, just three days after coming off his crutches, he had persuaded the Medical Board to let him go back to France in case he missed a battle.

So many soldiers' experiences seem to be straight out of the Boy's Own book of daring deeds, Gore-Browne wrote in his diary. Seeing the lads in the trenches, *humble people, often in as much good cheer as if they were just off for a Saturday outing*, he felt guilty that he was not in so much danger himself. One of his most dreaded tasks was to pack up bloodstained kits of the dead and send them to bereaved parents with a note that tried to offer some feeble words of comfort, and he feared having to do that for these young men. Not that there was much time to dwell on things. He was in his office from 7.30 to 10 every morning then out in the trenches till 7 p.m. or later, then back at the office doing more work usually till 1 or 2 a.m., and he would often be woken two or three times in the night. Not only was he responsible for finding billets for the 3,000 or so men and making sure rations were distributed, but there seemed to be a constant demand for maps, intelligence reports, defence schemes, charts of fire, plans of bridges, and lines of advance and retreat, as if those in charge thought that paperwork could compensate for lack of trained men. His mapping experience on the Anglo-Belgian Border Commission was invaluable, and since Nunk had sent him a set of calligraphy pens and Indian inks in blue, red and black, he enjoyed making the careful drawings, though admitting to his uncle, *Sometimes I think that just as we lost the Boer War for not having enough maps, this one could be lost for having too many*. Still, at least most nights he had a real bed to sleep in.

The division headquarters, where they were staying, was a château belonging to a retired diplomat. It was a huge place like a Monte Carlo hotel, and as far as Gore-Browne was concerned, *full of every abomination that misspent wealth could purchase*. The drawing-room had pink cupids on a blue ceiling, a gold grand piano, marble chairs with ebony arms inlaid with mother-of-pearl, and pink velvet curtains. When he and the other officers were there in the evening he fancied they must look like *a scene in a play, all in uniform waiting in this extravagant room for dinner to be announced*. His office was in the billiard-room, which had a stained-glass window through which the sun would shine in the mornings, making a kaleidoscope of colours on his paperwork. Each bedroom had a bathroom, which would have been a luxury had there been water, and it was cold at night, with the government ration of a scuttle of coal a day doing little to warm the huge rooms. He thanked the Lord – and Ethel – for George Lowrey, whom she had sent out from Brooklands to be his batman and who knew how to make a good fire from the most meagre resources (and who also kept her informed of her nephew's activities).

On fine mornings before breakfast he went swimming in the river Scarpe, down by the ruined mill. Often Hewson joined him. The water was icy, but Gore-Browne felt *it does the soul good to see the chestnut trees in flower, inhale the scent of lilac from the blossoms all over the ruins, and hear the birds singing*. There were still a few patches of snow around but the air was spring-like. Sometimes they would see a trout splashing in the water and try to catch it for dinner. *One can't forget the war because all the time the shelling is going on*, he wrote, *but it is a few minutes when the mind feels freed of cares*. The last time they had gone, as they passed the ruins of the Hôtel de Ville and entered the city by the Baudimont gate, they had seen rows and rows of poppies on the old walls. *Like scarlet women waiting to enter heaven*, he wrote. *It seems wrong somehow that these processes of nature should go on as normal despite all the devastation around but perhaps it gives hope . . .*

But the war had spread to more and more fronts over the last year and become more complicated with the introduction of gas by the Germans, and it was hard to be hopeful whenever the familiar whine of shells started up again, setting his nerves on edge. *The worst of it is that I know exactly what each can do,* he had once written to Ethel. *Oh Lord, how I hate that whistling sound like a kettle boiling. As it gets nearer and nearer, there are mean little pauses which leave heaps and heaps of time to think about where the shell will land and what it will be like when it bursts.* Clery, one of the captains, had once said to him he couldn't imagine hell being very different. *It's odd really,* wrote Gore-Browne, *I don't fear death and think I can bear pain, but the shells I dislike more than I can describe.* Sometimes 2,000 or more would fall in a single day and some days they would come from three different directions at once, so that the air *buzzed with them like fighting ducks*, reminding him of the music of Strauss. Then for ages afterwards bits of metal would fall sizzling into the mud and patter around.

That night was particularly bad, shells raining down for three hours, explosion after explosion, the three men huddling in the shelter taking the occasional swig of Hewson's cheap whisky, smoking Woodbines down to the butt, and sharing out some emergency chocolate Gore-Browne kept in his pocket. But finally the air stilled, leaving only the background roll of the guns like the tinpan drums of a far off orchestra, and for a moment he thought he could hear an owl hooting.

As soon as the shellfire seemed over for the night, Hewson disappeared into the blackness with a breezy cheerio. Gore-Browne looked over at Tremlett, who seemed to have sunk back into himself. He could think of nothing to say that would not sound trite, and decided it was better to let the lad work out his own grief. He took out his knife and sharpened the pencil in a few deft strokes, then returned to the letter he had been writing to Ethel.

Thank you for the chocolates, and cherries from the garden. Sometimes I wonder if I will ever see Brooklands again. Most of you at home have no idea what this is. The Boche has been putting up a strenuous show tonight, a rain of shells, must have been 1000 . . . And this gas business is loathsome, though our protection is now thunderingly good. Whatever happens I don't think we'll ever be able to regard Germans as anything but a people apart.

We lost one of our best today, Lt. Bowman. He was only a boy, curiously like Kerr and as good as they make them. He'd been through Gallipoli and come onto us and was doing A1. I don't know when I've thought so much of a fellow on short acquaintance. I saw a good bit of him and ran across him only this morning down in the trenches. He stopped and talked for a few minutes, laughed and was full of good cheer. He was one of those folk who do you good so everyone's the better for them. Then he went on his way and I on mine. Ten minutes later a shell hit him. He's still alive, most horribly hurt, and thank the Lord unconscious. One's only hope is that he'll soon be dead. Lord but it's hard, not for him for if ever there was a happy warrior it was he, but for the wife and child (he married a year ago). A fellow like that must leave a gap in scores of lives.

In a way it was those who would have to live on afterwards that he felt most sorry for, presuming the war would eventually finish. Not just the wives and mothers and children, but he often imagined being a French soldier who had fought for two years and come through it all, having to go back and find his house in one of these villages like Arras that were part of the line, left a heap of stones with not even a semblance of houses or streets. So much of the destruction was so wanton. When the Germans went through a place, they seemed to *pull out every single belonging and smash and spoil them.* He had seen one house which must have belonged to a community doctor where they had taken out all the instruments and stamped on them. Another one where the Sunday frocks of a young girl had been ripped into rags. And before they left, they used cooking pots and cupboards and bedrooms as latrines.

I can't imagine now how I could ever have thought of war as a splendid adventure, he wrote to Nunk. How excited and confident he and his fellow soldiers had been before that first battle of Le Cateau on 26 August 1914! They had all thought they would be heroes then. And even after the inglorious retreat at Mons, that time in Messines, when the Boche had shelled the eleventh-century church and all that remained was the wooden crucifix which somehow survived the blazing mass without even being singed, he had written, *we took it as a miracle, a sign that God was on our side and all would be over soon.*

It was the contrast which tore at him. Often the externals, the rows of trees, the white road into the distance, the cosy inns where buxom peasant girls served up vast omelettes and jugs of wine, and the fields in the orange and red sunset, were the same as if he had been making a motor trip in this land he so loved, with Ethel. Yet *not a mile away, or sometimes in the very villages themselves, were mangled bodies and rubble and blood.* His friend Kerr was just one of almost 10 million men who had lost their lives so far. *Numbers beyond comprehension*, he had written to Nunk. *Surely if men are sufficient masters of things to build a Howitzer they ought to know better than to destroy each other with it.* Of course he knew that if they didn't destroy, they'd be destroyed themselves, and not just them, but England and Brooklands and his beloved Ethel . . .

My dearest it's almost impossible to write to you. I can't put on paper the things I'd like to say. You know you are all the world to me and I long for you as a husband longs for a wife when they are really one.

He no longer knew what was going to happen. Even there in divisional headquarters they had little idea about the situation elsewhere. It was common knowledge that General Haig and Marshal Joffre had been discussing a major attack, but where and when was unclear. Kitchener's New Army plan of turning a fighting force of 150,000 into a 3 million-strong machine seemed an impossible dream, though there was no doubt that the recruits had been toughened by the heavy December fighting. All he knew was that when the slaughter came this time it would be pretty bad, worse than anything that had come before.

A few weeks earlier he had received a letter from Bulaya, scribbled in blunt pencil on a page torn from an exercise book. Written in Bemba, peppered with crossings-out, his servant was threatening to enlist, and Gore-Browne carried the letter in his inside jacket pocket, unsure how to respond. He had read and reread the last words numerous times. 'Bwana please let me come and die with you because if you are killed then I should be too.'

Sometimes, like Bulaya, he wondered if it really was the same moon and stars shining here on these battlefields as those reflected in the lake that used to disappear over the hill every night.

He had decided to send Bulaya and Kakumbi back to Africa in the end the previous year before he returned to France, when it was obvious that the show was not going to be over as quickly as everyone had hoped. The Boys had worked as his servants while he was based in Swanage training the 17th Division, and he had managed to take them to London a few times. He would never forget Kakumbi's *big round eyes* at the sight of the gas fire in the Criterion where he had taken them for lunch. 'Fire without wood. *Leca mukula wa na maka sana* – the Great God is very good,' the African had said in his gentle voice, feeling the warmth of wonderment and jumping from the flame as if it were real.

They are like children in many ways, he wrote to Ethel, *so easy to please and so open with their emotions.* He loved to order champagne for them, not to get them drunk – they could not hold their alcohol – but because the bubbles made them so happy. Ethel had already taken them up to town a few times to see the zoo and St Paul's Cathedral which he had suggested so that they could *see what great things men were capable of building once they got beyond the mud hut mentality.* They were no longer so scared of motor cars so he took them across town, showed them 7 Kensington Square and 11 Onslow Gardens, the white Victorian houses in Kensington where he had been born and grown up, and then the Natural History Museum. That was something of a disaster – he had taken them into the dinosaur hall, where Bulaya was so terrified he had tried to bolt. As Gore-Browne recounted later to Ethel, he had explained that before there were men there were dinosaurs, but Kakumbi was having none of it. 'In our land the royal crocodiles and spirits ruled,' he insisted, 'these creatures must be British.' Bulaya was almost hysterical, refusing to believe that dinosaurs had ever existed. Staring at the tyrannosaurus, he asked, 'How could they walk, *bwana*, the heads are too heavy and they would topple over?' The brontosaurus he found funny. 'Its head is too small to eat animals.

Not like the elephant, that is a proper animal.' Bulaya had an awed respect for elephants, having lost his own father to one in the forest near the lake. Then he had seen the pterodactyl, and started screaming, 'God will strike man down for creating such horrible creatures.' So much for education. At that point Gore-Browne had given up, bought them ices to calm them down, and taken them to see a moving picture. They had giggled so much that he had had to take them out before the end to escape the wrath of the frowning usherette and the rest of the audience.

The biggest success of the trip had been the tin soldiers in Selfridge's toy department. '*Wangu, tata*,' Kakumbi had whispered in an awed voice as he picked one after another up from a display and held them gingerly in his palm as if afraid that they would turn their miniature arms on him and run. 'Marvellous my father, how cunning men are.' After Gore-Browne had rescued a clockwork monkey with a drum from the attentions of Bulaya, and helped him choose some glass bangles to take back to his village as presents, he returned to the display and found Kakumbi still staring at the tin soldiers. 'Chief Chitimukulu would have given slaves and ivory and cloth for these. Will you bring some one day to the Bemba country? I would like my mother to see them, tears would run from her eyes.'

'Which ones are your favourites?' asked Gore-Browne, beckoning an astonished shopgirl to come over and serve them. Once he had got his package of soldiers, Kakumbi insisted on clutching it close to him as though it was the most precious thing on earth, and all day kept repeating, '*Wangu tata*, men are very cunning.' Gore-Browne found his simplicity touching.

When he told them he was sending them back to Shiwa, Kakumbi was so excited about all the tales he would have to tell that he rehearsed in great detail what he would say and how everyone would respond, over and over again in front of the mirror in his room in the Waldorf Hotel where they spent the last few nights, the Boys in a room several floors below Gore-Browne's suite. Unfortunately, the last night before he was due to take them by train to Southampton to meet Taggart, a colonial officer friend of Ethel's who was heading back to Northern Rhodesia, and had offered to escort them on board the steamer to Dar es Salaam, Bulaya slipped out of the Waldorf and disappeared. Gore-Browne didn't think he could get far on the fifteen shillings he had given him and went to Bow Street police station to give a description, then had to dispatch poor old Kakumbi on his own. As he boarded the Union Castle boat, Kakumbi bowed to him with a formality that had clearly taken some practising. 'Thank you very much indeed *bwana*, I clap my hands. And if I am not there to greet you *bwana* when you come back to my country then you will know I am dead.'

Some weeks later he received a letter from the police to say that they had found Bulaya working in the kitchen of the Strand Palace Hotel, earning £1 a week. Not surprisingly, shortly afterwards the *little blighter* had got tired of *working for a living and turned up back at Brooklands as cool as if he'd just been away for the day*. Ethel was supposed to arrange Bulaya's passage back to Northern Rhodesia, but Gore-Browne fancied she had become rather fond of the fellow. For all her often abrasive exterior, she was a soft touch and knew Bulaya had lost his mother at an early age, and he wouldn't be surprised if the African was playing on that.

On one of their last nights in London he had taken the Boys to Covent Garden to see *La Bohème*. It was his favourite opera and he had long wanted them to see the colourful costumes, hear the orchestra, *like a great sea of music*, and experience the emotion of the singers, to see whether it touched them in the same way. He had taken a box and enjoyed the way the Boys clutched their seats and the edge of the balcony, mesmerized by the action on stage though understanding nothing. Sometimes in the trenches, he thought back to that evening and tried to hear the music – *the three bars of the overture make one tickle all the way down the backbone* – and replay that haunting first act duet between Mimi and Rodolfo in his head which always made him think of Lorna. But rarely did his imaginary violins succeed in blotting out the shells. *God how I hate them*, he wrote. *I wish the waiting were over.*

Before sealing the letter to Ethel, he added a postscript.

If I am killed I would like a cairn to be put at Shiwa on the spot where our house was to be and the lime trees planted by the side.

5

Lt Col Stewart Gore-Browne
British Army of the Rhine, Cologne

19 October 1919

My very dear

Lorna died in Johannesburg on 27th September. She'd been ill all this year; in her last letter to me she told me of an operation which should have killed her but which had been successful. However it seems she had to have another a month ago and never recovered from it. It seems a week or two but really it's 14 years. She was so wonderfully beautiful and frail too that I expect it's all for the best but she didn't have much happiness in this life.

Do you remember the morning we went over to breakfast at Bingham's Melcombe from Nottingham in Redigonde, when she was just going out hunting? It was the first time I ever saw her and I think I can remember every moment we were together afterwards – after all it wasn't so long.*

The time at Rowners† was such a joy in the early spring. I drove her down from London and we lunched at Dorking and early on Sunday morning we walked to church at Billingshurst

* *Redigonde* was one of Ethel's cars.
†Rowner Mills was the house of Stewart's grandmother Lady Harriet Gore-Browne.

through the fields, all gloriously golden with buttercups. And that morning we went on the river in the canoe and talked such nonsense. She had on a large floppy hat from which some of her hair escaped and seemed flecked with gold in the sun. And once we went to Cambridge in Bird from London, in the same springtime, and picnicked in the meadows and she slept for a while on my shoulder, so close that afterwards my jacket smelt of jasmine – remember that scent she always wore? I took her to the opera one evening – La Bohème of course, watched the tears spill from her eyes at the sadness of it, and felt myself the envy of all to have such a pure unspoilt creature by my side. Then there was that glorious summer day when I went over from Salisbury Plain and found her alone at Bingham's Melcombe – I can tell you literally every moment of that day and night and see it all now as it was. Her dress was lavender, and as I helped put a shawl across her shoulders, her skin was like a pearl in the moonlight. And then that last time of all, at her wedding and our dinner side by side in the panelled white room and all that happened. That was the last time we spoke – except that we danced together once in the drawing room afterwards, it was a waltz but I don't think I even heard the music. I think selfishly that one is awfully lucky to have had this in one's life once anyhow. And as for her she's happy now. It's a very precious and sacred memory and now it can't ever be anything else but a memory. I'm sorry to write this to you, it is probably not appropriate, but you're the only one who knows.

Oh my dearest won't you come to me here? I have a Vauxhall motorcar and a box at the opera, and we can make trips along the Rhine which is just like a picture book with its black and white houses, and talk of the house we will soon build together in Africa.

You will come won't you?

Your S

6

Shiwa Ngandu, Northern Rhodesia,
1 October 1920

Gore-Browne stared at the blue water of the lake shimmering in the fierce sun and, picking up a pebble, tossed it with sudden violence to break the mirror-like surface. He knew the Bemba believed there to be a spirit dwelling in the lake's depths, and some even claimed to have seen it, a kind of beast with smooth dark body and a single ivory horn which they all feared disturbing, but at that moment he didn't care.

For six years he had longed for this place, day and night. He had dreamt of it in the trenches, yearning to shut out the roar of the German guns with its gentle backing orchestra of frogs, sparrows and crickets. He had clung to its image in the darkest moments of battle at Le Cateau and the Somme and all those other endless fields of death when sometimes it seemed as though his African paradise was but a mirage. And when the war was finally over, the Fifth Division wound up, and he had left the army, the brass pip and Tudor crown of a lieutenant-colonel on the shoulders of his uniform and a DSO for his work behind the scenes during the Battle of the Somme, but convinced the war had resulted in too many promotions for him to have a real career there, he wondered if Shiwa Ngandu was any more than a figment of his imagination.

But now finally, he was standing in front of the lake again, his lake, a neatly folded certificate in his pocket from the British South Africa Company, pronouncing Lieutenant-Colonel Stewart Gore-Browne the grand owner of 23,000 acres of land, 11,000 of which had been bought at a shilling an acre, and the rest in the form of grants to ex-soldiers. As he stood watching the concentric circles made by the pebble he had thrown, spreading across the surface, he found it hard to believe. *Here I am*, he wrote to Ethel, *an old Harrovian and graduate of the Royal Military Academy, holder of the DSO, mentioned twice in despatches, not a war hero perhaps but a distinguished war career nevertheless, starting a new life at the age of 37*, and it struck him that *in all those years of my existence and expensive education, I have learnt nothing that will be any use from now on.*

His last post had been as personal staff assistant to Sir William Robertson, the Commander-in-Chief of the British Army of Occupation on the Rhine. The old man had taken a shine to him, insisting Gore-Browne move in with him and his family in *the gilded cage* of their Cologne house, and when he had told him of his intention to leave to create a Utopian community in this isolated spot in Central Africa, had tried his best to deter him. *The C-in-C poured me a large whisky with a dash of soda, sat me down, then paced about the drawing room*, he recounted to Ethel. *Shaking his head, he looked at me and said 'I fail to see the wisdom, old chap, of building an English lifestyle in the wilds of Africa, when you can have a decent place in England. We all know the native will never change his spots.'* Eventually, seeing his assistant was not to be deterred, he had shaken his hand and said, 'Well, I shall be sorry to lose you, Gore-Browne. All I can say is if you do go, roll up your sleeves and don't look back.'

With the Commander's advice ringing in his ears, Gore-Browne had bid farewell to friends and family in England, and on 20 July boarded the P&O ship from Southampton to Cape Town via Madeira. As usual he was struck down with seasickness for the first few days, rarely emerging from his first class cabin for dinner at the Captain's table. He whiled away the long hours in his cabin or on deck by filling a pad with sketches of the beautiful palace and *royal park* with fountains, deer and peacocks that he would create at Shiwa Ngandu, and trying to clear his mind of the absence of the woman for whom he was planning all this and the death of another. By his bunk he had stuck a postcard of a painting entitled *Serenity* by contemporary Italian artist Giovanni Sottocornola.* A pastoral scene, depicting a girl and sheep in the sunlight, he had bought several of the cards in an old bookstore in Venice during a brief trip in March 1918, because it reminded him of Lorna.

From Cape Town he had travelled by train across South Africa and Southern Rhodesia to Victoria Falls, just as he had in 1911, and through Northern Rhodesia to Ndola, the mining settlement at the end of the line. Waiting for him on the platform, big eyes bright with tears, was Kakumbi, keeping his promise, made on Southampton docks five years earlier, to be the first to welcome him back. Clad in the uniform of the King's African Rifles, which he had joined for the latter part of the war, the African bent down clapping with his familiar laugh of delight, and asked, 'Did you have trenches in France, *bwana*?'

Alongside him, though more restrained in his welcome, was an Army colleague, Lt. Charles Austin, formerly of the King's Royal Rifle Corps and Gore-Browne's orderly in Cologne, who was just twenty-two and nicknamed Child for his fresh-faced appearance and sulky temper. They were to meet up with Major Walter Cowie, a twenty-seven-year-old former farm labourer who had served with Gore-Browne in the Fifth

*Giovanni Sottocornola (1855–1917), an Italian artist who specialized in pastoral scenes.

Division on the Somme and had come on ahead. Of very different backgrounds to his own – Austin was the son of a draper born above his father's shop in Romford – they were *not quite what one would have chosen as companions*, he confided to Ethel, *but one white man alone here would achieve little*, and they were the only ones eager to come on what they laughingly termed 'the Great African Adventure'. Austin was to look after the accounts while Cowie would be in charge of ploughing and planting. Not having Gore-Browne's kind of money, they had travelled out on cheaper routes.

So much of Africa is waiting, Gore-Browne had once written to Ethel during his days drawing up the border, and he was impatient, though not surprised, that it took some days to round up the forty porters he had arranged to accompany them, carrying his luggage the 400 miles to Shiwa Ngandu. Knowing it would be months before they saw a general store again, they stocked up on supplies such as flour and sugar. Eventually the party set off from Ndola, the white men dressed in khaki helmets, shirts and shorts, and white stockings, and the carriers walking behind. They followed a different route from the one he had used back in 1914, taking advantage of the water-passage that had been opened up by the Army for supplying troops to East Africa during the war. This involved a seventy-mile march across the Congo pedicle to Kapalala, his line of bearers in tow carrying on their heads all manner of trunks and household effects – bicycles, tin baths, wheelbarrows, crates of china, crystal glasses, chests of bedlinen, cushions and curtains, paintings, guns, a brass telescope, a chandelier, fine wines, boxes of biscuits, a typewriter and a Union Jack. Knowing he probably wouldn't get back to England for at least a couple of years, Gore-Browne had brought everything he could think of. Each morning as they set off there was a tremendous scramble among the porters to try to get the lightest load from the mountainous pile. Some things like the full-length antique mirror and the gilt-framed oil-painting of his grandmother took two men to carry, and Gore-Browne had harsh words for the porters when he caught them stumbling carelessly. *We must look quite a sight*, he wrote to Ethel, *the long procession of black men dressed in the red shirts and shorts I brought them, snaking along through swamps and over hills with all these packages on their heads, protected on each flank by others with spears and old Kakumbi of course in front with a rifle, spear and hunting knife.*

From Kapalala it was a ten-day trip in large dugout canoes up the Luapula river through a vast plain dotted with clumps of tree and park, and game which he had to refrain himself from stopping and shooting, knowing they should press on. There were four canoes, two for the white men with cushioned deckchairs to sit on and a sun canopy overhead, and two for the luggage and remaining porters. Each was rowed by six to eight natives, skilled in dodging rapids as well as hippos which occasionally surfaced and could easily upturn a canoe. At night they camped on the river banks, dining on the plentiful wildfowl and trying to identify the sounds of the bush. Eventually they reached Nsumbu on the shores of Lake Bangweulu, which lived up to its evocative Bemba name meaning 'where the water meets the sky'. It was a spectacular sight, with hundreds of little islands and inlets of water surrounded by marshland and papyrus grass full of shoebill storks, which Cowie said looked like dodos, and herds of black lechwe, a small antelope indigenous to the area. *There were so many that Child insisted there must be a million*, Gore-Browne wrote to Ethel. *It was tempting to linger but I told them there will be plenty of time for that later. So we watched a vast herd of elephants crossing the horizon in a long line, trunk to tail, then pressed on.*

Fighting off mosquitoes which hovered in clouds over the marshy land, they paddled up the Chambeshi river, disembarking at an abandoned rubber factory which had belonged to the British South Africa Company. The last seventy miles were again on foot, tramping across swamps, pulling off leeches and watching out for crocodiles which looked for all the world like black logs until they lifted scaly heads to show their glassy eyes. Eventually they started climbing, up over ridges and hills which Kakumbi told them were known as the mountains of the Sleeping Chiefs. According to legend, seven rival chiefs, meeting to try to resolve a drought which was causing widespread famine among the Bemba, had frozen to death lying on the mountain-tops because each was too important to light a fire and none of them trusted allowing up servants faithful to the others. As Gore-Browne and his party climbed, listening to Kakumbi's story, puttees protecting their legs from the spiky grass, as they stumbled over rocks scattered in a kind of moonscape, they passed through pockets of butterflies which fluttered alongside them for long stretches – *swallowtails, red admirals, peacocks, identified by Austin who has an interest in such things and all somehow larger and brighter than any one had seen in England.*

They approached the valley of the lake from the north side, just as Livingstone had done more than half a century before, the old explorer weary and sick with fever. As they mounted the last hill, Nachipala or Bareback, *the air all the time becoming purer and sweeter*, Gore-Browne felt his breath quickening with anticipation, and then *suddenly there it was*, the valley spread out below, a patchwork of light and dark squares of bush, drier and browner than on his previous visit. A grove of violet jacarandas formed a kind of wedding bower below, and shining in the centre was the lake, just as beautiful as he had left it, a little smaller perhaps, awaiting the rains. The wind lapped at the trees, and swallows ducked and dived across the valley as if it were their very own playground. *Without my needing to say a word, we all stopped and fell silent*, he wrote, *even Austin halting his ceaseless chatter*.

It had taken them three weeks to reach Shiwa Ngandu from Ndola, the nearest civilization *if indeed one can call it that*, and the three white men lifted their field-glasses and regarded the panorama for a while. To their right, to the west of them, a series of rocky hills went right down to the lake, a continuation of the range they had been crossing. Gore-Browne pointed out the Mansya river, flowing out of the west of the lake and through a gap in the hills to eventually join up with the Chambeshi, and told them of the cave, deep in the mountains, which the village people had taken him to see before he left, as a farewell present. Said to be a secret place of the Bemba spirits which no white man had ever seen, he had had to wriggle about thirty feet on his stomach to get in, and once inside there seemed to be nothing but bats and guano. *More pungent than spiritual*, he had written to Ethel at the time. Austin was excited by his tale, speculating that they might find hidden gold mines or treasures of ancient kings, prompting Gore-Browne to joke, 'You've been reading too much Rider Haggard!'

Directly across the lake, to the south, was a wide open space dotted with dark shapes, which through the lenses of the glasses could be identified as zebra, waterbuck, puku, and eland with their strange black corrugated horns, and which Cowie referred to as 'our very own on-site butchers'. Gore-Browne pointed out an area he had identified as good grazing land to keep cattle. The two men followed his gaze to their left, slightly to the east, to a stretch of green springy grass about a mile or so wide between the woods and the lake.

Cowie thought it looked too marshy, suggesting they might try growing rice instead.

Finally Gore-Browne showed them the spot where he planned to build his big house, on the north side, just beneath where they were standing, so it would be sheltered from the wind and rain by the hills and never get the sun directly. He wanted to make sure that the terrace, which would run all along the front, would always have shade. Below, where the gradient was gentler, going down in terraces towards the lake, would be the gardens.

As they started walking down the hill, laughing at the grey honeyguide bird calling insistently to point out honey in the bark of a thorny tree, they felt the ground thud with the pounding of drums. Messengers had gone ahead to the village a few days earlier to warn of their arrival, and when they reached the jacaranda grove at the bottom they were surrounded by small boys doing what he called the *Elisha before Ahab act, girding up their loins if they had anything to gird them with and running in front, laughing and chattering among themselves*. '*Mwasibukeni*', he said, using the Bemba expression for 'good morning', and the children fell about giggling, as they chanted back the usual response: '*Eyamukwayi!*'

The drumming got louder as they approached and a proud Kakumbi led them into a clearing of small beehive-shaped windowless mud huts. There was a sort of collective shudder and the villagers threw themselves on the ground, clapping their hands with a long scissor movement of the arms and rolling around. One man with an unruly beard stepped in front of their path, unleashing a shower of unintelligible words, not stopping to draw breath. Gore-Browne, having experienced this before during his work on the Boundary Commission, explained that the chief must have come to the village to greet them and this was his praise-singer who would lead them to him, singing their praises, much to Cowie and Austin's amusement.

They followed the praise-singer to the largest of the huts, that of Chikwanda, the headman, plastered with white clay and decorated with a row of diamond shapes fashioned from terracotta and brown-coloured muds. Outside, a group of bare-breasted big-lipped women were dancing, hips swaying sultrily to the drumbeat and strings of shells clattering round their ankles. The praise-singer stopped and gestured for the white men to enter. Gore-Browne pinched Cowie's arm to stop him gaping at the women and, following his lead, the two younger men removed their topees and ducked to enter the low doorway. 'Keep your right hands visible so they can see you don't have firearms,' he warned them. Inside they all blinked rapidly as they tried to adjust their eyes to the dark interior.

Chikwanda, the wizened little headman, who had worked for Gore-Browne on the Border Commission, greeted him, then led them to where the old chief Mukwikile was seated on a carved wooden chair. By one side was a platform spread with several reed mats, which was presumably the bed. With his palms together as if in prayer, the chief waved them to squat on the wooden stools around him, low to the mud floor. He looked *incredibly old and benign*, thought Gore-Browne, *like a black-faced drawing of God in a children's picture-book*, and on either cheek was a deep rectangular indentation. 'Welcome.' He and Gore-Browne exchanged greetings in Bemba, a lengthy process involving polite inquiries over fathers and fathers' fathers. The chief nodded, then clicked his fingers, and a villager appeared, crawling forward on his belly, bearing a large gourd of pungent brown liquid.

Seeing Cowie's look of alarm, Gore-Browne explained in

whispers that the liquid was *nsupa*, a special bowl of the local brew. Made at harvest time, around August, the villagers would waste half their maize on it, then wonder why they ran out half-way through the year. According to Bemba lore, if the *nsupa* is good, the gods are pleased and the next harvest will be good. Gore-Browne lifted the cup and supped noisily to show his appreciation. Cowie and Austin followed suit, the former rolling his eyes as he tasted the bitter liquid. Another mutual exchange of compliments followed between the chief and Gore-Browne, then a long silence while everyone looked at each other. Finally, at a nod from the chief, Chikwanda bustled them back out into the bright sunlight, where headmen from a few other nearby villages came forward with greetings and presents. *I felt pleased that my people were putting on a good show in front of my companions*, Gore-Browne wrote to Ethel.

Gore-Browne's delight over their elaborate welcome did not last long. As he walked around the estate, he saw with mounting irritation that all the careful preparations he had made in the three months he had spent there in 1914 had gone to waste. The avenue of fruit trees which he had planted had withered away and died; the thatch-roofed house he had built to guard his things had burnt down; the cow-shed had collapsed and the one bull and five cows he had left behind had mysteriously turned into ten small bulls; the irrigation channels he had dug to run from the stream were choked with weeds and, though he had planted many seeds bought from missions, there was nothing growing at all in the way of crops. About the only thing left to show he had ever been there was the footbridge he had constructed over the small Katete river between his house and the village. Africa was clearly not to be dominated easily, even by an English gentleman. Admittedly he had only expected to be away six months, not six years. Nevertheless he was furious with Chikwanda, whom he had left in charge and had intended to appoint his *capitao* or foreman. *I had to struggle to rein in my temper as I saw the extent of the neglect*, he admitted to Ethel. *I didn't want to frighten the bantu off just at the start of things. Instead I walked to the shore of the lake wondering whether people were right after all when they said you cannot trust the native.*

The lake at least was as enchanting as he remembered, *a giant sapphire nestling in a bed of green hills.* It was good too, to breathe the air of Africa again, that smell of *virgin land, of nature in full-force, of ancient earth and beasts that have passed through, and just a slight hint of threat.* But it was the end of the dry season and the green luxuriance which had so impressed him back in 1914 had been replaced by the brown scrub of land parched after seven months without rains. The sun beat down with a brightness which hurt the eyes and seemed to reflect off every leaf and blade of grass so there was no escaping it. The place seemed quieter too; there was a stillness, almost as if everything – bird, tree, man and even crocodile – was waiting to catch that first drop of rain.

As he thought about all there was to do and how ill-qualified he was for the task, Gore-Browne felt a growing despondency. He tossed another pebble into the water, and as it broke the surface the silence of the place was interrupted by a fish-eagle wheeling overhead, parading its broad black and white wings and yellow eyes. For a moment he seemed to hear the name Ethel, Ethel, Ethel in its haunting cry. *I wonder what you are doing now*, he wrote. *I wish so much you were here so I could show off the place, walk with you and feel that god-like strength your presence always bestows.* He suddenly felt very alone. He wasn't, of course. But having Cowie and Austin wasn't like having someone like old Kerr, *one of our own sort*, an old friend with whom he had shared motor tours, hunts and dances in their gilded youth and who he had hoped would be his manager but instead lay under the cold earth of a field in Ypres. Shaking off his gloom, he wandered up the hill to join the others where the bearers were setting up camp in a glade by the Katete river, a little way off from the lake shore.

A table had been set for tea under the shade of an acacia tree, and looking at it, the Minton china with the family crest, Gore-Browne thought it had definitely been worth the effort of bringing so much stuff from England, and set a good example to the native. *My gear looks so nice*, he wrote to Ethel, *the table with the clean white cloth, shining silver knives and the cockioly bird china cups, plates and teapot. They look like they belong to a person of substance. I loathe the kind of Englishman who travels with folding tables and enamel mugs as if he'd purchased all his things in a general store.*

The afternoon was hot with a strong dry wind, and finding Cowie mopping sweatbeads from his pink forehead with a grubby handkerchief, Gore-Browne reassured him that the temperature would drop considerably in the evening, Shiwa being about 4,700 feet above sea level, and that they would probably even need a fire, not just for keeping lions at bay. Cowie looked unconvinced, muttering about missing the English climate. 'It's the same every day here, Gorey,' he complained, 'hot sun, blue skies. Why can't we have the occasional grey sky or drizzle?' Gore-Browne had no such yearnings. Back in England it was now autumn – his least favourite season. *I can look back on autumn after autumn and remember with sinking dread the coming of each*, he had once written to Ethel. *I'm sure you and I are meant to live in warm places.* The only thing he missed was the smell of chestnuts roasting on the library fire, those dark afternoons at Brooklands while they sat round reading books, playing draughts or conversing with interesting visitors.

He found it astonishing how Cowie always contrived to look so crumpled, considering they had plenty of servants to shave them and wash and press their clothes. Cowie was of hefty build, his muscles evident through his sweat-dampened khaki shirt, and had been a farm labourer before the war so knew about ploughing and breaking in oxen. Although he was ten years younger than Gore-Browne, he had plenty of experience of life and was a no-nonsense chap, which Gore-Browne appreciated – *I detest insincerity above all.* But his language tended to be of the colourful variety with little use of the letter 'h' and, as Ethel would say, his was 'the kind of background that would not bear too much inspection'. Gore-Browne had been surprised when Cowie agreed to come, not just because of the difficulty in scraping together the fare, but also because he had once mentioned he was engaged to a girl back home in England.

Austin had been Gore-Browne's orderly for his last six months in Cologne, and they were well used to each other. Beanpole thin and living up to his Army nickname, 'Child', he had a tendency to sulk when he didn't like things and *can be rather jumpy, but otherwise he is full of energy and enthusiasm for life*. Both men were superb shots and had been awarded Military Crosses for their bravery in the war, with Austin leading a daring raid behind enemy lines.

His original plan had been to have three partners in on the scheme – a farmer, an engineer and a business manager. Cowie and Austin were none of those things, and by the end of the three weeks travelling from Ndola together he was already pondering the wisdom of inviting them. They weren't going to get much other company at Shiwa, so far from anywhere, with no roads, only porters' tracks and elephant trails, though for Gore-Browne its remoteness was one of the attractions. He liked the fact that they were far away from the racial policies of South Africa and Southern Rhodesia which he found *hard to stomach*. And he was not such a lover of his fellow men as to want to be constantly surrounded by them. *Better just to have those one really wants around, and make a trip back to London every year or so for music and shopping, and perhaps France for some fine dining*, he wrote.

His liking for solitude was just as well, as there were fewer than 4,000 white men living in the whole country at that time, and most of these lived far off, round the railway line which had been extended to Broken Hill in 1906 and Ndola in 1909, bisecting the country. The biggest employers were the lead and zinc mines at Broken Hill and the copper mine at Ndola. What white farming there was tended to be in the far east and north-east beyond Shiwa, growing tobacco and keeping cattle. The country's million or so natives lived as they always had on subsistence agriculture, growing finger millet.

He just hoped it would not be a problem running a farm so far away from any market. *I'm not expecting to make a fortune, just live in the way to which one is accustomed*, he wrote to Nunk. He thought his own income from his trust fund investments, his father, and Army pension would be sufficient, coming to about £1,000 per year, along with the occasional cheque from Ethel, who had been slipping him money since he was a schoolboy. Now he was heir to Brooklands, he had no qualms in taking more. Most of the materials they would need were to be found free all around – wood from the forest for building and fuel, clay for bricks and plaster from the earth, grass for thatch. Labour was cheap and plentiful – there were a hundred or so villagers living round the lake, the rest having been frightened off by the crocodiles, but he was quite sure others would come once they heard there was money to be earned. The British administration had set a hut tax of ten shillings a year, and for most of the Bemba the only way to pay was for the menfolk to go and work in the mines, which was no kind of life. He could train some of the better-looking ones as house servants and as long as there was some way to get hold of the stuff that really mattered in life, the fine wines, the port, the cigars, good books and *the beautiful things one likes to have around one*, then he couldn't see any real difficulty. It was not as though there was much competition.

Austin, who had been washing in the river, came over to join them, and after tea and biscuits Gore-Browne took them for a walk round the estate, commenting from time to time on his plans. They looked at the Katete, which seemed to come from a spring somewhere up the mountain, as a potential water and power source. *The water is so pure and clear and fast running that if it were not for the palm trees it would look like a highland stream*, he wrote to Nunk, adding that he hoped they might even be able to use it to power a sawmill.

Cowie was less than enthusiastic about the soil, which he said was so light and sandy that it would not endure more than a couple of years of staple crops like maize. Shiwa's vast distance from potential markets, 1,000 miles from any port, meant that whatever they produced would have to be something of high value and easy to transport, such as nuts and sunflowers to produce oils, or flowers and fruits for perfume essence.

Gore-Browne hoped money was not going to be a source of tension. The plan was for Shiwa to be run as a partnership, with him holding two shares as he had paid for the land, and the others one each. But Cowie had had to borrow money from his godfather and Gore-Browne just to pay the fare, and neither

Cowie nor Austin had had any capital to put into the scheme, the idea being that as money was made, their share of the dividends would be ploughed back to pay off their debts.

Discussing different possibilities, they walked more than Gore-Browne had intended, and by the time they returned to camp the sun was setting over the hills, leaving the sky like an opal with the evening star blazoned upon it. Darkness came suddenly and with it the usual hum of crickets, backed by the occasional bassoon sound of one of the hippo in the lake. Listening to the relaxing sound, Gore-Browne remembered the years of living under roaring guns and the scream of shells, and how he had longed for quiet. Considering war was one of the few things the three men had in common, he thought it strange how little they talked about it, almost as if there was a tacit agreement that some things are better left unspoken. Austin, he knew, had nightmares, and jumped at the sudden noise of a far-off roar, followed by an almost female crying, a hyena waiting for the remains of a lion kill perhaps.

Back at the camp a fire was crackling away, and finding themselves inadequately dressed for the sudden drop in temperature, they settled gratefully around it. Kakumbi appeared before them, kitted out in one of the smart uniforms of white calico shirt and scarlet Bermuda shorts and fez which Gore-Browne had spent £60 on buying for his personal staff.

'Cocktails, *bwana*?'

Gore-Browne looked at Kakumbi in surprise, then laughed. *He has Brooklands manners now*, he wrote to Ethel.

'I think we'll have some champagne to celebrate our arrival.' It would work out, he thought, looking out at the world of stars beyond the rim of the firelight and fancying that they were the first Europeans since Livingstone to see them from that point. It had to.

*

After dinner of impala leg grilled on the fire, tasting strangely like lamb, and served with redcurrant jelly which they managed to find in a big hamper that he had brought out from Fortnum & Mason, Gore-Browne retired early to his tent, tired by the long journey. He lay on his camp bed, rifle by his side, reading *The Life of Rhodes* by the light of a hurricane lamp. Finding it hard to concentrate with all the bush sounds, so different from those at home, his thoughts turned to Ethel and that last night at Brooklands. He had not wanted her to go to Southampton to see him off, knowing *walking away would be too unbearable*, and after Nunk had gone to bed, they had stayed up smoking and talking until the sky was streaked with morning pink. It was an odd night, chatting about acquaintances and trivialities *as if I were just off to visit the parents at Oakley, rather than the other side of the globe with no return date.*

He carried the lamp over to the portable writing desk which he had set up in the corner. On top was a photograph of Ethel in a silver frame, and a pack of writing paper embossed with the address Shiwa Ngandu, Northern Rhodesia, which he had had printed in London. He took the cap off the gold Mont Blanc pen which Ethel had given him as a farewell present, and addressed an envelope to Dame Ethel Locke King. She had been awarded the title for her work for the Red Cross during the war and as he told her at the time *there could be no one more deserving*. Writing quickly, the pen flying across five sheets in succession, he started recounting the day's events. Before signing off, he wrote one last line. *Oh dearest, do let's come out here and try to keep the little corner of the world we can influence, decent and upright and uncontaminated.*

He had no idea if she would come. He took heart from the fact that she kept hung in her bedroom the small painting of Napoleon which he had sent her for her birthday in 1916, just before the Battle of the Somme. It had been the only thing left hanging in a ruined house in Arras after massive shelling, and one of the battery commanders had fetched it for him, so that he could send it to her with a note: *There's only you . . . I'm with you all the time.*

On his last night at Brooklands before departing for Africa, when the small talk had finally run out and he knew he could not bear to go away leaving the most important thing unresolved, he had asked her when she would be joining him at Shiwa, pointing out as he had again and again in his letters how remote the place was, almost as if to say that no one would see them there. She had turned away, placed another cigarette in her holder, inclining her head as he lit it for her, and blown out a blue smoke ring as she loved to do.

'Stewart,' she said, 'you know you are like a son to us, the son Hugh and I never had.'

But from the endearments in their letters, it was clear the relationship had gone beyond this. Gore-Browne bowed his head, remembering how she had once written to him, 'Didn't they teach you anything at Harrow, young Stewart? Don't you remember your Seventh Commandment? One promises to be faithful, and if one is not, one is a liar and breaks one's word. I think we both know how we feel about that.'

A draught of chill air blew in through the open door and when Gore-Browne looked up, she had gone. He heard the sound of the fifth stair, the one that always creaked.

7

Shiwa Ngandu, 10 February 1922

He was woken at sunrise as usual by what he had taken to calling the *Valkyrie bird*. He had written to Ethel, *music is what I miss most out here in the bush*, telling her that the little orange sunbird in the magnolia tree outside the window of his thatch-roofed cottage, *delights in teasing me by singing Wagner's doom motif over and over as if it were the only tune it knew*.

There was a knock at the door of his bedroom and Kakumbi appeared with the usual morning tray of hot cocoa and biscuits. Gore-Browne rose from his bed and dressed in the long khaki trousers and white cotton shirt that had been laid ready as always. He fastened his leather belt, tucking in his knife, fitted his eye-glass, squinting a little, placed some pens and his notebook in his top pocket, shook his newly shined boots to make sure there were no scorpions inside, and rang the dressing bell. A small boy scuttled in to tie the laces, addressing him as *'bwana golo'* – the closest most Bemba could get to Gore, as, unable to say the letter 'r', they always pronounced it as 'l'.

Gore-Browne was in a good mood – it was Friday which was mail day and he was due a letter from Ethel. There had been nothing for the previous two weeks. *Perhaps the boat has been held up*, he wrote to her, *or maybe you have been busy with another visit from the King of Spain or some such dignitary . . . I never cease to marvel how a letter posted by*

Webster [one of the Brooklands staff] *in the little Weybridge post office can appear a few weeks later at my hut in the jungle in the brown hand of Kakumbi.* His own local post office was more than 400 miles away at Broken Hill, and he was still stirred by the sight of the mailman appearing in the moonlight on a bicycle in his scarlet uniform, a rifle on his back in case of lions, to take his letters through the forest and across the river.

Ethel had written that Bulaya was planning finally to come home to Northern Rhodesia and Gore-Browne was awaiting the dates of the ship. *I'm looking forward to seeing the little scallywag again and hearing all his adventures*, he wrote. After fleeing the kitchens of the Strand Palace Hotel for the sanctuary of Brooklands, the African had ended up enlisting as threatened, and had served with the Middlesex Regiment in France and then in Palestine. According to Ethel he had learnt to read and write English and become *quite a dandy* – a regular novelty at her dinner-table.

He opened the wooden shutters to let in the sun, watching its rays stretch across the room like a heavenly host, trapping the dust in its path. It was a lovely day with a light wind from the east. The Bemba called these calm periods between rains *chilalas*, and he wrote in his diary, *I had forgotten how wonderfully crisp the air can be.* In the living-room of his mud-walled cottage, which leaked when it rained, he could hear Elizabeth, the bushbaby he was trying to tame, chattering in her box. As he passed by she looked up with what he described as *her great big beguiling eyes.* The embers in the fireplace were still glowing and the clock on the mantelpiece was showing almost 6.15 a.m. During the rainy season, that was time for morning muster parade when workers would be assigned their daily tasks, and the bugle would sound at any moment.

The work-rate had improved enormously since he had replaced Chikwanda as head *capitao* with Peter Mulemfwe, his old hunter from the Border Commission, whom he had once described to his mother as *beautifully made with shiny black limbs*. Chikwanda was *a nice old soul* but Gore-Browne had completely lost patience with him after the first house had fallen down because the wrong sort of wood had been used as supports. Chikwanda's men had taken it from the trees in the grove by the village which were decaying, and it had all gone rotten and collapsed. *Chikwanda must have known that the mushitu wood wouldn't last*, he wrote to Ethel. Wandering around with the zebra-tail whip and assegai he always carried, Peter seemed much more thorough. An expert hunter and tracker, he had taught Gore-Browne much of what he knew.

As it was, the first house had been something of an experiment and would only ever have been a guest-house in the end. This time round he decided to start work directly on the manor house of his childhood dreams. It would probably take some years, but in the meantime he, Cowie and Austin could live quite comfortably in the thatch-roofed cottages they had built – a four-roomed one for him and a smaller one shared by the other two, as well as a separate kitchen hut. Mulemfwe's men had measured out the ground for the big house, and were currently building the wooden structure as well as beginning the bricklaying of the foundations. The house was to face south on a slight raise in front of Bareback Hill, or what they sometimes referred to as Livingstone's mountain – the place from which both they and the great explorer had first descended into the valley. *It is set back from the lake but with a spectacular view*, he wrote to Ethel, *and on the right side of the lake not to blow any mosquito*.

He still hadn't really decided what style the house would

be. Almost every day he looked through the sketchpads filled with drawings of houses from his travels round the Loire and Tuscany and his favourite English and Scottish estates, and experimented with new designs comprising parts of each. It had to have plenty of arches, a large terrace for sundowners and a grand library. He planned to have a courtyard in the centre, perhaps with a fountain, and imposing drawing- and dining-rooms with large stone fireplaces. He fancied the idea of a tower where he could set up his telescope, and a billiard-room like Brooklands, but wasn't quite sure of the logistics of getting a billiard-table out to Shiwa. In some of his sketches he had included a family chapel alongside.

Shiwa's vast distance from anywhere made it impractical to import building materials, and they were having to rely on what they could find on the estate for everything other than glass for the windows, which he had ordered from the store at Broken Hill. But he was determined the place should have as English an air as possible, like Brooklands or Bingham's Melcombe, so they were making red bricks from clay taken from the vast pinnacle-shaped anthills dotted around, and roof tiles from the white clay in the mud by the Mansya river, following instructions in the Army building manual he had brought with him, along with *Mitchell's Advanced Course in Building Construction*, and doubling the quantities to make walls thick enough to withstand the African heat and rain. The two books had become their bibles and, using them, they had successfully built a kiln to bake the bricks and tiles. He wrote to Ethel that he found the work quite rewarding, *a whole new side of the universe, having come from the class of people who always have things grown for them and bred and killed and cooked, without ever having to worry about how*, and he laughed to think of all those useless Greek and Latin declensions that had so tortured his mind at Harrow.

A fellow who had spent his entire life on board ship and never seen or tasted anything that hadn't come out of cold storage, would hardly be more ignorant, he wrote.

As on most days, Mulemfwe was the first to greet him, tipping his fez, and wishing him a good morning.

'Morning, Peter. Work going well?'

'Oh yes, *bwana*, we are going to make here the most wonderful house in all of Africa. Chiefs will line up to visit. People will come from all round the world to see.'

'Glad to hear it,' he smiled, pleased with his foreman's keenness. *The house will be wonderful*, he told Ethel. *Or at any rate it won't be in anyway commonplace.* He had written to her more than once of his horror at *the commonplace houses the white man manages to construct in the tropics*, criticizing farmers, colonial officers and missionaries alike.

'How many bricks are we up to a day?' he asked, taking out his notebook.

'Almost a thousand, bwana. Nine hundred and eighty-four it was yesterday.'

'Good man. Now let's try and get it up to fourteen hundred.'

The whole village had turned out to make bricks, as well as some other Bemba who, to Gore-Browne's delight, had returned to the lake on hearing of the 'mad English *bwana*' and the chance to earn a few shillings. Having never seen a building made from bricks before, they were all intrigued by the process and everyone wanted to join in. 'We had seen Europeans before and knew they liked building houses,' recalls Paramount Chief Chitimukulu, who as a young boy worked as a brick carrier at Shiwa, 'but we had never seen anything like this and it was wonderful to see right in the middle of the bush.' Already the biggest employer in the whole Chinsali District, Gore-Browne had 110 people on the work register; men at 5d a day, and women and children at 2d. Two men cut the clay out of anthills and the river bed, then others took it to a pit where it was mixed with water brought from the river by small boys. The women mixed the mud and carried it from the kneading pit to the brickmaker who cut and levelled it into a rectangular mould. Once the bricks were made, the women then carried them on their heads to the drying floor, *making a jolly sight*, Gore-Browne noted in his diary, *walking with that classic grace which English women seem to have lost. Behind them follow the old chief and his wife, rounding them up, everyone singing all the while. By mid-morning the whole place is resonant with harmony as different work-gangs go back and forth in various directions, all singing.* Some came with bundles of grass for thatching, others with poles and blocks of wood which they took to Cowie and Austin who were in charge of the carpentry, building the wooden frame for the house as well as furniture. Gore-Browne smiled as he saw a group of children, none of whom looked older than five, carrying spears, returning from an expedition to search for lime. They had obviously been successful and had chalked their faces with it, causing the dogs to bark in fright.

I feel like a missionary but without the hymn singing, he wrote, watching the scene. He assured his aunt and uncle that he was not about to start urging the natives to copy white man's ways, and give up their beer-drinking, drumming and polygamy, though he had no qualms about dressing them in European clothes. In fact he hoped that in years to come the skills he was imparting would be passed on, so that the children and grandchildren of his workers would be building their own red-brick houses rather than primitive mud huts. He told Ethel:

It seems a wonderfully right state of affairs and a very desirable kind of socialism. I am cleverer and better equipped than these people so they all work to provide me with what I want, a roof and a garden, but I get them meat and protect their crops from marauding eland and find them money for their tax and few luxuries they can't get otherwise . . . Also if an enemy came and burnt their houses or carried off their women, they'd expect me to take up their cause. It's a fair arrangement and we don't pretend we're all equal which we obviously aren't and when I pass through the village, they fall down and clap their hands and shout my praises. But I know that if I renege on my side of the bargain and take their crops or rape their women, they would soon rise up. In the old days they would have killed me, now I suppose they would go to the magistrate. Or maybe not.

After a quick check on progress on the goat-house and Austin's vegetable patch, where there was still little sign of growth, he walked round to what would be the front of the house where the terraced gardens were being laid out. A family of monkeys were leaping from tree to tree, prancing along the branches with their tails standing erect like question marks, chattering in delight, while down below Kakumbi and twenty small boys hacked away at the long grass. As usual Kakumbi was talking *the most utter rubbish in Bemba*, to which the children paid not the slightest bit of attention, and Gore-Browne noted it down to recount to Ethel later.

'There you are, you'll cut your fingers with the sickles . . . you can't use the mess knives . . . if you don't cut your own fingers you'll cut each other's legs . . . I never saw such a lot of useless children. The chief's dog is watching you, she's the right sort of overseer, you'll see . . . the chief'll just tell her the name of anyone who's not working properly and she'll run off and bite him straight away . . .'

In the end Gore-Browne couldn't keep quiet any longer, telling him, 'Kakumbi, you don't stop for breath!'

The servant hadn't seen him and scrambled to his feet, while the children sniggered. 'Oh *bwana*, sorry *bwana* . . .' he said, 'but it's the only way to get these terrible children to work.'

Gore-Browne stood for a while watching the children whom he described to Ethel as *looking like little Pucks as they skipped around.* Once the house was ready, he planned to build shops and schools and order them books from England. *I really feel I can do some good here in a way I never could back home where I am so utterly subordinate*, he wrote to his aunt. *There is so much to teach the black man and pitching him into the mines isn't the way, nor is making him sing hymns.* But his usual contempt for missionaries had been confounded by the local Presbyterian missionary, the Reverend Macminn, a scholarly middle-aged man, and his wife, who were his nearest neighbours, living at Lubwa Mission some sixty miles away. *They are well-meaning people and educated too*, he told Ethel, *the sort one doesn't at all mind having at one's dinner table.* It was just as well, as there were only eight Europeans in the whole north-eastern district of Chinsali including himself, Cowie and Austin, a Native Commissioner and a storekeeper, though not far to the south there was a mission of French Roman Catholic White Fathers at Chilonga. Macminn was from Ayrshire so knew the Campbell branch of his family – relatives of his grandmother, Lady Harriet, and had surprised Gore-Browne by being very supportive of what he was trying to do at Shiwa, telling him that he was always hearing natives discussing them and their ways and marvelling at it all. *I wish Father could hear that when he talks about my 'useless life' and writes such disparaging letters*, he moaned to Ethel, *or Mother when she reminds me of Father's knighthood and important work and then says 'I never thought I'd have a son who was a farmer', or Aunt Mabel who keeps insisting to everyone back home that this place is the abode of the Devil.*

Jotting a few notes in the estate book, he set off the mile or so to the lakeside to have a look at the ploughing. It never ceased to amaze him how much there was to do. He laughed when he remembered how Father had always derided farmers for doing nothing but sitting and looking at the crops coming up. *I'm not exactly a farmer yet*, he wrote to Nunk in his regular progress report. *I have no crops as such, yet I get up before sunrise and don't seem to have a second spare each day.*

The sky was clearest blue, a wintry chill in the air tingling the skin, and the lake still. Down by the shore a few sitatunga were grazing, strange dark antelopes with webbed feet, long legs and high hooves which made them look as if they were walking on stilettos and elaborately curled horns. He had told Cowie that he fancied a few sets of those on the walls of his future dining-room, but they had yet to bag any. The sitatunga fled as soon as they sensed his approach, shy as ever. A white heron paddled elegantly in the shallows, tipping its long curved neck into the water every so often to pluck out a fish. There were hippo tracks down to the water, the animals presumably having been out on one of their nocturnal excursions to munch their way through another hundred pounds or so of vegetation, and a little way out he thought he could just see a pair of pink-rimmed eyes and two grey ear tips disappearing under the dark water. He waited for a while for them to surface, knowing that hippos could only stay five or six minutes fully underwater.

The lake never failed to raise Gore-Browne's spirits, and, listening to the lively 'cheechoo-wee' cries of a band of violet sunbirds, he hoped that the rains were over and they could get back to ploughing on a regular basis. They now had twelve oxen, and Cowie had taught Austin and some of the lads how to plough. Ox-drawn ploughs were rare in Northern Rhodesia, and completely new to the Bemba, who were traditionally hunter-gatherers, and it was a slow process – about a quarter of an acre a day with a small boy leading the oxen, one man driving them and another man ploughing. They could only do it from 6 a.m. to 11 a.m. because after that it got too hot. The previous year they had managed to plough and plant a grand total of forty-one and a half acres, a drop in the ocean on an estate of 23,000 acres.

He had brought many seeds and seedlings out from England, and Nunk had sent others. Cowie was in charge of planting and, having no idea of what would grow in this soil and climate, they were planting just about anything to see what would take – some for decoration including his long-dreamed-of cypress drive and rose garden, and others for essential oil production. Before the rains they had planted eucalyptus, cypress, junipers, honeysuckle, hibiscus, mulberry, azaleas, oleanders, limes, hydrangeas, sunflower, orchards of apple, plum, peach, lemon, orange, quince and apricot, as well as beans and sugarbeet for food. They had tried digging irrigation channels to the orchards but without much success, hitting a hard layer of rock just below the ground surface.

That was not the only setback. The rice they had planted the first year had been a disaster, and it looked as if the mealies and groundnuts were going the same way. Their plans to keep cattle had been dealt a blow by the discovery of some tsetse fly on the estate. He had thought that they were too high, and the fact that Shiwa was not in a tsetse belt had been one of its attractions. *Now I suppose we'll have to rely on pigs and goats*, he wrote to Nunk, *and use what cows we have just for our own milk and butter supplies*. They had some chickens but these kept being killed in the night, by lions if the spoor was anything to go by, and the poison they had tried setting seemed to do nothing. So far, what with the money given by Nunk and lent by Father as well as his own savings, they had sunk £5,000 into the enterprise, and, however much he pored over the account books at night, the figures were all in the input column. Everything cost so much to bring out. It was clearly going to be some years before the estate would make any money.

With cattle ruled out, Shiwa's immense distance from any market, and Cowie continuing to complain about the poor quality of the soil, their main hope was to produce essential oils which had a high market value in proportion to their weight. Gore-Browne's brother, Robert, had gone to France to talk to factory owners and perfume makers, and had written that if they set up their own distillery they could command high prices for oils such as essence of rose, geranium, peppermint and eucalyptus, which would be easy to transport. He had laughed when he read Robert's letter suggesting they should plough and plant 2,000 acres to have a reasonable return on their capital. The most they had ever done was ten acres in a month, so they would be lucky if one day they had 200.

He had ordered geranium seeds from Corsica and they were waiting for plans to be sent from England on how to build an oil-press and a distillery. There was plenty of timber for firewood and an abundant water supply, and they had even acquired some machinery to power the steamroom. The big event of the previous month had been the arrival of a gleaming green and brass steam-engine, a 19-tonne Fowler Compound Road locomotive from Leeds, which had been imported in 1913 by the British South Africa Company for the rubber factory which they had passed by in the canoe on their journey over. It had taken eighteen months for the steam-engine to get all the way through the jungle to the factory, and shortly after it arrived the factory had closed, the wild rubber not proving economically viable in competition with the plantations of Malaysia, and the workers needed as porters for the Army.

The engine had been lying idle ever since, and, learning of its existence, Gore-Browne had managed to purchase it from the administration. He wrote to Ethel of how its arrival, huffing and puffing along the track, had caused an enormous hullabaloo in the village, everyone coming out to watch, eyes saucer wide. Apart from Kakumbi and a few of the men who had worked in the mines, no one had ever seen a car before, let alone a steam-engine, and some of the women were terrified.

'What is it?' people had cried.

'Some kind of monster!' others replied.

'A chariot of the gods,' said someone else.

'It is an engine,' pronounced Kakumbi importantly. 'It is stronger than twelve oxen. It can pull a train.'

'*Chituchuchuchituchuchu*,' chanted the children, copying the sound of the engine as it puffed. When the chief came and gave his blessing, they christened it Chitukututuku, and all stood around discussing it, daring to touch it and feeling proud because theirs was the only village in Africa or so they believed, with a Chitukututuku.

Seeing the steam-engine in pride of place, a group of children gathered round staring wonderingly at it, gave Gore-Browne confidence. Things had to get easier. All over Africa, pathways were being cut into the bush. Roads would improve and multiply, and railways be extended. The natives would become better off so there would be more of a market, and more white people would come out when they realized the opportunities. Already at Shiwa they would soon be less cut off, as a motor road was being built from Chinsali south to Mpika which would pass east of the lake, about three miles away from the estate at its nearest point. Hector Croad, the District Officer, had told him it would be twelve feet wide and would join up with the Mpika road down to the railway at Broken Hill. Once it was finished Gore-Browne intended to ship over a car from England. He missed driving.

To make an access road from his estate to the new motor road, some of Gore-Browne's men had been building a bridge, a kind of causeway across the Mansya river. After checking the ploughing, he decided to have a look at how it was holding up in the rains. To his annoyance much of the wood had gone, presumably stolen for firewood. His throat constricted as he felt anger rising, and he patted the large stick he'd started wearing from his belt. He had never expected to have to use it when he first arrived, but he wrote sadly to Ethel that *beating seems to have become a regular necessity to keep my men in line*. Increasingly, when the natives referred to him as Chipembele, the Bemba word for rhinoceros, it was no longer to commemorate his heroic feat of killing the rhino back in 1914, but because of his own fierce temper. 'I remember him smashing workers against trees or putting his hands round their necks and almost strangling them,' recalled Chitimukulu. 'We actually called him *Chipembele abutabele abamkombo mkwa*. *Mkwa* was the treebark we used as cloth before the Europeans came, and when people were out in the bush gathering this, *chipembele* would all of a sudden appear and destroy everything.'

Feeling the sun hotter on his back, Gore-Browne took out his watch chain. At ten thirty he always went back to the cottages to wash and shave. Passing the outbuildings, he decided to look in on the cowhouse where two calves had been born earlier in the week, a heifer and *a jolly little bull*.

Inside there was some commotion. Saini, the cowherd, looked up in terror as he saw his master approaching, coal-black eyes fixed on the big stick. '*Bwana*, Phillip the cow has died. I didn't touch him, *bwana*. Don't beat me, *bwana*, don't beat me.'

Damn, that's all I need, Gore-Browne wrote in his diary. *Rotten knave, almost as bad as Kawimbi* [the shepherd boy], *who keeps grazing the flock on swampy ground despite repeated orders not to, no wonder they keep getting infected with fluke.* Sometimes he felt as if he had to be everywhere at once, watching everyone, if he was going to get anything done.

'Stop snivelling, Saini, you little worm,' he told the boy, slapping his cheek. 'I will come back this afternoon to see why Phillip died and whether anyone deserves to be punished for this. And in the meantime, keep a close eye on those calves.'

They could not afford to keep losing animals, and his usual hearty breakfast of four eggs and porridge did little to improve his temper, particularly when he spotted Austin wandering around with his butterfly net. Gore-Browne couldn't understand the younger man's obsession with pinning down the beautiful creatures – to him it seemed cruel and pointless. *If they are all around you*, he complained in a letter to Ethel, *why should one need to trap them behind glass?* The butterflies of Shiwa seemed so tame, often fluttering about him as he walked, and he feared Austin's doings would destroy that. Thinking about it after breakfast, he could hardly sit still as Kakumbi shaved him and the servant's unsteady hand and endless chatter got on his nerves.

I often wonder how wise an idea it was taking Kakumbi to England, he wrote in his diary. The year-long trip had given the man an elevated status in the village and he kept *getting above himself.* One day he had disappeared, saying he was going to see a sick friend, then coming back drunk two days later; another time, on a trip up north to look at cattle with Austin and Cowie, he had refused to carry baggage; and one night he had almost set fire to the estate. Gore-Browne had been sitting outside with Cowie and Austin, smoking an after-dinner cigar, when they had suddenly seen flames leaping sky-high just a few hundred yards away. Almost everything they owned, from foodstores to cattle, was in thatch-roofed huts and they were terrified the whole lot would go up in smoke in what they thought was a bush fire. In fact it turned out to be Kakumbi burning his 'gardens'. Gore-Browne had not been able to stop the Bemba from continuing their traditional agricultural methods of making what they called 'gardens' by lopping off boughs of all the neighbouring trees, piling them on the land to be planted and setting them alight. After a couple of seasons of growing millet, the land would be worn out and they would move elsewhere, until there were no trees left in the vicinity and the whole village had to move. When Gore-Browne grabbed Kakumbi by the shoulders and asked him what he thought he was doing lighting a fire so near to so many inflammable things, the servant replied, 'As it was night, *bwana*, I didn't like to disturb you by asking if I might burn.'

What drivel, he wrote in his diary. *I'm getting fed up of natives lying every time they open their mouths.* He had never been one to suffer fools gladly, and found himself getting very violent-tempered with the Bembas' tendency to make up a hundred excuses for not doing something. *I want to help them*, he complained to Ethel, *but it's hard with their utter disregard for truth.* The previous year he had lent many of them money to pay their hut tax, and given out grain because they had none to plant, having used it all to make beer for the harvest celebrations. They were supposed to pay back with a quarter of the mealie crop after harvest, but few were making any attempt to do so, and some had even been caught stealing from the foodstore. *Sometimes I think the whole idea of us all living together peacefully and cooperatively is hopeless*, he wrote to Ethel. *They might be fundamentally good people but they are temperamentally lazy and easily led into bad ways*. The only thing they understood was force. As Austin said, 'Sometimes it seems the native would accept everything and do nothing in return.'

I suppose it would be a poor show if one didn't have to fight, Gore-Browne mused, but he found it very trying what with financial worries and tension with Cowie and Austin, both of whom still owed him their £250 initial share of the capital, and constantly fretted over the lack of likelihood of making any money in the near future to pay him back. Cowie kept talking of a plan to go off and run shooting trips, and Austin was increasingly sensitive to criticism. *That is the problem of people not used to the discipline of public school or regular army training*, Gore-Browne complained to Ethel. In the small world of Shiwa, trifles tended to get magnified. Austin had sulked for days just before Christmas when rain had burst through the drainage channels which he had been in charge of building, and Gore-Browne had joked to him, 'If you can't plan a better drain than that, you better go home.'

Sometimes he thought the only thing that kept him going was Ethel and her weekly letters full of wit, no-nonsense advice, and tales of the latest glittering party at Brooklands or of a lively Bank Holiday meet at the racetrack. It was like a lifeline to the other world. He hoped life at Shiwa would be better when his brother Robert and sister-in-law Margaret came out, though he found it hard to imagine a woman at Shiwa, not one of those stupid flapper types at any rate.

Anyway, he knew at least they wouldn't make fun of him for getting the kitchen boy to strike the brass gong for dinner, or for donning a white dinner-jacket for the evening meal. Cowie and Austin complained bitterly about this, not seeming to understand how important it was to do things right in order to maintain the natives' respect for the white man. Several times, when he had come to the dinner-table and checked the silver and china was all properly laid out, the family crest on the Minton plates the right way up, and told a boy to light the candelabra, he had heard Austin muttering under his breath, 'In Xanadu did Kubla Khan, a stately pleasure dome decree . . .'

That afternoon, thinking of what to do about the bridge, he caught sight of Chikwanda sitting picking jiggers, a kind of worm, out of his feet with one of Aunt Ethel's hatpins, which she had presumably given to Kakumbi, when he was supposed to be supervising the building of the house they were preparing for Robert and Margaret. *The natives can't seem to see the difference between crooked and straight bricklaying*, he had complained to Ethel, and he thought the roofing looked dangerously precarious. Telling him that the chimney looked like *the leaning tower of Pisa* and receiving a blank look, he ordered Chikwanda to get his men to take it down and start again, then told him to go with him.

The African's shorter legs meant he had to run to keep up with the *bwana*, and was gasping for breath when they arrived at the remains of the bridge. Gore-Browne recounted to Ethel how Chikwanda affected complete horror at the missing wood, saying, 'It is most incredible, *bwana*, how wicked men can be!'

'Yes, Chikwanda, and in this case it is your people.'

'Oh no, *bwana*, not my people.' The old man rocked back

and forth on the balls of his bare feet, wringing his hands in agitation.

'How many other people are there living round here?' Gore-Browne patted his stick and raised his voice. 'No, Chikwanda, it was your people and they will immediately rebuild the bridge and keep it in repair ever after with no pay. Do you understand?'

'Yes, *bwana.*' Chikwanda scurried off.

At the end of the day, after the workers had been signed off at 5.30 p.m. and received their daily wage and food ration, Gore-Browne returned to the bridge and saw that the missing timbers had all been replaced. Satisfied, he went to see the pigs fed, then back to the estate office to enter the day's work in the estate book. He was pleased to see that they had, as Peter Mulemfwe had promised, hit the 1,000-brick target, and smiled at Cowie's note that the first rose blossom had bloomed.

Back at the house, the house-boy had already prepared a steaming bath. *Not quite Brooklands standards*, he wrote in his diary, *but glad of it all the same*. He was looking forward to reading more of General Calwell's *Experience of a Dugout* which had recently arrived from the Times Book Club. *The more I read about the Great War*, he had recently written to Ethel,

the more I realize the chaos that reigned in government decision making right from the beginning. Only Kitchener, it seems, realized what a national war was, and for that the man should be blessed. Everyone else persisted in regarding it as an overseas expedition like Egypt or Ashanti. It was just a pity Kitchener had not gone further and let that conviction allow him to start right away with conscription, and of course that he was killed so early on.

The gong sounded for dinner, and he dressed quickly in the white wing-collared shirt, white bow-tie and dress suit laid out by his house-boy. Austin and Cowie were already seated at the table, napkins tucked under their chins, helping themselves to a plate of cold guinea-fowl, and complaining about eating zebra cutlets again. They preferred eland, or crocodile tail stew on the rare occasion that they killed a crocodile, as the villagers were terrified of them, believing them to harbour spirits, but Gore-Browne had become quite partial to zebra meat. He poured some red wine into the crystal glasses and swirled it around a little in the flickering candlelight. Like Austin, he used to have qualms about shooting zebra, charmed by their exquisite patterning, every one different, their equine nostrils and their long eyelashes. But there were so many of them round the lake and with so many mouths to feed it seemed senseless not to, though he had to admit it was a bit tough and rather strong in flavour. *Useless beasts though, except for ornamental value*, he had once written to Ethel. *Once the house is finished I'd quite like to keep some tame ones.* He had not given up on his royal park of deer and peacocks.

To accompany the zebra, the cook had made *an interesting kind of coquette* of potato and mashed haricot beans, and *excelled himself with a dessert of sweet omelette with apricot jam* recently sent out from Brooklands. Gore-Browne felt calmer after the good dinner, and, as it was a clear night, the three men took their coffees and brandies to the fire outside to wait for the postman. It was a long time since it had been warm enough to sit under the night stars. They did not talk much, having long before run out of pleasantries. Neither Cowie nor Austin shared Gore-Browne's literary tastes, having left school at fourteen, and the estate, which was all they had in common, was too depressing to dwell on. Even Cowie, who always had some opinion to venture on something and an endless supply of stories which Gore-Browne found *coarse in the extreme*, had quietened down in recent weeks, and both Gore-Browne and Austin had noticed that the once frequent packages of knitted socks and elaborate letters from his fiancée which they used to tease him about had become few and far between.

One evening after a few whiskies when Cowie seemed particularly morose, Gore-Browne had asked him if he was missing her.

‘’Ow can I miss someone I don’t properly know, Gorey?’ Cowie had replied.

‘I thought you were engaged.’

‘It’s not really an engagement, it’s something my godfather arranged. I told you before, she jumped in the train as I was on the way to Southampton the last time I went out to France and threw herself at me, proposing and everything. It was hard to refuse, being wartime and all that. She’s all right, but I won’t marry a girl I don’t know, nor one who has more money than I have, whatever the family say.’

‘I wish I’d got a girl, someone at home waiting for me,’ said Austin wistfully, ‘particularly one with a bit of money.’

‘Well you ain’t going to find one out here, that’s for sure,’ said Cowie.

8

Shiwa House, November 1926

Gore-Browne wound the handle of the gramophone, placed the last part of Act I of *La Bohème* on the turntable and rested the needle on it. For a long while he had resisted having a gramophone, writing to Ethel, *the idea of the lonely exile sobbing over tin-whistle reproductions of ditties of his far-off home is so cheap and sentimental.* But Robert and Margaret had brought one out with them along with many boxes of records, and he had got so accustomed to having music in his life again that when they had returned to England a couple of years earlier, he had been delighted when they made him a present of it. Now he was alone, barely an evening went by that he didn't sit listening to records in the library, with an H. Upmann cigar and a glass of port, his terrier pup at his feet or on his lap. *La Bohème* was his favourite and the record set was worn from use. Scratched and fuzzy as the reproduction was, listening to Rodolfo singing of the icy coldness of Mimi's hand transported him back to Cologne Opera House with Ethel and his days in the Rhineland occupation army, or even longer ago at Covent Garden with Lorna, watching the wonder in her eyes.

He shivered. Bouts of fever were part of life in the tropics, and even though it was the hottest time of year, he drew his armchair closer to the fire, resting his feet on the head of the skin of the lion he had shot in his second year at Shiwa – his first lion. Peter Mulemfwe had removed the claws and presented them to him in a small wooden box which now sat on a shelf in the glass-fronted cabinet on the library wall among his medals – the DSO, the Order of Santiago e Espada and the Order of Avis, presented by the Portuguese after his year spent as liaison to their expeditionary force in 1917 when they joined the war – a period he had found extremely frustrating for being away from the main action, though he had struck up some lasting friendships. He amused the house servants by referring to the cabinet as his *babenye*, the Bemba word for sacred relics – special things kept by Bemba chiefs.

Waving his right hand conductor-fashion to the music as he always did, he let his eyes wander around the room. He was pleased with the house – *our castle in the woods*, as he always referred to it in letters to Ethel. It was not yet the royal palace he had imagined; there was no tower or chapel, no Oxford college style courtyard or fountain, but those could be added later. He had recently described it to her in detail:

The walls are good and solid – almost three feet thick, and with plenty of antiques and paintings around [mostly sent out from Brooklands] *as well as some Persian rugs on the floors, and it all looks opulent and ancient and established, not at all parvenu. The brass fittings gleam and the lampglass shines in the glow of the big open log fire, the light flickering on the buffalo horns above the mantelpiece and making the black shadows in the arches even blacker.*

The library was his favourite room. His carpenters had embossed the Gore-Browne coat of arms over the doorway, an eagle aloft above a shield bearing three lions, beneath which was carved the motto 'Spero Meliora' – 'I hope for better things'. Heavy wood bookshelves ran from floor to ceiling on three sides, lined with volumes of history, biographies of leaders like Napoleon, Genghis Khan and Alexander the Great, military history, philosophical tracts, and some leather-bound classics such as the works of Sir Walter Scott from his childhood. A sofa and three armchairs stood in front of the fire, covered in eggshell-blue velvet sent by Ethel, and curtains of the same material hung at the windows. A padded red leather visitors' book lay open on the polished mahogany table, alongside copies of *Punch*, the *Illustrated London News* and the *Times Literary Supplement*, from which he frequently ordered books. Late at night, he often sat there writing his letters. The library was on the first floor of the house and french windows led on to a large terrace from which a Union Jack was run up the flagpole every morning while the household staff lined up for inspection. He took tea there in the afternoons, looking out over the gardens, and at cocktail hour loved to sit and watch the lake changing colours as the sun went down.

His bedroom and dressing-room were next door to the library and adjoined his bathroom, with its lavatory mounted on a wooden box, and large enamel bath on brass feet. A sweeping dark wood staircase ran up from the ground floor, carved wooden warriors with spears holding the banisters, and English landscapes in mustard and olive-shaded oils on the wall. Directly below the library was the dining-room. He still put on a smoking jacket and starched white shirt for dinner even though he was all alone. When he didn't have visitors he felt somewhat solitary when the gong struck and he took his seat at the head of the vast table, dining with Sheffield silver cutlery off white Coalport china, and being served from silver platters by servants in uniforms of white shirts and scarlet bermuda shorts with gold brocaded scarlet waistcoats and red fez style hats. But he was not about to change the habits of a lifetime. *The moment one gives up the niceties is when one stops being an Englishman*, he told Ethel.

He wasn't completely alone at Shiwa. Cowie and Austin had left, as had Robert and Margaret, and young Viscount Ockham, sent out for six months by his father the Earl of Lovelace to 'become a man'. But he had recently been joined by Joe Savill, a twenty-five-year-old fellow artillery man from war days whom he had first met at Arras, where Savill was a dispatch rider, and who had ended up serving as his batman. After the war Savill had worked as a handyman at Brooklands, and when Gore-Browne was left all alone at Shiwa he had readily agreed to come out to be his general manager. Although Gore-Browne was pleased of the company, the two men were of very different backgrounds and Savill was not someone with whom he could talk of music or books. An East Londoner who swore like a trooper, Savill had his own house on the estate where he usually ate, feeling uncomfortable in the formality of Gore-Browne's dining-table.

At the moment Savill was down in Livingstone, sorting out paperwork for the car, a Morris sedan which Gore-Browne had just had shipped over, and, he suspected, wining and dining a few women, if he knew Savill and his Cockney charm. *Oh to be 25 and carefree again*, he moaned to Ethel. Trips to the capital had become more frequent since the British South Africa Company had handed control of Northern Rhodesia over to the Colonial Office in 1924, retaining the mineral rights. He hoped that being under British government control would mean development funds and real political representation for settlers. The country was now a Crown Protectorate, administered by a British Governor and a Legislative Council with nine nominated and five elected European members. The council was supposed to have a consultative role, but, he told Ethel, *as far as I can see the Governor does as he likes*.

Since the completion of the road, several of the council

members had been up to Shiwa to pay him a visit, having heard of the grand house in the wilderness. The new Governor, Sir Herbert Stanley, and his wife had come for a few days the previous year and *really put the place on the map*, and he had enjoyed their stay, writing to Ethel that he found the Governor to be *a man of culture and intensely pro-native in a sensible way*. But for the rest, he thought they were *all Philistines and stuffed shirts, and a nuisance needing to be fed and entertained when there is work to be done*. His heart sank whenever he saw their long cars driving up to the gatehouse, stopping to marvel at the clocktower and pass through the arch, then up along the cypress-lined drive to the house, where they always apologized for arriving unannounced but said they were just 'passing through' and had had no way to contact him. Unfortunately the house lay only just off the route between Abercorn in the north and Broken Hill in the south, and was apparently becoming known as the best inn on the road. With nowhere else to stay within a day's drive, he felt he could hardly turn people away. He always showed guests the library straight away, hoping they would amuse themselves with the books, but he moaned to Ethel, *it is a rare visitor who lets me be*. Still, most of the time the administration was far enough away for it not to interfere with the peace of the days and never-ending beauty of Shiwa. And sometimes he had to admit he was glad of guests, when they were like the Stanleys, to be able to converse about books and plays and politics, as well as acquaintances back home. He had tried playing his opera records to Kakumbi and Peter Mulemfwe, but though they smiled and said, 'Oh, nice,' he didn't think they would ever share the same appreciation.

It had been a blow when Cowie and Austin left, but as he had written to Ethel, he supposed it had been inevitable. *Both of them were rather soft for this life and had no capacity for amusing themselves with books or letters or the like.* As one crop after another had failed in Shiwa's poor soil, the battles over money had worsened. Even mealies wouldn't grow, and the natives had been far more unresponsive to modern ideas than he had imagined. He had complained to Ethel: *Cowie is always wasting coin on things we don't need, then when I question his purchases, says I make him feel he's 'sponging'.*

Austin had been the first to go, more than four years earlier in 1922. Towards the end he had been getting increasingly edgy, complaining about dressing for dinner and reacting to the slightest criticism or raised voice, accusing Gore-Browne of treating him and Cowie 'like natives'. Then suddenly one evening, perhaps after a few too many glasses of claret, Austin had glared at Chitimili fumbling with the silver serving spoons which kept slipping from the white gloves Gore-Browne insisted were worn by those waiting at table. Slamming down his cutlery, he had turned on Gore-Browne, shouting, 'Do you know how ridiculous you look? Trying to build an empire in the middle of nowhere. You'll be organizing polo matches and hunts next! You're not in Surrey now.'

I told him, 'Yes, and that's all the more reason to maintain one's standards', Gore-Browne later recounted to Ethel. *We have a duty to educate the native.*

'You call this education?' Austin had replied. 'Dressing up little Sambas in shoes and gloves to wait on you. I've had it with this, Gorey! This place is cursed, nothing grows. It's not natural to live like this. You might enjoy playing the Great White Chief, growing old and alone here, but it's not for me. I'm out of this!'

Austin's remarks had stung, and Gore-Browne was upset when he stormed out, taking little comfort from Cowie's explanation that it was the high altitude doing strange things and that the lad would calm down after a good sleep. The next morning Austin had gone, *without so much as a farewell*, and leaving the estate accounts in *a complete mess* which only Margaret would manage to unravel later. *I don't mind the money*, he wrote to Ethel – Austin's two years of work had been well worth the £250 he had lent him – *it's the lack of courtesy I find hurtful*. He felt a little placated when he received a letter from Austin's parents, thanking him for all that he had done, and saying that they didn't consider Austin's time in Africa in any way wasted. *I think in time Austin himself will come to feel the same*, he wrote to Ethel, *but I still feel sore*.

After that it was only a matter of time until Cowie also quit. For a while, to assuage Cowie's constant refrain of 'I'm always sponging off you, Gorey,' they tried a new arrangement whereby he would be kept on not as a partner, but on a six-monthly contract, paid £20 a month to be in charge of the planting and carpentry. For the rest of the year Cowie planned to run shooting trips for rich visitors. But he was *getting stick from home* over the long-suffering fiancée still waiting for him to return, and eventually announced he was leaving too. Gore-Browne missed him more than he expected, *his strange turn of phrase* and the way whenever he was impressed by something he always said, 'You're a bloomin' marvel, Gorey.'

Robert and Margaret, who had arrived just after Austin's departure in 1922, stayed only two years. They had been very keen to start with, Robert bringing out an anvil and forge to set up a blacksmith's, and full of all the information he had garnered on the French Riviera about essential oils that they could produce to scent expensive perfumes. Margaret, who had given birth to a stillborn baby in England the previous year and been anxious for a change of scene, had turned out to be *a brick*, getting all the accounts in order. *I can't deny a woman's touch is useful with curtains and things*, he wrote to Ethel, though he wasn't sure about the pink wash on the walls of some of the bedrooms. But they hadn't acclimatized well. Both kept getting malaria, Robert was still troubled by the leg he had broken jumping a wall, trying to escape from a German prison during the war, and, though Margaret had learnt to shoot, even bagging a few buck for dinner at times, they weren't really outdoor types. Robert dreamt of being a novelist and found he had far less time for writing than he had anticipated, and Margaret clearly missed London life.

Gore-Browne suspected that their mother had played some part in his brother's departure from Shiwa. Their parents had never approved of Robert joining him. Sir Francis Gore-Browne, who had been knighted in 1921 for his work chairing the Civil Service Arbitration Board, had hoped his younger son would follow him to the Bar, and wrote to Stewart, 'Robert ought to do something of importance in the world . . . if you should find in the end that you have to chuck farming the delay in starting in life would have very seriously prejudiced Robert in taking up any other career'. Later, after Ethel's intervention, he wrote a more conciliatory letter, saying 'I quite recognize that to "make the desert blossom as a rose" is a great ambition and if you make your corner of Northern Rhodesia a success you will have proved my fears groundless.' But Sir Francis died a year later, in 1922, in bizarre circumstances, suffocating himself in his sleep, and their mother began working on Robert's guilt at leaving her alone. She made no secret of her displeasure not only that her eldest son was in Africa on some 'madcap scheme' as she called it, and that her daughter Sapphire was reduced to running a humble parish in Leicester with her clergyman husband rather than being the society lady she had hoped for, but that her favourite son had been lured out to the wilds of Africa too.

The brothers had had their differences out at Shiwa, Robert more than once accusing Stewart of being more concerned

SHIWA,

3. May. 1922

Dear Nunk,

Only a scrap this mail as its the end of the month, and as things are just now that means quite a lot of extra work in the way of adding up figures. My share is the Cash account, £127 this month to be made to balance, and the Estate accounts, and the ration account. Perhaps the figures will interest you:-

RATION ACCOUNT — 5,062 lbs of meal issued during April. value £15.16.0.

ESTATE ACCOUNTS

1. Ploughing.	12/-	(finishing off, 2 acres for windbreak and 7 acre field left uncompleterd)
2. Harrowing	17/6	24 acres.
3. Cattle	11/-	Breaking, two oxen.
	20/-	Upkeep of byres, grass, cleaning out etc.
	33/6	Herding.
4. Sheep and Goats	7/-	Herding
5. Pigs.	9/6	Herding.
6. Poultry.	5/6	Chicken Boy's wages.
	11/7½	New house and runs.
7. Timber.	24/-	Sawing (480 feet)
	74/8	Hauling in 50 trees.
	27/11	Felling 132 trees.
8. Carpentering		
	10/-	File cupboard
	24/5	Fittings S.G.B's bedroom.
	17/3	" " bathroom
	17/-	" Cowie's house
9. Buildings	38/5	new compound, (roof poles only!) £7.10.2 new grain store, (roof + foundatns)

Stewart Gore-Browne sent regular reports of the running of the estate back to his uncle Hugh Locke King.

with creating a palatial estate than a commercial enterprise, spending extravagantly on servants' uniforms rather than equipment, and planting trees in picturesque positions rather than where they would grow best. But Gore-Browne was sad

<u>BUILDINGS</u> (cont)

S.G.B. bedroom and bathroom £5.5.0 (tr. window frames etc see ~~below~~ above)
staircase walls, and ceiling, £1.6.10
Cowies house 7/1

<u>10. NURSERIES & GARDENS</u>.
New vegetable garden(irrigateable) 26/2
Fence repairs 24/4
New seed beds 23/3
Forestry 9/3
Garden staff (mostly nursery work) 15/-

<u>11. SURVEY</u>
Beacons 5/10

<u>12. DOMESTIC SERVANTS (Wages and Food)</u> £3.13.0

<u>13. NATIVE HUNTER</u>
Wages and food 23/6

TOTAL FOR APRIL £42.6.10

Its a considerable sweat keeping all those figures day by day with about 100 men employed but I think its worth it, as otherwise one can go right off the lines as regards expense.

I've just started brickmaking again. I'm wanting about 30,000 pr 40,000 at least for ~~bxxx~~ building a worker's compound and more for the forge, and for various small odd jobs as last year's supply is quite exhausted now. I'm also going to make more tiles, last years' didn't stand too badly after all, and we must have some for the roof of the forge and of ~~x~~ the still room.

I;m awfully sorry your pigs aren't playing up as they should however by now I hope they've settled to live in large numbers. How perfectly damnable abput the cattle feed.

I must get on with the other mail letters. Luckily there aren't a great lot of business ones this week.

Yours,

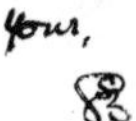

to see his brother and sister-in-law leave. Several times during their last weeks together, Robert had reminded him that at forty-three he was *well and truly middle-aged*, and suggested to him that he get himself a wife, saying, 'It's wrong to live all alone out here. Speaking from experience, I can recommend the married state. Don't you want someone to warm your slippers and bring you hot cocoa?'

'I've got servants to do that,' he had laughed drily. 'Besides, there aren't any suitable females in these parts.'

Robert had suggested various girls from his past, constantly dropping into conversation the name of Lady Diana King, who, he claimed, 'has always had a thing about you and she's a nice girl with lots of spirit'. Gore-Browne laughed at the idea, writing to Ethel, *Can you picture her in all her finery tripping about this place?*

He had driven the couple down to Broken Hill, a two-day motor trip, to catch the train back to Cape Town and, as he bid them farewell, Margaret, whom he had grown quite fond of, had put a gloved hand on his arm and asked him if he would be lonely.

'Don't worry about me,' he had reassured her. As the train steamed off across the African plains, they had looked back once from the carriage window, and then they were gone on a journey that would take them 6,000 miles away.

How could he tell them there was only one woman who could take that place at the other end of his table? Sometimes, despite his dislike for putting words to emotions, he longed to confess to someone. Robert and Margaret had stayed some weeks at Brooklands before coming out to Shiwa, and he had hoped for a clue from them that Ethel was planning to move to Africa. But nothing. Then, the last year or so, Hugh had got weaker, suffering gallstones on top of his chest problems, and he knew it was impossible that she would leave him. Finally, this January, Hugh's heart had given out. Reading the telegram, Gore-Browne had experienced a mixture of emotions. He would miss his clever uncle but at the same time it was as if a locked door had suddenly opened, which no one knew what was behind. He had expected that once a decent interval had passed, Ethel would finally come out to Shiwa. But to his dismay so far she had mentioned nothing in her letters. He had hesitated to push her, feeling it was distasteful and knowing she would have a lot to do winding up the estate. But this year would be her first Christmas alone, and once Joe Savill was back to take charge at Shiwa he planned to sail to England to be with her; perhaps they would even take a holiday together. In their letters they had discussed meeting in Sicily to see the ancient temples and have some private time together, before he went off on the usual round of friends and relatives.

He would not stay long in England, he decided, whatever Ethel's answer about coming to Shiwa. Despite what he had said to Robert, he had thought about looking for a wife. The companionship would be nice, but there had only been two women that mattered to him, and he thought he was too set in his ways now to adapt to anyone new. He had shown no interest in women since his arrival at Shiwa, unlike some white men who satisfied their physical needs with local village women. Africa had become his mistress, and such a demanding one. *I so want to do good here,* he wrote to Ethel, *to build a really grand estate that will be the envy of all and talked of even back in England*, and only she, he thought, could understand that. She herself seemed to agree, having recently written to him that any wife must be *one who has a longing after the life for itself and a strong feeling for you added.*

It was funny how deceptive a place could be. Often, when he looked out from the terrace, the landscape of Shiwa with its green hills and meadows speckled with pink and yellow flowers reminded him of the gentle beauty of home, of the Surrey hills around Brooklands or the Dorset downs encircling Bingham's Melcombe. But the peaceful exterior cloaked a land of poisonous snakes that devoured infants, diseases which could turn urine black and fell a grown man in less than a day, insects which could wipe out cattle, and terrible beasts of prey with growls that could freeze a man's blood. Africa sucked one in – his original idea of getting the estate up and running then spending every other year in England seemed laughable now.

That afternoon, he had gone down to the lake as always when depressed. Watching the water and the wildlife all around, a family of elephants and a herd of playful puku under an endless sky, never failed to put to rest all questions as to why he was there. As he walked, he thought proudly that the buildings he had constructed seemed to have put the final touch to the natural beauty – *The red brick and tiles are a perfect foil to the green vegetation*, he had written to Ethel, and he wondered if he would ever find another white person to share his passion for the place.

Peter Mulemfwe was down by the shore, fishing, his ebony assegai by his side. For a while they discussed how work was progressing on the estate. In order to finish the house and farm buildings, as well as staff houses, Gore-Browne had increased the number of permanent staff to 356. Some were Bemba who had come from outside, hearing that work was available, and some were people from the lake who had returned from working in the mines. Gore-Browne felt pleased that he was drawing people back and creating employment. One day, once the estate was in full swing, he hoped to have more than 1,000 people on his payroll.

He took the opportunity to ask his foreman if he had had any more problems with Kakumbi. As the two workers closest to Gore-Browne, Kakumbi and Peter had long been rivals. Matters had come to a head earlier in the year when Kakumbi's first wife, or rather the first of the second series, as the real number one was murdered, had miscarried. *This was hardly surprising*, Gore-Browne wrote to Ethel, *considering the number of children she had already had and the harsh life the local women lead, doing far more work than the men.* But local folklore held that miscarriage must be the result of adultery. The other women of the village, particularly her in-laws, kept nagging at Mrs Kakumbi to name the culprit, and finally she pointed the finger at Peter. Kakumbi demanded blood. Gore-Browne was appalled. Not only was Peter his trusted foreman, but he was also an excellent shot and one of his best trackers. Although he relished the power, he sometimes found his role as *de facto* local judge, resolving disputes between workers or villagers, rather complicated, and in this case it was particularly hard. He had tried to persuade Kakumbi that there was no proof of Peter's guilt and that the miscarriage was obviously the result of medical complications. Kakumbi had gone away grumbling, clearly not accepting the explanation, and he had since heard whispers among the house servants of a witch-doctor being consulted and black magic being used against his foreman. It wasn't the first problem he had had with Kakumbi and he was disappointed. Taking him to England had not had the educational effect he had hoped for. It certainly had backfired in the case of Bulaya – he had never returned and the latest news from Ethel was that the African had got involved with a white woman and was acting in a play in London.

Peter reassured him that any attempt by Kakumbi to give him the evil eye was bound for failure, explaining, 'It is hard to make the spirits stir trouble for an innocent man.' Instead, he seemed more concerned by a couple of other problems in the village. The young son of Mashilipa, one of the house servants, had been killed by a black mamba, his body found all swollen up when they went to take him dinner. The villagers were linking the tragic event to the presence of a leopard, said to be stalking the place at night. According to Peter, the Bemba were frightened to go into the forest, saying that the leopard was a supernatural being, inhabited by the restless spirit of a dead chief, which could never be vanquished, and that the death of Mashilipa's boy was the first sign of havoc to come.

Gore-Browne was worried by the news. The leopard had been hanging around the estate for some time. He thought it was responsible for eating Agnes the cow the previous week, and was sure he had seen it pass right in front of the doors of the dining-room at night, bold as anything. Leaving poisoned meat around at night hadn't worked. He asked Peter whether they should arrange a hunt, though he added it might have to be after the rains as he was planning to go to England as soon as they started.

He was about to go back to the house when a long cry sounded overhead. Both men looked up to see a fish-eagle flying low in the cloudless sky.

'Hear that, *bwana*?' asked Peter. 'That sound "*Nkoya, nkoya, nkoya, kupwa*"? We Bemba say, it means "I go, I go, I go to get married." Now hear that?' Gore-Browne could just hear a far-off response.

'A sort of "*Kaweeya, kaweeya, kaweeya, kupwa*?"' Peter mimicked the sound exactly. 'It is his mate saying "Go, go, go and get married."'

'And what do you mean by that, Peter?'

'Nothing at all, *bwana*. Just that is what some people say. You know we Bemba are people of many legends.'

The record came to an end, the needle scratching round and round on the empty groove. Gore-Browne stood up to put on the first part of Act II, sliding the 78 out of its brightly pictured sleeve and on to the turntable. As he wound the handle, he noticed the puppy had slipped into the room and was cowering by the side of the chair. Stooping over and rubbing under its chin, he picked up his most recent copy of *The Times* and sat down to read the latest on the General Strike back home. He had the newspaper mailed to him and though it generally arrived a month late, he tried to follow the news, knowing it would be very easy to get cut off from the world. On the front page was an article about Suffragettes. *Hard to believe sometimes what the world is coming to*, he wrote in his diary. His early life had been dominated by strong women – not only his mother Helenor, for whom nothing was ever good enough, and his father's sister Ethel, but his dynamic grandmother Lady Harriet, who, with her mass of shiny dark hair and gregarious nature, had been a great hit during her husband's governorship of New Zealand, despite Thomas Gore-Browne's controversial handling of the Maori, which many blamed for leading to a decade of Maori wars. But he thought giving women the vote was *going too far*, and he suspected that he and Ethel would have some heated discussions on the subject when he got home.

It was hard to concentrate on the newspaper when the puppy kept crying. Its ears twitched up like antennae and Gore-Browne turned the music down and tried to hear what was bothering the little creature. There was a sound. A kind of far-off roar which he always thought of as the voice of Africa. There it was again, closer this time, more of a bark than a roar. He wondered if it was the leopard that had been terrorizing the village. He and Peter would definitely have to arrange another hunting party. A leopardskin would look rather nice on the floor of the sitting-room.

He increased the volume of the record and sat down again. Although the fire was dying in the grate, the room was starting to feel uncomfortably hot, and he found it hard to get back into the music. The puppy wouldn't settle, and the francolin outside, which he'd put in the gardens as a temporary ornamental alternative to peacocks, were making a racket with their almost human screams. Feeling the need for air, he got up and opened the french windows. The velvet curtains blew in wildly in the force of the hot wind. He stepped out on to the terrace, really having to push against the wind, the little hair he had left whipped against his scalp. He walked to the edge, holding on to the brick parapet, and tried hard to hear the leopard again or identify a shape in the velvety blackness. High above, the stars were clearer than ever, and he picked out the Southern Cross, four bright points among hundreds, and listened hard to what Peter Mulemfwe had taught him to think of as the language of the bush. This time he heard something else, a rumbling or drumming, perhaps from the village. The wind dropped as suddenly as it had started, and the powerful perfume of the magnolia tree, just in front of the house, filled the air with its sweetness. For a moment the night was completely quiet. The francolin had ceased their racket, no birds were singing, and the usual night-time hum of cicadas had ceased. He wondered if the leopard was nearby, watching. He could see nothing. Not for the first time, he wished he had Mulemfwe's ability to scent an alien beast on the air.

Then it came. A bone-snapping crack of thunder, followed by a flash of lightning illuminating the lake momentarily with a silver glow. Gore-Browne felt a large drop of warm water burst on his bald pate, and then stood there enjoying the feel of one drop after another until he was dripping wet. Inhaling the new smell of greenness, he imagined his desert blossoming as a rose. No leopards tonight. The rains had come.

9

St Andrew's Church, Bingham's Melcombe, Dorset, March 1927

It was one of those crispy wintry days that he sometimes missed when he was in Africa. Late snow lay thick on the ground, crunchy to the tread.. The trees lining the estate drive were stark and naked of leaves, stretching up into sky blue and clear as a window. The fallen snow coating the Dorset downs, which swept up either side of the small hamlet, seemed to swallow the morning sounds, the clip of horses' hooves and the rattle of wheels of a passing carriage. Just over twenty-one years earlier, Gore-Browne had watched another carriage pass this way, bearing a girl in a white lace veil the short distance from the house to the church. A young man then, he had lingered at the end of the path by the gate, watching Lorna step out to be somebody else's bride, that of a well-to-do medical professor famous in his field of cancer research, with whom he, as a lowly subaltern in the Royal Artillery, could never hope to compete. Now, both she and her husband lay in African graves and he was here to attend the funeral of her mother, Flora. It felt very final, saying goodbye to his last contact with Lorna's family, almost as if he were laying to rest their romance after all these years.

Inside the chapel the service was already under way. Gore-Browne was usually a stickler for punctuality, but he had had some problems with the gearstick of Ethel's car on the way down, so he slipped quietly through the side door and on to the end of the right-hand row near the front as the congregation rose to sing the first hymn. The quavery English voices intoning 'The Lord's My Shepherd' made him long for the rich African harmonies of his workers at Shiwa when they sang 'Nkosi Sikeleli Afrika', the Bantu anthem, and he peered around the small fourteenth-century church. On the left wall was a newish marble tablet inscribed 'Lorna Lawrence Bosworth. Born Harrow 3 February 1881, married at Bingham's Melcombe February 27 1906 to Edwin Allen Goldman. Died September 27 1919.' Gore-Browne remembered the first time he had caught sight of her at Harrow, a long white pinafore over her clothes and laughing up at her father. All the boys had been a little bit in love with her. *What a terribly short life*.

He looked around to see if there were any familiar faces. Sunlight streaming through the stained glass made dappled colours on the stone floor, and caught in its golden reach a few strands of hair escaping from under the wide-rimmed hat of a young girl on the edge of the left front row. Even with his poor eyesight, Gore-Browne noticed something strangely familiar about that slight figure, the tight pose of the head, and square boyish shoulders. Without meaning to, he found himself staring. Feeling his gaze, the girl suddenly turned and looked across the church, her eyes searching until they fixed on him. Her brow wrinkled as she obviously wondered why the tall balding stranger with the tanned face and eye-glass was watching her. For a moment their eyes met, then a burly man in a black suit next to her tapped her arm and she turned back. *I had to concentrate hard to keep my hymn-book from shaking and the words from jumping round the page*, Gore-Browne later wrote. It could not be. The same serious face with its smooth flat brow and wide bluebell eyes of the picture that he had carried round in his head for all those years. That *all-knowing look of a Madonna in a Renaissance painting*. It could not be Lorna. The plaque on the wall said she had been dead eight years.

The service seemed interminable as he tried his best not to keep looking at the mysterious girl. The vicar, a new fellow by the name of Harry Caryl, droned on about the great loss to the community of Flora Bosworth Smith, and Gore-Browne tuned in and out, picking up odd phrases: 'a noble woman' . . . 'with strong faith' . . . 'who made the joys and sorrows of others her own . . .' He usually enjoyed church, in fact as a youth had been *somewhat priggish about religion*, and he planned to build a chapel at Shiwa where he would have both Protestant and Catholic services, Catholicism having always appealed to him, though not all the gold and garish bleeding Christs. He liked this church with its wooden rafters and stone pillars, its elegant simplicity very different from the ornate churches in Sicily where he had just been holidaying with Ethel. He wondered again why his aunt had not agreed to come out to be mistress of Shiwa. Now he supposed he would have to look for one of his mother's so-called 'suitable' young ladies, though all the ones he knew were either long married off, or if they weren't there was a good reason. He did not worry too much about looks, he was well-aware he was *no oil-painting*, though he fancied he had improved with age and had a certain bearing, but as he told his brother, *one wants someone one can be proud of*. And above all, she would have to care about his African house.

Finally the middle-aged woman on the harmonium, whom he recognized from one of Mrs Bosworth Smith's musical afternoons in aid of her nurses' fund, plunged into the first chords of Verdi's *Requiem* and the coffin was borne slowly outside, the congregation filing after it. As they shuffled out, their breath steaming in the bitter air, Gore-Browne glanced across to the vast honey-coloured house with all its roofs and chimneys, somewhat reminiscent of Hampton Court. He wondered what would happen to Bingham's Melcombe. *It has always been one of my favourite spots in England*, he was to write to his friend Roy Welensky many years later. *The main house is such a blend of styles yet somehow pleasing to the eye*. Parts of the house and gardens dated back to the twelfth century. The dark towering yew hedge running the length of the lawn, where he had first taken Lorna's hand and then bid her a final farewell, was more than 500 years old, and he had seen nothing like it elsewhere. Other parts were Tudor, with a bit more added in the time of Queen Anne. The feature he liked best was the wonderful round oriel window in the hall where years before, he, Lorna, Joan and Neville had done amateur dramatics, putting on scenes from *The School for Scandal* for the élite of the county and one night shows for the village people. He had often sat in the alcove there with Lorna, talking of books and music and walks or drives they could make together. The window was stained glass, featuring the coat of arms of King Philip of Spain, who had stayed at the house on his way to marry Queen Mary. Gore-Browne thought he would like to build something similar at Shiwa.

Tearing his gaze away from the house and turning up his collar against the cold, he followed the crowd, trying to pick out the girl with the Madonna eyes. He spotted her black-ribboned hat as she wended her way through the mossy tombstones and age-worn crosses, clutching a few white lilies in one hand. She walked like a schoolgirl, struggling in heels she was clearly unused to, looking as if she would like to kick them off and run.

In the churchyard the coffin was lowered into the grave and the vicar began to murmur the last sacraments. 'Ashes to ashes, dust to dust . . .' Standing at the edge of the grave, the girl stepped forward and threw her flowers inside. She looked skywards, where a V-formation of birds were flying over the edge of the downs, almost as if bidding farewell to Flora. Gore-Browne could see her face quite clearly now, devoid of cosmetics and as waxenly pale as the lilies she had thrown. Her hair was the colour of autumn hazelnuts and parted dead centre, to hang down as heavy wings either side of her brow. As the vicar sprinkled some earth on to the coffin in a final gesture, saying 'Her children shall call her blessed', a choked sob came from somewhere deep within the girl, reminding Gore-Browne of a wounded hartebeest on one of his hunts. The burial over, people started drifting away and he watched the middle-aged man with the moustache and black Homburg, who had been sitting next to the girl in church, put his hand on her shoulder and say something.

Seeing a lady he vaguely recognized from past gatherings at Bingham's Melcombe nod him an acknowledgement, he tipped his hat and after some brief small talk took the opportunity to ask if she knew the identity of the girl. To his astonishment, she told him it was Lorna Goldman, the orphaned daughter of Lorna Bosworth Smith, and that the man with her was the Honorable Major Charles Sydney Goldman, her uncle and guardian now that her grandmother was dead. The woman, who turned out to have been a close friend of Flora, pointed out Goldman's wife, a thin woman with thick furs, daughter of Lord Peel, and told him that the couple were 'well-heeled', with a place in Park Street in London, just off Park Lane, but had little time for Lorna, whom she had heard was 'treated like a housemaid'. According to her, young Lorna was a 'bit of a troublemaker' who had been expelled from various boarding schools and was now at Sherborne. Gore-Browne was hardly listening. He had quite forgotten that his Lorna had had any children, and it had never occurred to him that they would be back in England and almost grown-up.

Seeing the girl make for the gate, he strode quickly to block her path and held out a leather-gloved hand. Introducing himself as a friend of her mother, he scanned her face for signs of recognition of his name, but she kept her head down. Estimating that the girl was sixteen or seventeen, he realized she would have been too young when her mother died to have known anything about him.

'I'm Lorna Goldman.' Shyly, she stuck out a hand, with those same long white pianist's fingers he remembered so well, though unlike her mother's well-kept digits, so often clad in long silk gloves, these had chewed fingernails and the right index finger was ink-stained. 'How do you do?' she said in that polite but disinterested way one addresses a wearisome uncle.

Her hand felt fragile in his grasp, and he fumbled for some adequate words of sympathy. *I wish I wasn't always so hopeless on these occasions*, he had once written in his diary. *It is so hard for one to feel comfortable with matters such as illness and death, and this poor creature has suffered more than her fair share in her short life.* He could just see the lower half of the girl's face under the hat, and noticed that the cold, which had put vivid dots of colour on the cheeks of the other females standing around the churchyard, seemed to have sucked all the colour out of hers.

Without meaning to, he told her how much she resembled her mother, and she looked up from under her thick eyelashes, head slightly tilted to one side like a bird to reveal violet tear-puffed eyes. *How well I recalled that look*, he later wrote.

'Did you know Mother well?' she asked, with new interest.

He started to tell her that they had been part of the same set long ago, but was interrupted by a call from her uncle summoning her.

She turned to leave, and Gore-Browne, who was usually

the most proper and unspontaneous of men, realized that simply to watch her walk away would be like losing Lorna twice. As she put out that childlike hand again to say goodbye, he asked if he could pay a call on her in London, adding that he was only in town for a short while as his real home was in Africa. The mention of Africa made her lift her head and look properly at him for the first time. She saw a tall expensively dressed man with a ramrod back and a silver-topped cane, long face dominated by a large hook nose, skin weathered by years in the tropics, thin lips and watery grey-blue eyes with a monocle over the right-hand one. He looked, she later told friends, like a character out of the adventure books her mother had read her as a small child when they were living in Johannesburg, her father having died when she was a toddler after operating on himself as part of his research, before her world had been plunged into darkness and boarding schools and being passed from one relative to another, separated from her brother Bosworth, who had been sent off to the Navy, where he was now a midshipman. His years in the war, then running Shiwa, had given him a commanding air, that of someone not to be trifled with. She imagined the tall stranger whisking her on to a large white horse and riding off into the far horizon, slaying any beasts that might cross their path.

'I grew up in Africa,' she told him, adding that she longed to go back there. Her happiest memories were of going to the Kalahari when her mother's coughing was bad and she had been told to go to a dry climate. There, with her mother and brother Boz, they learnt to put their heads to the ground like bushmen to listen for people coming. But back in Johannesburg, the consumption really took hold, leaving the elder Lorna with bright eyes, flushed cheeks and wracked by coughing which even opium could no longer relieve. She had died when her daughter was just eleven, bequeathing the younger Lorna shadowy memories of a serene, beautiful figure and a dressing-table drawer of things from her young dancing days in Dorset such as long white gloves, jewelled brooches for the hair and pearls.

Gore-Browne opened his wallet, where he still kept the *Serenity* postcard which reminded him of the first Lorna, and took out some photographs of Shiwa Ngandu, pointing out the house and the lake of the Royal Crocodiles which she looked at in awe. 'Maybe I could show it to you one day,' he said, as her uncle called out to her again in exasperation, and started heading towards them. Lorna turned to go and Gore-Browne pressed his visiting card on her. 'The name is Gore-Browne,' he called after her. 'Lieutenant-Colonel Stewart Gore-Browne'.

Back at Brooklands that night, he couldn't get the girl out of his mind. He was sure he could smell a trace of jasmine on the sleeve of his jacket, which her hand had just brushed against as she reached to take his calling card. He had to pay a call on her, he decided. She was so like her mother. Not classically beautiful, at times plain even. But somehow so alluring. He thought about the long white fingers, the heart-shaped face with the blue-violet eyes so direct in their gaze. And this Lorna had something else. Whereas her mother had viewed the world through trusting eyes, this Lorna, while equally fragile in her appearance, had something harder in her expression. It was difficult to imagine her as the girl with the sheep in the Sottocornola painting. *More of a Pre-Raphaelite than a Madonna*, he wrote. And even something cheeky, as if she were laughing at them all and their social niceties. Tragic yes, but *somehow one felt she was a survivor*.

To Gore-Browne's relief there were other guests present

for dinner at Brooklands that evening, including two *extraordinarily verbose* politicians, so his own conversational skills were not much called upon. The usual polite questions about his life in Africa elicited so little detail that the table soon desisted. He usually found people didn't really want to know anyway, *it was all too alien for their own comfy existences.* How could people whose daily worlds revolved around petty gossip and the latest antics of their spoilt infants begin to conceive of lions on the lawn and snakes in the bath, of families who dwelled in mud huts and considered themselves blessed if there was a bowl of corn porridge at the end of the day? *I find it droll*, he once wrote to Ethel, *that I can walk into a London drawing-room unknown and unnoticed, people completely unaware that back in my own place, hundreds of men prostrate themselves at my approach.*

But his aunt knew him too well to let his preoccupied air go unremarked, and after dinner, when the guests were moving into the parlour for coffee, she took the chance to ask him what was ailing him, surprised that Flora Bosworth's funeral would have so affected him. He told her he was feeling under the weather, perhaps because of the long drive and not being accustomed to the cold English mornings, and excused himself, letting her get Annie the housekeeper to make one of her famous hot toddies. As Gore-Browne lay in his bed that night, a fire in the grate, the peacocks mercifully quiet outside, he realized that it was the first time in his life that he had ever lied to Ethel.

Part Two

1927–1967

Lorna the Second
by Thomas Hardy

LORNA! Yes, you are sweet,
But you are not your mother
Lorna the First, frank, feat,
Never such another! –
Love of her could smother
Griefs by day or night;
Nor could any other,
Lorna, dear and bright,
Ever so well adorn a
Mansion, coach or cot,
Or so make men scorn a

Rival in their sight;
Even you could not!
Hence I have to mourn a
Loss ere you were born; a Lorna!

Winter Words, Macmillan, 1928

10

Shiwa Ngandu, October 1927

Lorna had fallen asleep in the car against Gore-Browne's shoulder, and he tapped his new young wife softly on her wrist to wake her, noticing as he did that she was wearing the ivory beads which had been his first present to her back in April. They had been married just three months, and his manner towards her was still somewhat stiff, but he was anxious for her to see the estate and the first view of the lake.

Lorna opened her eyes sleepily, stretching herself cat-like against the leather seat. The Morris sedan was no longer on the mud carriageway they had been driving along last time she woke. Instead they were jolting over a sandy track through trees and bushes in shades of red and green. It seemed an age since they had disembarked from the steamer with their fifty-one trunks at Mpulungu on the southern shore of Lake Tanganyika, the previous morning. Gore-Browne had originally planned a more leisurely trip, but the moment they had stepped on to Northern Rhodesian soil after their long honeymoon, to be met by James, his driver, he had suddenly felt eager to be home to start their new life. So they had left their luggage in store to come on later by truck and oxen carts, and, taking just a few cases and Lorna's precious violin, they had set off, stopping only at the provincial commissioner's house in Kasama to overnight and pick up some supplies such as sugar, flour and butter.

They had departed from England in September after a few

weeks at Bingham's Melcombe, and a few days in London for shopping at Fortnums and the Army & Navy Stores, and a round of farewells. Overjoyed to have someone to share his favourite places with, Gore-Browne had then taken Lorna on the Orient Express to Venice, where he took her for her first gondola ride and checked himself from entering the small bookshop where he had bought the postcard of the girl and sheep which reminded him of her mother; Egypt, where they had stayed in Ethel's Mena House Hotel and he had shown her the Pyramids and the Sphinx; and then caught the Union Castle steamer to the East African port of Mombasa and the spice island of Zanzibar, where they stayed a while as guests of the British Governor. Throughout the trip they were frequently mistaken for father and daughter, young officers on board ship and at a ball in Zanzibar asking Gore-Browne for permission to dance with his 'lovely young daughter'. Such comments made him bristle with irritation, though to anyone looking at the wedding pictures they were easy to understand. He was forty-four and looked ten years older with his balding head, distinguished air, and skin leathered by years in the sun; she was nineteen and appeared much younger, despite his attempts back in London to get her to buy more sophisticated clothes for their honeymoon.

Even so he described himself as *as happy as I have ever been*, and as they got to know each other, found himself more and more intrigued by his young wife and her soulful expression. *Lorna I do truly think one in ten thousand*, he had written to Ethel the day after the wedding, and arriving in Northern Rhodesia, he repeated these sentiments, writing, *I still find it hard to believe that Lorna agreed to marry me.*

He had proposed when they were out walking the dogs at Shropham, the home of her aunt, Lady Grogan. It was less than a month after their first meeting at her grandmother's funeral, and initially Lorna had been shocked, saying she would very much like to accompany him to Africa, but as his housekeeper, not his wife. Caught up in his own wonder at the unexpected reliving of his first love, he tried to be understanding. *I expect she's too young to feel deeply about anyone yet*, he wrote to Ethel, *and she's all mixed up with bits of ideas partly out of books . . . Poor girl, it's a bit rough on her trying to decide.*

Lorna told him that she was against marriage in principle, and that she had hoped to study music, medicine or languages, though she doubted her uncle would permit it. But Gore-Browne persisted, taking her to Brooklands, dropping the charms of Shiwa into conversation, showing her photographs of the house and the lake, telling her how it changed colour with the seasons, and recounting stories of hunting, and the Bemba people to whom he said she could teach so much. Something, perhaps her yearning to see Africa again, and his repeated assurances of how useful she would be in his 'mission', persuaded her. One evening in late May, after they had been to see *Tristan and Isolde* at Covent Garden and he had seen her home to the Goldmans, he received a note at his club, the Army & Navy in Pall Mall. Recognizing her loopy handwriting, he opened it nervously, then saw the one word answer he so longed for. The following week he had swept into Sherborne school one evening and told Lorna's headmistress he was taking his 'fiancée' out for dinner. 'We don't have fiancées here,' said a shocked Mrs Mulliner. 'You do now,' he replied.

Yet he worried she would change her mind, right up to the morning of Saturday 23 July, when, resplendent in cream chiffon, she had walked up the aisle towards him in the society church of St George's, Hanover Square and said 'I do' in front of Lord Portsmouth, the Earl of Lovelace, General Purvis, his commander from his time training the raw recruits of the 17th

Division at Swanage, and a host of his titled friends and relatives. Bach's 'Toccata and Fugue' and Purcell's 'Trumpet Tune and Air' were played during the signing of the register, and the couple spent their wedding night at Bingham's Melcombe. Gore-Browne kept *The Times* cutting reporting the wedding in his wallet, almost as if he didn't believe she was really his. He found it odd to have the name Lorna on his tongue again after all those years, a name he thought lost to him for ever, and to start with in his diary referred to her as Lorna 2. Lorna herself apparently had no idea what her mother had been to him, but he knew behind their backs people talked disapprovingly about him marrying the daughter of his childhood sweetheart. Lady Grogan, Lorna's aunt and sister of the first Lorna, had not attended the wedding, claiming to be ill-disposed, and Thomas Hardy, the writer, who had been a friend of her grandfather, the late Reginald Bosworth Smith, and often spent time at Bingham's Melcombe, where Gore-Browne had met him back in 1905, was so taken with the story that he wrote a poem entitled 'Lorna the Second'.

Now, seven months after meeting Gore-Browne at her grandmother's funeral, Lorna was about to see the magical lake he had told her of that first day. He asked James to stop the car, then leaned over to roll down her window, and pointed reverentially, nervous of her reaction. It was important to him that she understood its charm and cared about it as he did, so that she could share his vision of the place. Lorna poked out her head, her emerald engagement ring flashing in the sunlight as her hand rested on the window, and happily inhaled the warm dust and woodsmoke smell of Africa that unlocked memories of her childhood. Far below, where the trees ended and the earth met the wide blue canvas of the sky, she would see a strip of water glinting deeper blue in the afternoon sun, and behind it a distant line of purple hills.

'It's beautiful, my Man,' she said, using her pet name for him, 'exactly how a lake should be. Like something out of a fairytale.'

I always think it looks like a little bit of Italy transported here to the middle of Africa, Gore-Browne had once written to Ethel. *It's a Mediterranean colour, not an African blue in the least.*

James restarted the motor and continued along the track which was now heading downwards, though still with no visible end. Gesturing towards an area of trampled bushes and mopani trees stripped of leaves, he remarked that elephants had been passing. They had seen only the odd puku darting into the bush on the two-day drive to Shiwa, though it often felt as though there were eyes watching them, and the couple looked eagerly out of the car windows. Gore-Browne recounted the story of how he had got in trouble with the local magistrate during one of his first years at Shiwa for inadvertently killing a bull elephant that was charging some of his men, not for killing it but for his failure to obtain a licence beforehand.

The Morris slowed as they reached level ground, and bumped heavily on some tree roots and into a grove of tall blue gum trees casting long purple shadows on the ground. A wind had got up, making rustling sounds of the leaves, and a cluster of pink brick cottages with tiled roofs and chimneys came into view, a marked contrast with the mud hut villages which they had seen along the way. These were the workers' houses, and Gore-Browne pointed out some larger buildings on the right which he said were farm buildings and workshops, and beyond those the oil-press and still-room where they had started producing essential oils which would end up in eau-de-Cologne and lavender water. He had told Lorna about Chitukututuku, the steam-engine which produced the steam for distilling the oils. On the left, he pointed out the village store which he rented out to an Indian gentleman called Mr Shem, who he said would try to swindle her out of vast amounts of coin in return for a bar of carbolic soap and a box of matches.

A little further on they came to the estate office and gatehouse – a high brickwork arch supporting a tiled clocktower in the style of an English schoolhouse. Just over the arch was the date 1920, when the building of Shiwa had started, and a carved black rhinoceros. Gore-Browne explained how he had shot a rhino by the lake on his very first visit there in 1914, providing meat for the whole village, and they had given him the name Chipembele. He did not think it necessary to explain any other significance the name might have – he had described his relations with the natives on the estate in rather glowing terms to his new bride.

The car turned through the arch and up the long drive, the engine protesting noisily as always at the gradient. Dark spindly Italian cypress trees lined either side, and Lorna felt a stab of panic about her new life. Always highly strung and still somewhat awed in her husband's presence, up until now there had been other people around, places to visit, familiar settings. Now it would just be them, far from anything.

And then, there it was, the house. He had shown her black and white photographs of it back in England and she knew it was majestic, but nothing could have prepared her for the shock of actually seeing it there in the bush. Red-bricked and rambling, with a huge heavy wooden arched door and arched windows, orange honeysuckle and deep pink bougainvillaea climbing up the wall, and a Union Jack flying from the first floor terrace. Rising up behind was a wooden hillside dotted with clumps of grey rock. In front the garden was bursting with colour, as if nature was trying to show what she too could do. The flowers were larger and brighter than they would be in England, with waxy petals forming bells, stars and trumpets in brilliant pinks, deep purples, vivid yellows and bridal whites. The birds which flew in and out of the bushes and trees seemed to come in every colour of the rainbow and sing in every tone of the harmonic scale. It was how Lorna had always imagined the Garden of Eden when her mother had read Bible stories to her as a child. No one could fail to be impressed by the building of such a house in the middle of nowhere, yet as other visitors were to note, *there was something incongruous about it, like coming across a mud hut or a herd of buffalo in Piccadilly Circus.*

As the car drew to a halt, a loud clapping started and Lorna looked at her husband in surprise. On either side of the path to the main door, the household staff and *capitaos* were lined up in their uniform of white cotton shift tops, scarlet bermuda shorts and scarlet waistcoats or cummerbunds, some with shining medals pinned on to their chests. Round faces in shades from copper to mahogany grinned out at them from under scarlet fez hats.

Pleased to see that his servants had arranged a welcome as instructed, though disappointed that there was no sign of Joe Savill, his general manager, Gore-Browne got out and walked round to Lorna's side to give her his arm. She worked her feet back into the tight black winklepickers, shook out the calf-length sky-blue gingham skirt and cape he had bought her in London, and tried to plump some life into her flat brown hair, which had been shaped into a shiny flapper-style bob for the wedding but was now back to its usual lifeless self. She pulled on her blue felt cloche hat and stepped down on to the running board, trying her hardest to look dignified but stern, the way she thought befitted the mistress of such a house.

Arm in arm, the couple walked forward to be greeted by the line of servants, who, to Lorna's embarrassment, had prostrated themselves on the ground and were rolling around. As they got nearer she could see they were small wiry people. Some had decorated their faces with red ochre markings. A loud drumming started, sending a family of speckled francolin scooting noisily across the lawn, their blue and red necks working up and down as they ran. Women in boldly patterned dresses came forward, ululating to the rhythm, and urging towards her a small band of children with black shining eyes. Frowning with concentration, a tiny girl presented her with a handful of flowers, and they all burst into giggles as Lorna accepted it. She smiled distractedly and tried to fix the scene in her mind to stow away, but it was hard to take in so many heady sensations at once, the loud birdsong in the trees, the sweet perfume of orange blossom, and the house dominating everything like a feisty old mother-in-law.

Gore-Browne waved his hands impatiently to halt the drumming, and gave a short speech in Bemba, a strange language with a warm fruity sound. Perhaps because of having been born in Germany, and brought up in South Africa, Lorna had a good ear for languages and she hoped she would be able to pick this one up soon. She stepped forward as he began to introduce everyone, starting with Peter Mulemfwe, his chief foreman, a middle-aged man with a rifle on his back, an ebony assegai and a wide grin, who Gore-Browne told her had been with him since 1911 and had taught him to hunt. Next in line was Kakumbi, a tall, beaming man, slightly hunched, with grizzled hair and a chest full of medals, whose adventures in London Gore-Browne had already amused her with. Then came James Mwanza, his trusted chief clerk who did the typing, kept the accounts and handed out the wages; Polleni and Reuben, the butlers; Kalikeka, the chief cook; Mashilipa, his assistant; George, the pudding maker, and various kitchen and serving-boys; as well as room-servants. After these came the *capitaos* – Walimaposo in charge of building, Sam who ran the orchards, Massiti, the head gardener, and Henry, the chief carpenter, who her husband said could run up an Elizabethan cabinet in no time.

'*Mwasibukeni*,' said one after another, putting their palms together as if in prayer, bending their knees low and bowing their heads low in greeting.

'*Eyamukwayi*,' she replied as her husband had taught her, despairing that she would ever remember their names, apart from Livingstone and Stanley, the laundry-boys. Gore-Browne assured her she would have no difficulty in remembering once they started causing trouble. *Give them an inch and they'll take ten miles*, he had written on more than one occasion to Ethel.

Finally they reached the end of the line and stopped under the gabled porch. Either side of the front door was a black wooden rhino head and on top of the plinth a long carved crocodile. One of the butlers opened the doors and Gore-Browne's young terrier Kim bounded out, jumping around them, its pink tongue hanging out. He wondered if he should carry Lorna over the threshold, joking that he was not sure that his old bones could take it. He had initially been proud to have captured such a young wife, and generally made light of the fact that he was more than twice her age, but despite his tough appearance, he was a highly sensitive man and hurt by outsiders' comments on the subject. He was never to frame their wedding picture and was angry when, at a ball in Zanzibar where the couple were fêted by the island's top white officials, Lorna had daubed her face with cosmetics in an obvious attempt to make herself look older.

Lifting Lorna in his arms and into the house, to the clapping of all the servants, he wondered at her lightness. *I felt as if she could be borne away on the breeze*, he recounted to his aunt, almost as if she were an exotic bird that might fly from its cage. He placed her on her feet inside the hallway. Although Lorna did not realize it, he too was nervous. He had written from England to ask his manager, *to have the house white-washed and so on against our arrival. I think it worth spending a few pounds lest my wife should be so overcome with horror that she demands to be returned at once to England . . . Seriously though, a great deal depends on first impressions, don't you think?*

Lorna looked around curiously. Her first impressions were of cool stone, white walls, lofty ceilings and a grand wooden stairway leading upwards with heavy banisters either side, each guarded by a carved wooden warrior bearing a knob-kerry. She followed him into a series of large rooms. It was hard to take everything in but she had the impression of dark masculine furniture, red damask drapes, silver-framed photographs, and a vast silver candelabra. Dominating the drawing-room was an enormous lifesize oil-painting in a gold frame, of a slender, glamorous lady with strawberry hair and peachy complexion, dressed in a gold and white satin suit and clutching a white ostrich feather fan. Lorna stared at it for a moment, finding something familiar in the direct blue-eyed gaze though not recognizing it as that of the now matronly grey-haired aunt Ethel dressed for her presentation at Court, until her husband told her.

As they walked around corridors and courtyards and room after room, she lost all sense of direction. The house seemed even bigger inside than outside, and was filled with marble busts and paintings of lords and ladies, most of whom seemed to be relations of her husband. Along the corridor were coloured engravings of various regiments, and in the library a glass case of his medals. On the round mahogany table in the library stood a silver-framed photograph of Ethel at the wheel of a car, and another on the desk in his bedroom of Ethel in her Red Cross nurse's uniform during the war. To anyone seeing the house, it must have looked as if it had been built with Ethel in mind. Surprised, Lorna asked why his beloved aunt had never visited the place. Gore-Browne told her that his uncle had been more or less an invalid whom Ethel could not leave, and that she was always busy with her charity work, her 'salon' in Surrey, and the Brooklands racetrack, which had reopened in 1924 after being reconcreted to repair damage caused by its use as a base for the Army Flying Corps during the war, and was now flourishing again. In fact, he had asked Ethel to come out to Shiwa as 'companion' to Lorna, but she had refused, though he still hoped to change her mind and in fact had even written to her from Bingham's Melcombe, four days after their wedding, to ask her to join them on their honeymoon. On her advice, he had not told his wife of the invitation.

Seeing that Lorna was looking pale, he realized in his eagerness to show her around the house he had not offered her tea or let her rest, quite neglecting his usual impeccable manners. *I've become so used to bachelordom that I'm forgetting how to treat a lady*, he wrote to Ethel. *Poor thing, I think she must have been affected by the altitude, it's almost 5,000 feet you know and many people find it hard to adapt to though I've never had a problem with it myself.*

He led his young wife past the library to her rooms – a large dressing-room and a front-facing bedroom overlooking the gardens. An oval mirror hung on the wall, a Persian rug lay on the wooden floor, and an armchair and table stood in front of a fireplace where a small fire had been prepared in the grate, though not yet lit. Her few pieces of luggage that had come with them were piled in one corner, the treasured violin case balanced on top. Gore-Browne apologized for the lack of decoration, explaining that he had not expected to return from England with a wife, and promising that Joe Savill's carpenters would make her a dressing-table to any design she chose from one of his books, and that they could order new curtains and carpets from the Army & Navy Stores. He suggested they hang on the wall the Canaletto-style oil-painting he had bought her in Venice at St Mark's Square.

Picking up a brass bell from the mantelpiece, he rang it three times. A young boy came running whom he introduced as Lameki, her room-servant, who would bring her tea or fresh orange juice, prepare her clothes and heat water for a bath. Taking out his watch, Gore-Browne said he would meet her in the library at six o'clock sharp for sundowners, then left, his brisk footsteps dying away on the stone floor.

Lorna turned her attention to her eager-faced new assistant, who addressed her as Mama and told her to take off her shoes for a foot massage, something he said he regularly did 'for the *bwana*'. She declined, asking instead for tea and a bath. Lameki cast a curious look at the violin case and scurried off. Lorna walked over to the windows set in deep arches, alcoves in the thick walls in which one could sit. Outside, women in bright dresses were sashaying along the grove of feather-blossomed jacaranda trees, some with babies in slings on their backs and all with baskets on their heads. Beyond she could just see the lake, turning pink in the late afternoon light. So much beauty.

11

Shiwa House, that evening

The darkness which fell on Shiwa was so complete that even as Lorna's eyes adjusted she could make out little. The window was slightly ajar and there was a sweet fragrance coming from outside – something between lavender and frangipani. Becoming aware of a repeated tapping at her door, she realized that she must have dozed off after her bath, and fumbled for the handle to find Lameki standing there clutching a lighted candle and looking worried.

All the servants knew better than to be late for the *bwana*, fearing his 'big stick' that he kept on his belt, but Lorna laughed at Lameki's concern and shooed him away once he had lit the hurricane lamp. She slipped into her dressing-room and carefully put on a mustard crêpe suit with a calf-length pleated skirt and long jacket, conscious she still looked far more like the schoolgirl she had been a few months earlier than a married woman.

She found her way along the dark corridors to the library, where a lively fire was burning. Her husband was nowhere to be seen. Instead a servant whose name she had forgotten appeared as if from nowhere and led her wordlessly downstairs to the dining-room, where the long table had been set for dinner with one place setting at either end. Gore-Browne was standing at the window with his back to her, one arm folded behind his back and one hand in his pocket, but turned and came forward to take her hand as she entered. He was dressed stiffly in black lounge suit and white tie and looked as if he was fighting off an urge to look at his watch.

Nodding to a waiter who held out a chair for her at one end of the long table, Gore-Browne took a bottle of Pol Roger from a silver bucket on a side cabinet to celebrate their first night. There was no ice in the bucket and he apologized for it not being chilled, though the cellar kept bottles fairly cool. He always opened champagne himself, as the house servants tended to get so carried away shaking the bottles that guests ended up having a shower. Popping the cork with the suavity of one who has done so many times, he wrapped a white cloth round the neck of the bottle and poured it into two crystal flutes. Taking his place at the opposite end of the table, he waited for Jackson the servant to serve them, then lifted his glass in a toast. 'Chin, chin, my dear Lorna. To life at Shiwa.'

'Chin, chin.' She raised her glass and drank, the tiny bubbles tickling her nostrils.

Another servant entered, mincing uncomfortably in the black patent shoes which Gore-Browne insisted all waiting staff wore, and bearing a silver tray in his white gloves from which he served slices of chicken liver pâté on to their gold-rimmed Meissen plates. It must have made an odd scene, the husband and wife so far apart, the large silver candelabra in the centre casting shadows on the white linen cloth, the room silent except for the grind of their cutlery on the plates and the loud tick of the grandfather clock in the hall. Various oil-painted ancestors looked down on them from the walls. In the centre was Gore-Browne's grandfather, Sir Thomas Gore-Browne, Ethel's late father, who had been Governor of St Helena, New Zealand, Tasmania and Bermuda, and whose prominent nose had clearly been inherited by his grandson. Next to him was a chubby-faced man in bishop's robes, Gore-Browne's uncle Wilfred Gore-Browne, the first Bishop of Kimberley. On the other side of Sir

Thomas was his wife, the beautiful raven-haired Lady Harriet, Gore-Browne's late grandmother from the Campbell family of Craigie in Ayrshire, whom he had always called Grammy.

Having cleared away the first course, Jackson and another servant entered with silver platters of wild duck in orange sauce, sweet potatoes and green peas. The servants were always forgetting to warm up the plates, to the irritation of Gore-Browne, who found cold plates a particular dislike, even noting the event in his diary. His rebuke unnerved Jackson, who was already having difficulty manipulating the serving fork and spoon with the tight-fitting gloves. Nervous herself, and not used to champagne, young Lorna must have found it hard not to giggle, but she had been warned to behave by her uncle Major Goldman, who had always complained that she was an unruly creature, and she was eager to impress her new husband and show him that she was a worthy mistress of this great house.

Gore-Browne told her that his general manager, Joe Savill, was back and would come over for lunch with them the next day. While she was sleeping he had been catching up with what had been happening on the estate in his ten-month absence. The leopards which had been causing trouble before he left had continued raiding the farm, stealing ducks and chickens, getting twenty-two in one night and terrorizing the village, killing the wife of one of his builders while she was out fetching water. Lorna's eyes lit up at the news. Leopards were rather more exciting than boarding school in Dorset, and in years to come she was to develop her own leopard traps. She asked why they didn't use poison, and he explained that they had tried all sorts of things but these leopards just ignored the poisoned bait, and seemed incredibly arrogant, often passing right by the windows of the dining-room where they were sitting. He had told Peter Mulemfwe to arrange a hunting party.

A fussy eater, Lorna picked at her food, brightening only

at the sight of dessert, which was a plate of pink shape, made from milk and strawberries from the estate. Unlike the first few years when Shiwa produced almost nothing, far more was now home-produced – all their meat and milk, fruit, sugar and cooking oils, though not enough of anything to sell. Butter and cheese was bought from Kasama, and tea, coffee, biscuits, flour, candles and blankets came from Thatcher & Hobsons, the store 400 miles away in Broken Hill which sent a lorry up north, stopping at Shiwa, every two weeks. The only household items imported were luxury goods such as chocolate and fine soaps from England, wine from France, sherry from Spain and port from Portugal. They were still far from making money, but Gore-Browne was hopeful that the essential oils would soon take off.

He promised to show his wife round the estate the next day, though doubted she would be up early enough to accompany him on his usual pre-breakfast walk. Lorna was keen to go out on the lake, and he warned her that the natives were terrified of it and would tell her all sorts of legends about a terrible beast inhabiting its depths. There had been an enormous outcry when he had put a canoe on the water for the first time a few years earlier, the villagers all convinced he would be devoured by either the beast or one of the famous crocodiles, huge creatures twelve or thirteen feet long which emerged every so often and ate a staff member. *Natural wastage, I call it*, Gore-Browne had written to Ethel.

The servant returned with cheese and biscuits, a plate of roasted groundnuts and a silver coffee-pot. Taking two tiny cups from the glass-fronted cabinet, he poured the bitter Turkish coffee, a taste which Gore-Browne had acquired from Ethel. After coffee, he usually went upstairs to the library terrace for a glass of port and a cigar, and he suggested that Lorna accompany him.

The library was lit by candles and Gore-Browne opened the doors to the terrace to let in the warm fragrant air and the buzz of cicadas. The moon was almost full and cast a silvery finger across the floor. On the table, a crystal decanter and two glasses had been set out on a tray, full of ruby port from his friend Victor Delaforce in Oporto, with whom he had stayed several times. Gore-Browne had retained a link with Portugal since training some of their men in the war. *Funny people the Portuguese*, he had written to his aunt. *A little like Africans in the sense that they're as lazy as anything and only work if watched, but well meaning*. He had kept in touch with several, including General Hipólito, *a charming old buffer who always keeps one hand in a purple glove for reasons no one seems to know*, and had recently learnt that a Portuguese explorer, Dr Lacerda e Almeida, had been the first white man in the Shiwa area, even before Livingstone, though he had died while waiting months to be received by the Kazembe king.

Lorna enjoyed listening to her husband's stories about his travels, longing to see the whole world herself, and he loved to tell them, sucking occasionally on a large cigar and watching his young wife indulgently as her eyes sparkled in the candlelight. *I do hope she won't be bored here*, he wrote to Ethel. *You and I with our love for books and the big things in life would fit in very well but it is not for everybody as I have learnt*.

Seeing the gramophone, and the large pile of records alongside, she asked if they could have music and began to search through the pile, looking for something to dance to and finding mostly boxed sets of opera. Lorna was extremely musical, with a lovely singing voice and an ability to play almost any instrument she picked up from flute to guitar, though violin was her favourite, but the couple had married so quickly that they did not really yet know each other's taste in music. Lorna drew out Beethoven's 'Sonata Pathétique', exclaiming that her mother used to play it on the piano. 'No, not that,' he told her, his sharp tone making her look up. Instead, he asked her to find *La Bohème*, and placed Act I on the turntable, winding up the gramophone and recalling that the last time he had listened to this music in this room was just before the rains the previous year when he was feeling quite alone.

Lorna went outside on to the terrace, and from the french windows he watched her leaning against the parapet, silhouetted against the moon. She turned towards him with that Madonna look in her eyes, so much like her mother that for a moment he was about to recall the time they had gone to Covent Garden to hear *La Bohème*. He stopped himself just in time, instead suggesting she get out her violin and play for him one evening.

'Why not a musical evening?' she asked, excitedly. 'We could invite some people.'

But at Shiwa there was no one to invite. Joe Savill had no ear for classical music, and they had no neighbours. *Dinner guests have to stay a few nights and tend to be of the stuffed shirt colonial officer variety*, Gore-Browne had once written to Ethel. *Do nothing but run down the Bantu.*

Knowing his love for music, Lorna was surprised to find that her husband had no piano at Shiwa. He explained the difficulty of getting one all the way out there, but she retorted that there was a road now, and that he had managed to get a four-poster bed out. 'Touché!' he laughed and put an arm on her shoulder, stroking her hair gingerly. In those early days they were still awkward in each other's company, she for youth and inexperience and he for his own upright manner.

Hearing a noise in the blackness, Gore-Browne pulled away and looked out. In the garden below, one of the hunters was standing holding an oil-lamp.

'Here is Jeffrey, *bwana*,' he said. 'I've come from Peter Mulemfwe, *bwana*, he's out hunting over by Mansya river and says for you to come quick quick.'

Gore-Browne turned to Lorna. He did not like to leave her on their first night but he knew Peter wouldn't summon him unless it was urgent. Telling her not to wait up, he left to change and get his guns and hip-flask of whisky.

Lorna sat on the terrace wall and watched the moon and immense sprinkling of stars, Sirius, Orion and the Southern Cross. After a while her husband appeared on the lawn down below, and with a quick wave and call of 'Go to bed!' he was swallowed up by the velvety darkness. She sat for a while longer, listening to the competing sounds of the African night, the cry of nightjars and a pair of hippo lowing at each other in the lake. Inside, she flicked idly through the visitors' book, where her husband had noted details of every guest in perfect black copperplate, so very different from her own childish untamed scrawl. There were months at a time when nobody came to the house.

Later, lying in the unfamiliar bed, clad in her long-white *brodérie anglaise* nightgown which had been a wedding present, all manner of thoughts ran through her mind. Lorna always had problems sleeping and it must have been even harder sleeping in this strange new house in the middle of nowhere, her head spinning from the wine and the unaccustomed altitude. The house seemed much bigger at night, full of all sorts of unidentifiable noises as if it had taken on its own life. In the distance she heard barking and wondered whether it was the ghost of Livingstone's dog Chitane, which Gore-Browne had told her was buried on the hill behind the house.

She thought about her husband's faraway expression when listening to *La Bohème*, and remembered her aunt Ellinor's cryptic warning, 'Don't forget, child, there's always a snake in paradise,' in a letter after she had told her excitedly of her engagement to this dashing colonel and how she was going to be mistress of his big house by the lake in the remote African valley. She knew many people raised eyebrows at the age gap, and she was sad to have abandoned her dreams of studying medicine to be a famous doctor like her father. But ghosts or no ghosts, life at Shiwa was going to be an adventure, and had to be better than living with the Goldmans, who had been clearly only too anxious to get rid of her.

I always feel more alive hunting, Gore-Browne had once written to Ethel, *particularly at night when all the senses are on alert and all sounds magnified*. In some ways it reminded him of the war. Peter and his men had made camp on the bank of the Mansya where it ran under the wooded cliff which always reminded him of the Thames at Henley. As he and Jeffrey approached, his headman put a finger to his lips and pointed. He followed the man's gaze to the dark forest on the other side of the river.

'*Mbwili*,' whispered Peter. 'Leopard.' For a long time they waited in complete silence, conscious of every crackle of twig and rustle of leaf, and the pant of their own breath. *I began to wonder if Peter had imagined the animals*, he later recounted to Ethel, though years of hunting together had taught him to trust the African's instincts. *Then at the very moment three leopards glided across, coming out of the river bed, looking like dappled ghosts amongst the trees in the moonlight*. As they padded forward, he could see the muscles rippling beneath their pelt and he tensed in excitement. *It was the first time I'd seen a leopard so close up, outside a zoo*. He watched for a moment, captivated, then, at a nod from Peter, lifted his rifle and aimed. The sound of the shot ricocheted around the clearing and one leopard rolled over, the others disappearing into the night. Covered by Jeffrey and Peter in case the other leopards returned to their fellow, he moved cautiously towards the injured animal. Leopards kill their prey by breaking their necks and he had no desire to suffer such a fate. *When I got to it, the beast was all but dead*, he wrote. *Though it couldn't move, it opened his mouth and cursed me with its amber eyes and sharp fangs, and its claws contracted as if it were about to tackle.*

Gore-Browne drew back, but with a long shudder the animal breathed its last, its eyes turning to glass. 'Good show,' Gore-Browne said to his foreman as he gestured for the men to come forward to deal with the dead animal. 'We'll skin it back at the house.'

So heavy was the leopard, presumably from having feasted on so many Shiwa chickens, that it took three men to carry it, raised above their heads. Their arrival in a strange procession caused great excitement back at the village, the whole population of which seemed to have woken up for the great event. Women twirled around them, cheering and singing, and the headman came forward, proffering a gourd of celebratory beer, saying, '*Bwana*, you have unbound the forest for us.'

Gore-Browne liked the phrase, and thought proudly of the magnificent beast he had slain and the good luck it would mean for his new life as a married man. He wondered what to do with the skin, writing to Ethel, *I fancy it will look rather fine in the corridor outside my bedroom.* Extracting himself from the celebrations, after reminding his workers there would be no excuses for turning up late the next morning, he walked up to the house alone. Inside, noticing it was almost four in the morning, he picked up a candle and made for the study. Seating himself at his desk, despite the late hour, he dipped his pen in the black ink and began to write. *My dearest Ethel, I'm feeling pretty bucked tonight. Once again I only wish you had been here . . .*

12

Shiwa Ngandu,
Christmas Day 1930

Gore-Browne had been a keen photographer since the age of sixteen when Nunk had given him his first camera one summer at Brooklands, and he used the medium religiously to document life at Shiwa and progress in building his grand house, filling album after album with black and white photographs, all carefully labelled in his neat writing. Since Lorna's arrival he had started the tradition of a Christmas Day photograph of the household staff, works foremen and wives, assembled on the steps of Shiwa House after Christmas morning service in the library. He told them to wear their uniforms, but predictably some of the men turned up in T-shirts and the women in their Sunday best with large head-scarves tied in complicated knots. Everyone from the area wanted to be in the photograph, having seen the *bwana* around the estate with the strange machine, and there was an excited crowd of onlookers pointing at the camera on its tripod, some of whom kept trying to sneak into the shot. Among those who shouldn't be in the picture he spotted Shem, the Indian storekeeper, his white turban revealing his presence.

It was almost impossible to get everyone to keep still, and he complained to Ethel, *Sometimes it is like dealing with children, even the most basic instructions go unheeded*. Such difficulties made him wonder about the future of the country. While he abhorred the South African credo of racial supremacy, he was by no means ready to see Africans in positions of superiority. *I can't believe you really feel that we settlers should be prepared eventually to live according to the law of the land as administered by the Bantu*, he had written to Ethel in July after she said she supported the controversial Memorandum issued by Ramsay MacDonald's Labour government back home, making it clear that in conflicts between the interests of whites and Africans in the colonies, those of Africans would prevail. Yet as his aunt was quick to remind him, only the previous month he had admitted, *I used to have ideas of conferring patriarchal benefits on the Bantu but that's I'm afraid all moonshine. The natives don't want to be patriarched.*

Even so, Shiwa was very much his own mini-state where he acted as banker, judge and provider, and he clearly relished his role as local squire, clapping his hands and issuing directions. Lorna appeared from the front door cradling a large sleeping baby, and took her place in the centre, an island of pale calm amid all the bright movement.

'Lorn, try and get Mark to look at the camera,' called her husband.

'She's asleep,' she replied firmly. The infant's name was Lorna Katharine and she had been born at Brooklands in April of the previous year by Caesarean after a difficult pregnancy, but Gore-Browne insisted on calling her Mark, claiming it was to avoid the confusion of having two Lornas about the place, and because she was Lorna mark II (or III, as his wife now realized). Yet he wrote the little girl's name as Mark in the photo albums and made no secret of desperately wanting a son and heir to be the next laird of Shiwa, and he was delighted when she told him she was pregnant again.

Gore-Browne looked through the lens one final time then ran round to join Lorna in the centre. Despite the crush of bodies around them, there was a good few inches of space between them and the staff. For a moment there was silence, the Africans all staring ahead, and when the shutter clicked neither he nor Lorna were smiling. He repeated the process twice more until the group started to shift, and the baby, which was teething, began to cry.

Dismissing the crowd with a clap of his hands, Gore-Browne summoned Peter Mulemfwe to call out the register for gifts, wishing the staff all Merry Christmas and warning that if people crowded they would get nothing. One by one names were read out and permanent staff members came forward to receive presents of blankets. With military-style efficiency, Gore-Browne had categorized the blankets from A to D, depending on their quality, and the best and most senior workers got thick woollen A class blankets in cheerful tartans, while lesser mortals were given thin D class worsted blankets in dull brown or hospital blue. No one seemed to mind the discrepancy, wrapping themselves in the blankets and dancing round in delight. For a few privileged souls like Peter there was a bottle of whisky or brandy too, and some shotgun cartridges, everything noted in the estate books.

Lorna had little patience for what she called 'the lord of the manor stuff', and she looked on from a chair on the terrace, her heavy body already dull and slow though the birth was still some months away. Her first pregnancy had been hard, and the second seemed even worse. She avoided catching sight of herself in the mirror because her skin was pasty and blotched and her ankles thick and swollen. She found looking after baby Lorna exhausting and handed her over with relief to Miss Hatwell, the stern English nanny chosen for them by aunt Ethel. She would have preferred someone young and frivolous with whom she could gossip, chatter about clothes and play tennis on their newly built tennis lawn, which was the fascination of the local children who fought to act as ball-boys and changed ends with the players in their eagerness to keep them supplied with balls. Miss Hatwell, whom she referred to as 'that stolid harridan', preferred backgammon. 'Still, she is efficient,' wrote Lorna to her sister-in-law Stella, 'and having her means someone else to deal with the infant's constant bawling. Pity she can't do breastfeeding as well.'

Relieved of the baby, Lorna wandered round the back of the house where the servants' party was under way and took her place by her husband's side. Beer, buns and fizzy drinks had been laid out on trestle tables, and the carcass of an ox hung from a tree, ready to be dismembered and the meat distributed among the staff, each of whom would receive 3lb. The sound of drums started, three pairs of hands patting out the unswerving beat, just as they had in the annual torchlight procession the night before. Colourfully clad women came forward, their large hips swaying fluidly to the rhythm like ships bobbing on a wave, followed by their blanket-clad menfolk. Lorna often felt tempted to cast off her hat and shoes and join in, but her husband was fastidious about maintaining one's dignity.

Just as they were in their own homes, though not in African society, the women were in charge of this dance, a kind of courtship ritual where they chanted and skipped back and forth, clapping and swaying round the man of their choice until he agreed to take to the floor. All sorts of women were dancing – some old with sagging breasts and bellies and masses of petticoats, yet still possessed of a strange grace; others young and lithe with babies in slings on their backs which stayed motionless and doll-like, despite all the movement. One man coaxed into the dance was so fat that as his belly flapped so fast one could hardly make out where it was. The audience roared, and as Lorna joined in the laughter, a small child ran up to her shyly proffering a bottle of orange soda, sent by old Sam, the *capitao* from the still-room. She sipped the sticky sweet liquid, smiling and nodding, as the drumming stopped and Peter and Sam made effusive speeches thanking the *bwana* and his wife for all their kindness and 'bringing joy and prosperity to the Bemba'.

Thanking his staff in return for all their hard work over the year, Gore-Browne reminded them that next day was a working day – well aware that if previous years were anything to go by few would turn up – then left them to their party, which would get louder and livelier as the day wore on and probably move to the village. Lorna followed him to the front of the house where a few servants and a line of donkeys awaited them, which he described to Ethel as *saddled up and laden like a Moorish cavalcade.* As always at Christmas, providing it was fine weather, Gore-Browne had planned a trip to the hot springs at Kapishya, his favourite place on the estate, where only favoured guests were taken. In the dry season they often made the ten-mile journey by *jinga* or bicycle, but at this time of year the ground was too soft and the spindly wheels would stick in the thick red mud. Because of Lorna's condition he had arranged for James to follow them in the Morris, so she could jump in if she got tired.

Riding along the avenue of jacarandas on to the track beside the lake, it was easy to forget the discomfort of sitting atop one of her rather spirited Shiwa donkeys in a long skirt amid the humbling beauty of the place. They were having one of the clear spells that sometimes occurred in the middle of the rainy season. The vast bowl of sky above was a diaphanous blue and the lake a cobalt mirror in which the purple hills were perfectly reproduced. Far off to one side, a dark herd of *sitatunga* cavorted by the shore, and the air seemed filled with the happy chatter of cormorants swooping and diving over the water with the black and white pied kingfishers the village boys delighted in catching to tie on strings. In such fine weather Lorna loved to go out on the lake in *Venus*, the canoe Gore-Browne had bought her for her first birthday spent at Shiwa, and in which he would row her in the moonlight, discussing their dreams of the previous night and interpreting them for each other.

As they rode on, over sand ruts and past swamps dotted with tall razor-edged reeds and white, yellow and pink water-lilies which looked artificial, like Chinese paper flowers, the track widened enabling them to ride beside each other. As always they talked about plans for the estate and all that needed doing. They were intending to start a proper dairy herd so that they could make their own butter rather than fetching it from Kasama, which was a day's drive there and back and where it cost the exorbitant amount of three shillings threepence a pound. They were also planning some extensions to the house, a new guest wing, chapel and another storey, which would mean building some more furniture. Gore-Browne had been going through some new books he had ordered from England, trying to find designs to copy. They had planted some new orange and lime trees and were debating experimenting with coffee and tobacco, both of which were grown further north. Lorna thought they ought to get the natives to plant some sweet potatoes on their small plots as security against a flood such as that two years earlier, which had wiped out their maize crops.

However early they rose and late they slept, there never seemed enough hours to fit everything in, though as Lorna often remarked, there would be more time if her husband didn't write so many letters – 100 or so a week, not counting the almost daily detailed epistles to aunt Ethel into which the trip to the springs would be recounted as everything else. Gore-Browne had tried to insist that she also write a weekly letter to Ethel. Most weeks she pleaded some excuse, and when she ran out of excuses, she dashed off scrappy efforts which she suspected caused the pair some amusement.

Lorna felt hot, sticky and donkey-bruised by the time they arrived by the bend in the Mansya river at the grove of raffia palms enclosing the springs. They had erected a bamboo screen as a changing-room, and she slipped behind to unpin her hat, and cast off her long beige crêpe shirt and calf-length skirt and her muslin bloomers. At least in Africa no one worried about corsets. Naked, she stepped on to the fine white sand and entered the clear turquoise water, lowering her body into its relaxing warmth. The couple floated on their backs, surrounded by little puffs of rising steam, lulled by the tinselly sound of the palm trees overhead and the rush of the river just behind. The warm water lapping round produced a womb-like sensation. A pair of gossamer-winged dragonflies hovered close by, performing a kind of waltz just above the water's surface, and Gore-Browne opened a bottle of champagne and floated a tray towards Lorna, bearing a crystal goblet and a bone china plate of some of the odd-looking mince pies she and the pastry cook had managed to make.

Most romantic of all was spending the night by the springs, floating under the stars like an enchanted princess, picking out Jupiter and the Milky Way. She had suggested to her husband that they build some huts and make a permanent camp there. Since the previous year, with the damming of the Katete river, from which pipes were run into Shiwa House, and the installation of woodburning water heaters, they had had hot running water for baths, no longer having to go through the laborious process of heating buckets of water. But nothing could equal the magic of lying back watching the lattice of leaves against the sky. Sometimes a grey parrot would alight on a branch, regarding them with amused eyes, or a pair of tiny psychedelic violet or bronze birds. All cares seemed to float away, and Aggie, Lorna's personal maid (Gore-Browne having finally acquiesced to having a female servant in the house), would soap her body and knead her shoulder muscles with strong fingers, while one of the men servants did the same to Gore-Browne. Whenever Lorna thought she was being lulled too far into oblivion, she would rise dripping and wander through the mud to the river, where she would jump in to cool off, apparently oblivious to the threat of snakes or crocodiles.

It was an idyllic time in their own personal paradise, far from thoughts of negative bank accounts and failing crops, and Gore-Browne regarded his pregnant young wife with both affection and alarm, worried about the baby which he was sure would be a son. Despite her nervous disposition, Africa seemed to hold no fear for her. He had written to Ethel the previous week that he could no longer imagine a time when Lorna wasn't there, adding, *I don't know why Lorn married me, but I thank the Lord daily and hourly that she did.* He had always thought of himself as very self-contained, but he had to admit, *It's nice to have someone to share things with – the good and the bad.* She seemed to believe in the project and had taken on a lot of the work of the estate, overseeing the kitchens to produce the fine food he adored, even if she ate like a bird herself, and was never fazed by the guests who turned up unannounced, enticed by the idea of an English country house weekend in Africa. *Unfortunately very rarely people of our own type*, he moaned to his aunt.

But the three years since Lorna's arrival at Shiwa had not been easy. Their first year together, when they could have done with some calm to adjust to each other's ways, there had been terrible floods, washing away the bridges and cutting off the estate completely from the outside world, as well as waterlogging the nurseries and orchards, wreaking havoc on their crops, and they had had to buy in emergency grain to stop villagers from starving. As for the essential oils for perfumes which had been his great hope for the estate, the experimental phase had taken much longer than he had ever envisaged and they were still not making money. In fact a thorough going-over of last year's accounts in yet another attempt to see what might actually generate money had shown that the geraniums, which had once been his biggest hope of all, had produced only 8lb of oil last year and cost five times as much to grow as their return. Far from his dream of self-sufficiency and creating a model for both natives and settlers, Shiwa Ngandu was still eating up over £4,000 a year, more than twice the return on his entire worldly capital, and if it wasn't for the flow of funds from Brooklands he would not have been able to carry on. Although the Brooklands racetrack was going through a sticky period, Ethel regularly sent him large cheques, faithful as always to the need to support 'big ideas'. Gore-Browne realized now how naïve he had been at the start of this venture, trying to produce essential oils with information from Provence and the Côte d'Azur, which were hardly similar to tropical Africa. 'It is quite useless to think of starting to manufacture essential oils without a considerable amount of capital,' he wrote in the *Rhodesian Agricultural Journal*. But even so, white farmers with more conservative crops, far more experience, and in less isolated places like the European enclaves of Fort Jameson and Abercorn upcountry, were going bankrupt.

One problem with essential oils was that the market was very speculative – peppermint oil, for example, which had been £6 per lb when he started growing it in 1925, was now down to 7 shillings. 'Essential oils are not money for nothing in any sense of the phrase,' he stated in the same article. He hoped the coming year would be better. He felt relieved that they had finally decided to give up on the geraniums – as he wrote to Ethel, *they are a blasted nuisance that have never grown well and need intensive weeding*. One acre of geraniums with 10–15,000 plants yielded less than 20lb of oil a year, which was worth under £16, and most of the plants seemed to die off in their first year, eaten by white ants or killed by the excessive damp of the rainy season. Instead, they planned to concentrate on producing lemongrass, lime and eucalyptus oil, and neroli from oranges. Thomas Durrans, his oils expert in England, had recently sent him his first favourable analysis, reporting both the citriadora from eucalyptus and lemongrass as 'good marketable oils'. He was also experimenting with spearmint, coriander and fennel. But his main hope now lay with citrus, and during the year they had planted another 10,000 lime trees and 3,300 orange trees, and if they didn't start getting a good yield and price soon, he wasn't sure what they would do.

So much of what they needed still had to be shipped from England, or brought up from Bulawayo or Johannesburg on the appalling roads. Sometimes he thought the whole scheme crazy and ill-fated. The biggest disappointment was the complete lack of interest of the Bemba in the success of the project. Even the brick houses he had built to replace their huts seemed a failure: 'While they did not actively resent living in them, they appeared to feel absolutely no responsibility for keeping them in a decent condition,' he later wrote in a paper on his experiences. But Ethel was unflagging in her support, and every so often things happened which made him feel he was really doing *something worthwhile for the native* and making his presence felt in a way he never would have in England. Bunker Willis, the provincial commissioner over at Kasama and *rather a decent fellow as colonial officers go*, had asked him to attend a special conference on the future education of Africans in the Northern Province. *I'll have more than a few words to say about that*, he told Ethel, adding that it was time they tried again to open their own school at Shiwa, his first attempt having failed. The Reverend Macminn and his wife over at Lubwa Mission did their best, but they were getting on in years, and were missionaries after all and thus could never be entirely trusted in his view.

With so much to think about, the skilful fingers of the masseur to relax him, and a bottle of champagne to finish, the hours slipped past, and it was only the cry of a fish-eagle flying overhead that alerted Gore-Browne to the streaks of mauve in the small window of sky visible through the palms. He was always careful not to stay in the water too late in the afternoon, and to be out and covered up by mosquito time when the risk of malaria increased ten-fold, and he roused Lorna, who was floating on her back, eyes closed, hair spread around her in the water in dark fronds, looking for all the world like a swollen Ophelia.

Gore-Browne was a great stickler for tradition, having happy memories of festive parties at Brooklands, and he tried to keep Christmas dinner at Shiwa as faithful to the British model as possible. There was spurwing goose from the lake instead of turkey, but it was stuffed with apricots and figs, and served with green beans, peas and sweet potatoes. For dessert they had the Christmas pudding Lorna had made in November, which was *not at all bad*, particularly after he had doused it in brandy and set it alight, then served it with brandy cream sauce, though neither of them found the lucky sixpence, and Gore-Browne wondered if the cook had pocketed it. To make the table more festive they had placed red candles in the silver candelabra. In place of a tree Lorna had planted large branches of cypress in a pot and decorated them with glass baubles sent out from the Army & Navy stores.

After dinner they went out to the porch to listen to songs by some of the local children in the moonlight, their small faces white-eyed and earnest. Gore-Browne felt in his pocket for some coins to give them, and called one of the house-boys to bring mince pies and cocoa. He and Lorna then went up to the library, where in the morning he had read the lesson and they had sung carols. A fire had been lit and they sat listening to 78s from the set of Bach cantatas which Lorna had bought him for Christmas, and roasting chestnuts sent out from Brooklands. Christmas cards were strung on ribbons all round the room, but as usual most would arrive in the New Year. Gore-Browne had sent out 300 that year. He poured some of his special 1896 Martinez port which Ethel had let him have from the Brooklands cellar, and sat back contentedly, listening to the music and the crackle of the fire. *All in all a pretty good show*, he wrote in his diary, adding, *I can't remember when I enjoyed a Christmas more.*

He wondered if he should have invited some young people to make it more lively for Lorna, knowing how much she loved dancing, but she had insisted that she didn't mind a quiet Christmas. Sometimes he thought he caught a longing in her eye and he hoped that the isolation and loneliness of the place, which he so revelled in, wouldn't become too oppressive for her. *Actually these evenings alone together are my favourite time*, he wrote to Ethel, when Lorna would do mending or sewing of clothes or the overalls she wore round the estate (and he hated), and he would read aloud from books, usually biographies of famous leaders and military heroes like the Duke of Wellington which he ordered from London after reading the *Literary Review*. That night he planned to start reading the new biography of Napoleon which had come in his Christmas box from Brooklands. Describing the scene to his aunt, he wrote, *It's all very dignified and very quiet, rather like a Dutch picture, and as if the earth were standing still.*

13

Shiwa Ngandu,
29 January 1932

The heavy rains cleared as suddenly as they had come, leaving the afternoon air so clean and fresh that it reminded Gore-Browne of northern Italy and the Apennines in the long-ago days of his motor tours with Ethel. *Each year I forget how beautiful this time of early rains can be*, he jotted in pencil in the small notebook he carried with him from which he would later write up his diary, putting order into the day, as he liked to think of it. *'Ille Amarum mihi, super omnes angulus ridet' and never more so.* Shutting the much-hated accounts book, he locked up the estate office with its huge drums of meal from which workers were given their weekly ration, and wandered across the track to the still-room where a procession of ebony-skinned women were arriving in boldly coloured dresses, babies in slings on their backs and large woven baskets on their heads filled with golden coloured limes or waxy white orange blossoms for essential oil production. *How graceful the women look*, he wrote to Ethel, *and how well they fit in the overall picture.* '*Mwasibukeni*', he nodded in the usual greeting, eliciting a giggling chorus of '*Eyamukwayi*' as they bobbed down respectfully, hands together as if in prayer, while careful not to upset their loads.

The still-room was a long brick shed, inside which, amid all the clamour and steam, old Sam was overseeing the distillation process, barking instructions as little boys ran in with logs from the woodpile in the yard and delivered them to men who opened the boiler doors then rammed them into the flames. Balanced up above, on narrow boards, other men were oiling machinery, checking the pipes to ensure they were steamtight, and tipping the baskets of fragrant white flowers into vast copper vats where they would be turned into a pulpy mass which Gore-Browne told Ethel, *looks like sludge but is worth its weight in gold*. Out of it came the essence used to scent expensive soaps and perfumes that would be worn by *grandes dames* in Paris and London. He had bought the distilling equipment in France for £50. The vat was fitted with a perforated tray and when it was almost full, a jet of steam was directed in from underneath. As the steam passed through, the oils in little sacs inside the orange blossom petals turned to gas and were driven off with it. The steam was then cooled, condensing into water, and the oil, being insoluble, would rise to the top. Finally the water was run off, leaving liquid neroli, as attar of oranges is known, a vital constituent of eau-de-Cologne and lavender water. The quantities needed were enormous: 2,500lb of blossom – about 130 trees in full bloom – would yield less than 2lb of oil. This was the first year that Shiwa had produced enough orange blossom to distil, and Gore-Browne vowed his neroli would be as good as any that came out of France.

Extracting the oils was a simple process in theory, but it had to be right, and it was not always easy to retain the oil's fragrance. Picking was supposed to be done shortly after daybreak because the rising sun causes evaporation of oil from the petals, but it was now the height of the season and blossoms were gathered without interruption, distillation continuing all through the night. 'It is not the case,' wrote Gore-Browne in the *Rhodesian Agricultural Journal*, 'that an ordinary native is quite capable of taking charge of the process.' In previous years they had experienced problems because oils had been overheated: once they had lost lemongrass oil because they let the grass sit too long before distilling it, and another time a special implement, laboriously designed by Joe Savill to extract oil from lime peel, turned out to be penetrating too deep and they had ended up with lime juice rather than oil.

This year the lime crop was looking good, which was just as well as Gore-Browne was hoping to take advantage of the crisis in the West Indies where the citrus trees had been devastated by hurricanes, pushing up the world price of lime oil despite the Depression, which had sent all other commodity prices tumbling. They used no fertilizers because of the cost of obtaining them in such an isolated spot, so everything depended on good weather. In theory an orange tree blooms and bears fruit when it is six years old, but Shiwa's poor soil meant it was taking longer. The estate had yet to earn more than £135 a year from oils – a tiny fraction of its annual outlay. When Gore-Browne had first started out the only essential oil he had ever heard of was attar of roses, but after his brother's research in the main producing areas of France and Bulgaria he had planted peppermint, camphor, lavender and all manner of things. However, only eucalyptus had taken to the Shiwa soil, and the citriadora oil produced from its leaves had never fetched a very good price. Since the previous year the market had collapsed altogether, while the Depression had sent costs soaring. What with Lorna's trip to England to give birth to their second daughter, Angela, the previous June, the year's expenses for the estate looked set to top £5,000.

Mostly at Lorna's instigation they had been trying to cut costs, reducing the amount of labour on their books, which at times had gone above 1,200 people. The construction of an elaborate irrigation system with brick sluices and a dam across the upper Mansya river meant plants no longer had to be watered by hand during the dry season, and abandoning the geraniums had cut down on the seventy or eighty people they had employed for weeding. But Gore-Browne found it hard to say 'No' – he felt responsible for his little corner of the world. 'His people', as he thought of Bemba, needed jobs, and he liked to give presents to reward those who did well, or money for educating their children to give them a chance in life.

A lot of the expense had gone on extending the house. Over the last couple of years they had added a proper wine cellar, a cloistered courtyard with additional guest-rooms, a swimming-pool for the children, and the tower he had always dreamed of, as well as a covered loggia outside Lorna's room on the first floor where she had taken to sleeping. He had built arches over the front terrace to give it the appearance of a grand Tuscan manor house, which he thought no one could fail to be impressed with. He knew some settlers referred to it derisorily as 'Liverpool Cathedral', but walking quickly back up the lawn he looked at it with satisfaction. *It is the sort of home one would be proud to leave for descendants in generations to come*, he had written to Ethel, though he still didn't have the male heir he dreamt of. *It's silly to be cramped in Central Africa*, he added.

Noticing dark banks of cloud gathering again in the Mpika direction, he started walking back up to the house, stopping just in front to admire the white lilies from Brooklands which were flowering either side of the path. He smiled as he saw Lorna coming towards him, returning from overseeing the vegetable gardens which were her latest obsession, and was about to ask her how things were coming along when he heard what sounded like the whirring of a propeller not far off. Recounting the episode later to Ethel, he wrote:

I said to Lorna it sounded like an aeroplane, but of course it couldn't be [there had been a few attempts to start aviation companies in

Northern Rhodesia in the 1920s, all unsuccessful], *so I thought perhaps it was someone coming up on a motorcycle. She said it sounded like a mechanical flying flea, and we both laughed, and then the noise got louder and we saw a silver twin-engined bi-plane fly right overhead, then back again lower, circling the house.*

The plane was heading down low over the trees, almost brushing the tops, and towards the lake, apparently making for the flat meadow area near the shore. Realizing it was trying to land, the Gore-Brownes started to *run like hares* down through the avenue of jacarandas, jumping over gnarled tree roots, and scattering villagers who had come out of their huts and were pointing upwards at the strange beast in the sky and putting their hands over their ears as the throb of engines grew louder. As they came out on to the meadow, the ground seemed to be vibrating and there ahead of them the aeroplane had landed and was drawing to a halt, narrowly missing a large red cathedral-shaped anthill.

It was a Hercules with an open crewpit and the name *City of Baghdad* painted on the side. Seeing the legend 'Royal Mail' with a crown above, Gore-Browne realized it must be one of the new Imperial Airways mailplanes which he had read about in the *Bulawayo Chronicle*. The first Imperial Airways service in Africa had started the previous February with a successful flight from Croydon to Mwanza in Tanganyika, and ironically, when they announced they were extending the weekly Croydon–Mwanza/Nairobi route on to Cape Town and starting an African air-mail service, he had tried to get Shiwa Ngandu designated one of the stops, and a runway built. But the surveyors who had come to inspect the previous year had decided the *boma* at Mpika was more important, and built a small aerodrome there instead.

The engine shuddered to a halt, the door opened, and a tall

uniformed pilot jumped out of the cockpit, removing his goggles and leather flying-cap to reveal movie-star looks. He appeared as astonished to see two white people in the middle of the bush as they were to see him, and for a moment seemed lost for words. Then he peeled off a glove and stuck out a hand, introducing himself as Captain John Sheppard of Imperial Airways, piloting the maiden voyage of the African Air Mail from Croydon to Cape Town. He apologized for 'landing on the lawn', but explained that the weather had closed down on them at Mpika and it would have been dangerous to cross the hills. Having failed to find an opening, he had turned back but did not have enough fuel to return to Chinsali, so had been looking for somewhere to land when he spotted the Shiwa estate. 'Saved our lives,' he told them.

Delighted by the unexpected visit, and always keen for the chance to see the latest in technology, having inherited his aunt and uncle's fascination with aircraft and mechanical things in general, Gore-Browne began to introduce himself and Lorna. He had just finished when the passenger door swung open and a strident female English voice rang out from inside the plane.

'Captain Sheppard! Are you going to stand there all day gossiping or are you going to help us out of this infernal machine?'

Looking a little sheepish, the pilot lowered some steps and held out a hand to a substantial woman in her fifties, aristocratic in bearing and dressed for northern climes with a mink stole over a tweed suit, a large floppy hat, a string of pearls and a furled umbrella in her hand.

'This is Lady Vyvyan,' said the pilot. 'Colonel and Mrs Gore-Browne.'

Watched by a gathering crowd of bemused locals, jabbering excitedly at the plane and 'the people who had descended from the heavens', they all shook hands. *Lady Vyvyan was very relieved to see white people,* Gore-Browne later wrote to Ethel. *She told us that when they started hurtling down through the jungle, she and her husband had been imagining cannibals and witch doctors and all sorts.*

Air Marshal Sir Vyell Vyvyan, director of Imperial Airways, Mr Francis Bertram, the deputy director of the Civil Aviation Department, dressed in dark suit and bowler hat, and a wireless mechanic followed Lady Vyvyan out of the plane, and soon the whole party was making for the house, where tea and fresh orange juice was served in the library and Lady Vyvyan was persuaded to remove her fur stole. It was agreed that they would stay the night as the plane could not take off until the weather had improved and a runway been cleared. The Vyvyans and Mr Bertram were shown to guest-rooms and Gore-Browne called Peter Mulemfwe to accompany him, Captain Sheppard and the mechanic back to the plane so that they could clear a runway. The crowd of villagers had grown even larger, some children daring each other to touch the strange beast, and everyone asking how it stayed up in the sky. After a good look round, the pilot told him that he would need a runway about 800 yards long and seventy yards wide, which would mean taking down several large anthills and two of Gore-Browne's treasured ornamental fir trees. Quite liking the idea of a Shiwa aerodrome, though so obviously distressed about the trees that Captain Sheppard would apologize about them in Christmas cards years later, Gore-Browne issued some instructions and soon there was an army of 100 or so men at work, clearing and levelling the ground under Mulemfwe's supervision. With no mechanical equipment, it was a hard task. Some of the anthills were as high as twenty-five feet tall and forty feet in diameter, and as one cubic yard of anthill weighs more than 2,500lb, this meant carrying away large amounts of earth, in baskets, and the two Shiwa wheel-barrows.

Back at the house, Lorna was busy organizing dinner. Gore-Browne was pleased there were some new people for her to talk to, and hoped she would dress up for the evening. He had, he wrote to Ethel, felt a little embarrassed introducing her to their titled visitors in the baggy dungarees she had designed for herself, a pair of secateurs pushed through her belt, and no stockings or hat, though she had been wearing shoes, which was not always the case. *Sometimes I wish she would be more feminine*, he complained. He himself wore khaki shorts round the estate, exposing his long hairy legs which because of his red hair and pale skin stayed surprisingly white despite all the sun, as well as a blue cotton shirt with notebook and pen in the pocket, and a leather belt from which his keys hung in a big bunch, but he always dressed for dinner.

In some ways, Lorna had taken to life at Shiwa far better than he had expected. Gore-Browne admired the way she had picked up Bemba, already speaking it more fluently than he, and even sitting like the village women, crouching cross-legged on the ground. Mrs Macminn, the missionary's wife, had shown her how to manage the house, and she took a load off his shoulders on the estate by running the dairy, where they now made their own butter and cheese, and taking charge of growing vegetables. She had even got involved in building, staying away down at a camp on the Mansya river, supervising the production of tiles for the new roof, and corresponding with her husband by scribbled notes sent by message boy. Under her instruction a gang of men dug clay from the bed at a bend in the river, putting the finest silt in trays which were taken to clay pits where women pounded it with their feet. The clay was then baked in kilns and covered with fine sands of different hues to give a variation in colour.

Although the pair of them worked on the estate, there was so much to do that after the 7 a.m. drum sounded for morning roll-call and the raising of the flag (6 a.m. in summer) they barely saw each other except at mealtimes, and not always then. Gore-Browne was always up at 5.30 a.m. for his morning walk with the dog but Lorna rarely accompanied him any more. He was often away, first building a proper bridge over the Mansya river which he was very proud of with its three brick arches, and he was shortly to become involved in full-scale road building with the new government project to build the so-called Great North Road, which would be part of the Cape to Cairo road. The scheme was something he had long advocated, and the Secretary for Public Works had asked him to oversee the Mpika–Chinsali section, which would pass a few miles from Shiwa and replace the current rather convoluted route through the estate which had been based on an old elephant track.

When she wasn't busy with the everyday running of the estate, Lorna occupied herself with various projects. She was currently trying to make marmalade from the oranges, and was always on at her husband to open a real clinic or cottage hospital, something he had to admit they needed. She had designed wooden leopard traps, though these had yet to be a success, and she often helped at the small dispensary he had set up, run by Aaron who had been trained at the Presbyterian mission. The nearest expert medical attention was 120 miles away at Kasama, more than half a day's journey, which could be fatal if someone were critically ill.

But increasingly Gore-Browne suspected she was no longer happy at Shiwa. Ever since she had come back from England after the birth of their second daughter, Angela, the previous year, she had seemed miserable, often staying in bed for days, and he had noticed her looking out wistfully towards the lake – the cobalt colour of the water reflecting in the pools of her eyes. A few months ago, after the latest round of building work on the house was completed, he had got a carpenter to carve their initials in white wood and nail them above a door at the front of the house either side of the date. When he took her to see the L 1932 S, she had reacted with horror, asking, 'What does that mean? Does it mean we have to live here for ever?' She often spent hours alone on the lake in *Venus* or one of the other dugout canoes, or in the boathouse on stilts she had organized the building of, sitting there in the moonlight. Occasionally she would take their two young daughters, but for the most part she seemed to have little interest in them, leaving them with Inga, the new governess, or the servants' wives to play with. Already three-year-old Mark was dancing like an African and speaking Bemba better than English, which he tried to correct by reading to her in the library after tea every afternoon. It was no good trying to discuss it with his wife, as they always ended up having a row.

The previous year a young anthropologist from Cambridge, Audrey Richards, had come to stay to study the Bemba, and Lorna had volunteered to act as her translator. Although he instinctively distrusted academics, Gore-Browne initially admired the no-nonsense Richards, but soon became jealous of the bond she formed with Lorna. The pair of them had been off together the whole time, Lorna going for walks with her rather than her husband, *gossiping and giggling like schoolgirls* even in front of important guests like the Governor, and making fun of his gun-drills, where he tested them on loading rifles without which no guest was allowed to leave the house at night because of the danger of lions and leopards, but which had to be unloaded on entering the house. Recently *the Richards woman*, as Gore-Browne referred to her, had written to say she wanted to come back for another few months to study Bemba women and wished to employ Lorna as her field assistant, which, he wrote to Ethel, *I am not at all happy about, as I think she gives Lorna all sorts of ideas.* During her first stay he had often suspected they were laughing at him, and noticed that his wife had started answering him back.

In letters home from Shiwa, the thirty-one-year-old Richards described Gore-Browne as 'wanting to be the Great White Chief with all the advantages and disadvantages that implies', adding:

> He is very egotistic . . . rather inclined to talk of his brilliant posts in the war and all the titles he is connected with. He has great ideas about how he should be treated and flares up over some lèse-majesté in more than boma style . . . Both are a curious mix of being extremely indulgent and very severe . . .

She had kinder words for Lorna:

> I like her better than him . . . She is very young in all her cut and dried theories of life but as she cheerfully remarks 'when the natives let you down for the hundredth time you just retire to your room and weep and then you start again'.

Lorna had much greater faith in their workers than her husband and found it hard to take when they disappointed. Recently she had started criticizing how he treated them. She didn't like him giving them presents, accusing him of playing the feudal lord, and she had been furious the first time she had seen him losing his temper and beating one of the natives almost into unconsciousness. *She needs to be here as long as*

I have to understand that sometimes force is the only thing that works, he wrote to Ethel.

But he thought the real problem was the loneliness of Shiwa, which he so loved but had already learnt to his cost was not for everyone. He had hoped that she would become as passionate as he about his mission and this would compensate for missing other things. *Perhaps I was wrong to think such a young girl could adapt*, he wrote in a note to her. She was still only twenty-two and other people her age were at dancing parties and theatre outings. Aware of his fears, the notes she sent him when they were apart were full of remarks like 'Dear Man be peaceful' and 'I hope to be a comfort instead of a burden to you my dear good Man.'

He had bought her a piano, but since the tower was completed she had spent more and more time there, playing her violin late into the night with only the hyenas, down on the meadow where the plane had landed, as an audience. He hated lying in his bed, hearing their supernatural howls, knowing it meant Lorna was up in the tower again.

Sometimes she did not even get up for days at a time, lying out on the loggia and complaining of feeling ill. Page after page of Gore-Browne's diary started with the words *L unwell* or *L in bed*. She had four teeth out and had had to go to Bulawayo in Southern Rhodesia for treatment, and would have to have crowns fitted on their next trip to London. *I know about toothache*, Gore-Browne wrote to Ethel, *having suffered viciously at the hands of London dentists in my youth*. But since recovering from the abscesses, she seemed to have more or less stopped eating. She tried to keep it secret from him, but the servants told him that first she had been eating only oranges, and now she was surviving on a cup of tea without milk or sugar for lunch and afternoon tea, and a plate of porridge for dinner. When he tried to convince her to eat properly, she complained that ever since the second Caesarean, anything else gave her indigestion, and insisted that she was getting fat, which he told Ethel *is patently nonsense.*

Hoping that having interesting guests would cheer Lorna up, Gore-Browne opened a couple of bottles of his best champagne at dinner. He proposed a health to King George before eating, the crested family china was laid out on the table, and to his delight it was *a most convivial evening*. The Vyvyans knew Ethel and they had mutual acquaintances in England. Lord Vyvyan had served in the Great War, and Lady Vyvyan was the daughter of the late General Sir Aeneas Perkins, and Gore-Browne discovered that he had been with her brother as a young gunner at the Shop. All the guests were pleasingly impressed with the house and staggered that he had built it himself. He hoped they hadn't noticed that the fleur-de-lys carved on the top of the bookcases were upside down – *Joe's fault*, he complained to Ethel, *stupid fellow I gave him the designs and he did them all the wrong way up*. They didn't say anything if they had noticed, but admired the carved coat of arms, the framed pen-and-ink sketches of Venice in their dressing-room, the tapestries on the walls of the corridors, the vast cavernous stone kitchen hung with copper pots and pans, and the Moroccan lamps in the dining-room. They were complimentary about the dinner too – guinea-fowl in Madeira, one of Kalikeka's specialities – and Gore-Browne boasted that everything was home-grown. Dessert was figgy pudding, prompting Lady Vyvyan to exclaim, as she later told the *Evening Standard* journalist who interviewed her about their adventure, 'I have to keep pinching myself to reassure myself that I'm not dreaming. It's such a miracle to be here in the middle of the jungle with people of one's own kind, fine books by Byron and Carlyle on the shelves and fine food on the table. People from Surrey of all places!'

Lorna questioned the pilot enviously about their journey, which had taken them from Croydon, leaving on 20 January, to Alexandria, Luxor, Wadi Halfa, Khartoum, Entebbe, Nairobi and Mbeya and would now go on to Broken Hill, Bulawayo, Johannesburg, Kimberley and Cape Town, where they were programmed to arrive on 2 February. The new Croydon to Cape Town air-mail service would take eleven days, and halve the time it took letters and newspapers to reach Shiwa from England. Imperial Airways already flew to India and, according to Captain Sheppard, the company was negotiating with the government to carry all the Empire's air-mail. The plane they had flown in was a three-engined De Havilland 66 Hercules which could carry fourteen passengers, but the service would get even faster later in the year when the company would be introducing specially built four-engined monoplanes which could cruise at 120 m.p.h. rather than 87 m.p.h. He told them that in its first year of flights to Africa, forced landings were so common that pilots carried emergency rations of a tin of bully beef, a packet of biscuits and half a bottle of brandy, but that the machines were improving rapidly. Aerodromes were clearly going to open up the Protectorate and interior Africa in general. Originally Gore-Browne had been against them, cherishing his isolation, but as he wrote to Ethel, *I have learnt the value of good communications, not least for obtaining supplies and getting one's produce to market*. They were soon to have telegraph at Mpika, as well as the proper road which would make it easier to get to Lusaka.

Lady Vyvyan was astonished to learn that it took a month for *The Times* to reach them, saying, 'You really are in the back of beyond!' and begging Gore-Browne to tell them how he had found the place. Explaining it was a long story, he suggested they adjourn to the library for coffee and port. He rang the bell for the servants to clear the plates, then, as was his custom, poured a glass of wine for each of the serving staff, as well as one for the cook who had come in from the kitchen. As the guests looked on in astonishment, the servants each solemnly took their glass and filed out.

Over port, cigars and Shiwa cheese in the library, Gore-Browne confessed to Sir Vyell Vyvyan that he was thinking of going into politics. *One would like to feel one had made a difference*, he had recently written to his aunt. *I know the problems of this place by now and would like to be involved in some kind of system where black and white can work together.* Like other people with whom he had broached the idea, Sir Vyvyan was surprised, as most white settlers were known to be keen on what they called 'Amalgamation' – joining up with neighbouring Southern Rhodesia and Nyasaland and having some kind of white home rule. Like other white settlers, Gore-Browne had little patience with *rule from Whitehall*, feeling the Colonial Service officials who ran the country had no real understanding of it, and he could see the attraction of the Amalgamation idea. There were fewer than 11,000 whites in Northern Rhodesia – a territory three times the size of Britain – compared to an estimated one and a quarter million Africans, and everyone feared that one fine day a Labour government would simply hand them over to black rule with no safeguards, and they would lose all they had worked for. But he believed that Amalgamation would mean *government by not very competent settlers*, and that more importantly Whitehall would never agree to it, so felt it was pointless pushing for it and that it would be better to look for another solution entirely. *From what my experience has shown me, hope for Africa lies not in segregation, repression by a dominant race or even some form of benevolent white autocracy though of course this is the tradition we were brought up in*, he had told Ethel, *but in a kind of partnership between the white and black races, however long that might take*. He repeated these ideas to Sir Vyvyan, who was interested, though cautionary in his response. 'It's all very well talking about equality until one has to face the black as a social and professional superior.'

Some years later Captain Sheppard wrote to Gore-Browne, recalling the visit, and saying, 'I couldn't ever live out in those parts like you. You've got a good set-up, your people obviously like and respect you. But as far as I can see they're a race apart and always will be.' In particular he recalled how over port they had talked about an incident which the air passengers had been told of during their stop in Chinsali, involving Gore-Browne's friend John Peacock, the local District Commissioner. Apparently Peacock had entered the sacred burial grove in Shi Mwalule's village, where all the Bemba senior chiefs were buried. *A kind of Westminster Cathedral for Wemba* kings*, Gore-Browne described it to Ethel, *a rather remarkable place actually, surrounded by thick foliage and wonderful great palm trees about 60 feet high*. Inside was a sacred hut containing relics of past chiefs, forbidden to all except senior chiefs and certainly to white men. No one was sure why Peacock had entered – whether it was for a dare or that he had got lost shooting snakes and entered accidentally, realizing too late. Anyway the locals were saying he would be cursed and some terrible fate befall him, and the keeper of the grove had supposedly told him he wouldn't live another year.

Gore-Browne was worried by the news. The last white man to enter the grove had been a man called Ford, D C for Kasama,

* 'Wemba' is sometimes used instead of 'Bemba'.

in his first year in Africa. The incident had lost him the trust of the local people and he had had to be transferred to another district 600 miles away. The first day he went to his new *boma*, the flagstaff fell on his head and killed him. Sir Vyvyan laughed at the story, describing it as mumbo-jumbo and saying 'these fellows will never progress while they go on thinking like that'. But Gore-Browne wasn't so sure. *In my eleven years living out here I have come across some rum things,* he wrote to Ethel, *and no longer make light of dealings with the spirits.* He told them how he had once purchased a small herd of cattle from South Africa and ignored the local villagers' advice to pray to the spirits. The cows all perished. Lorna suggested they go to bed before he scared everyone, and reminded him of her first night when he had told her of the spirit of Livingstone's dog haunting the hill behind the house, which had then kept her awake half the night while he was out hunting leopards.

The next morning dawned clear and bright and, after a large breakfast of eggs, sausages, toast, porridge and orange juice, the unexpected guests set off with their baggage in Gore-Browne's Mercedes. The pilot and mechanic met them at the new runway, pronouncing everything ready for a 9.30 a.m. takeoff. Captain Sheppard thanked Gore-Browne for his hospitality and promised that when he got back to England he would be recommending to the airline to build an aerodrome there, as the lake and house made such good landmarks. They all shook hands and Gore-Browne took a photograph, before the passengers got in and took their places in the wicker seats. He stood watching as the mechanic wound the engine and jumped in, the propeller turned faster and faster until the blades were no longer visible, and the pilot executed a perfect takeoff, waving from his open cockpit. Leaving his driver to take the car, he walked slowly back towards the house, smiling to himself as the plane circled round once as if in salute, sorry that Lorna had not got up again this morning to see them all off. As he looked up, a slight movement at the tower window caught his eye, and he saw her face watching the small grey plane disappear into the distance.

14

Stewart Gore-Browne, diary entry

Lusaka, January 21st 1936

Heard that the King died peacefully last night at midnight. One is v. glad he had the triumph of that Jubilee.

Lunched at Government House. All in deep black.

Sir H walked on the terrace with me and after lunch took me to his study and we talked till 4pm. Hard to feel really at ease with the fellow. Discussed my screed on Native Development and Constitutional Reform. Sir H doesn't like my territorial divisions. Won't have anything savouring of segregation. He wants a white community and a black community each with local self-government and not usurping any of the functions of central government till they are fit to take it over in its entirety.*

Wonder why we go on.

Lusaka, the new capital, was a hot dusty one-street town with the railway station on one side, shops, Lusaka Hotel and Barclays Bank on the other, and a ditch in the middle which filled with water during the rainy season and into which people occasionally fell. Gore-Browne didn't much care for colonial life there, with its endless rounds of sundowners, musical evenings, treasure hunts, church bazaars, cinema outings, and

* Sir Hubert Young, Governor of Northern Rhodesia.

talk that never seems to achieve anything, and its few shabby stores on Cairo Road, where whites were welcome while Africans had to stay on the pavement outside and be served through a hatch. He still wasn't sure it had been a good idea to enter politics. *I'm the last person in the world to be a successful politician*, he had written to Ethel, though he admitted that he liked *being in the know* and having a role on the national stage rather than just his *own little northeastern corner*. He enjoyed receiving the gold-eagle crested cards summoning him to the Governor's white colonnaded mansion on the big green lawn fringed with red and yellow canna lilies and the Union Jack flying from a pole. But when he and the other members of the Legislative Council met in the gilded-ceilinged room in the Central Offices, the civil servants in their white uniforms with swords, medals and epaulettes, surrounded by paintings of Cecil Rhodes and other eminent persons, a ceiling fan slowly stirring the thick air, he couldn't help feeling that they were all just *playing at parliament*.

Although he had often toyed with the idea of becoming a politician even in England, it had been a complete surprise when the Broken Hill Political Association had sent him a telegram the previous year asking him to stand for the LegCo elections in September 1935. At the time he had been staying at Morris Hall in Perthshire, where his mother Helenor had grown up, touring Scotland with Ethel, visiting friends and family, while waiting for the results of Lorna's medical tests and hoping to persuade his wife to come back to Shiwa and him and their two daughters after her two-year absence. In a way the invitation had been a welcome diversion from all that, but he really hadn't thought he stood much chance. Northern Province was a large constituency, stretching from Broken Hill in the south right up to Abercorn in the north, and, apart from a few missionaries and coffee or tobacco farmers in Abercorn, the rest of its 600 white voters were mostly working-class, employed in the lead or zinc mines or on the railways. Since the Depression had sent the price of minerals plummeting, wages had fallen and men been laid off, and though things were picking up again and people talking excitedly of the untold riches of the Copperbelt, some of the white workers were living in makeshift shacks little better than the Africans. Apart from the managers of Thatcher & Hobsons store and Proctors garage, Gore-Browne did not know a single person in Broken Hill. *Not our sort of people at all*, he wrote to Ethel, *and one has little patience for their anti-native views*. For a week he brooded over the matter. Then, he received a letter from Mackenzie Kennedy, the colony's Chief Secretary, urging him to accept the nomination. Feeling that perhaps he could do some good in his adopted land, he had agreed and returned to Africa without Lorna.

The month-long campaign had been exhausting. It was the hottest time of year just before the rains, clouds of red dust billowing everywhere. As he had feared, the railway workers, locomotive drivers, mechanics and miners mistrusted him the moment he opened his mouth, regarding him as some kind of tropical squire, and he intensely disliked canvassing, *the indignity of having one's name up on trees like some kind of music hall spectacle*, and having to sell oneself at public meetings. Although he never fooled himself that he was a brilliant orator, he found that on the platform he was able to put his views over clearly and convincingly, rediscovering the confidence he had developed during wartime when he used to address everyone from sappers to generals on artillery training. He was careful to leave out the Latin and Greek quotations which usually peppered his conversation, and his forceful manner made his prospective constituents see him as someone who could stand up to the Governor, in contrast to his opponent Arthur Davison, whom he described as *a railway man of little personality*.

But what really swung things in his favour was the unlikely friendship he had struck up with Roy Welensky, the twenty-nine-year-old leader of the Railway Workers' Union, who had originally been backing his opponent. The gruff-spoken engine driver and former Rhodesian national heavyweight boxing champion was a six-foot-tall, seventeen-stone bear of a man with a moon face and huge eyebrows, *bad vowels* and little education, having left school at fourteen to work in a store. His father, Michael Welensky, was a Polish Jew, one of the early pioneers, who had made a fortune in the South African diamond mines in the 1890s, lost it all and ended up an alcoholic, running a humble bar in Salisbury's Pioneer Street with his Afrikaner wife Leah. Their thirteenth child, Roy had worked as a barman, butcher and in the mines before marrying Elizabeth, a waitress in a Bulawayo café, qualifying as an engine driver and being transferred to Broken Hill. Having successfully reorganized the moribund railwaymen's union (largely to counter a fascist campaign against his Jewish blood) and become known nationally as champion of the workers, Welensky was the key opinion-maker in the constituency. But with not a drop of British blood in his body, he couldn't have been more different from the perfectly mannered aristocrat with the stiff bearing and crystal-cut accent.

The first time Gore-Browne had addressed the workers at Broken Hill's Railway Club, his sponsors begged him, 'Don't wear your monocle!' Ignoring them and walking out before the crowds, he had seen Welensky scowling at him like a bulldog from the floor. Yet something made them hit it off that first evening – perhaps mutual recognition of a deep-rooted insecurity, Welensky about his lack of schooling, which he tried to hide with the brawn, quick wit and campaign of self-education, reading everything from Shakespeare to Marx, and Gore-Browne about his inadequacies at Harrow and his parents' disappointment in him – and the pair would write to each other every week for the rest of their lives. Gore-Browne dealt unperturbed with the fire of questions, and looked up to see a big smile from Welensky. With his help, and that of the local women who turned out to drive and canvass for him, Gore-Browne had been duly elected by 253 votes to 112. Afterwards, passing the African market by the big *mupapa* tree under which not so long before slave auctions used to take place, he reflected how odd it was that most people living in his constituency had no say at all.

During the campaign Gore-Browne had been careful to hide his increasingly liberal views, knowing they would find little favour with his constituents. He avoided speaking about Amalgamation with Southern Rhodesia, which had become an ever more popular theme among the white settlers, particularly after riots on the Copperbelt earlier that year by African mineworkers who were angry that they were receiving much inferior pay and housing to Europeans. The police had opened fire and five Africans were killed. Worried about repercussions, Leopold Moore, a drugstore owner and the leader of the seven elected members of the new Legislative Council, proposed a motion for Amalgamation. Gore-Browne had little time for Moore, whom he referred to in letters to Welensky as *that dreadful pharmacist*, and in his maiden speech at the LegCo session in December he set the record straight. In a long discourse which made headlines in the *Bulawayo Chronicle*, he proposed decentralization and provincial autonomy, and attacked the government's failure to look after the welfare of Africans, claiming they were being left at the mercy of frequent famines because of lack of attention to agricultural development, and were still almost entirely dependent on missionaries for education. He criticized the hut tax as forcing rural Africans to leave their villages and go and provide cheap labour in the mines as the only way they could raise the money. Controversially, he proposed 'regarding the native as a partner . . . a potential partner but still a partner'.

He followed this up with his 'Memo on Native Development' to Sir Hubert Young, which they had been discussing that afternoon. In it he had suggested appointing what he called a Superman Director of Native Development who would coordinate all organizations linked to African welfare and make policy recommendations, and it was obvious who he had in mind. From the Governor's reaction, it looked unlikely ever to be more than a memo. *Why these people can't see that the future of the Protectorate would be far more secure if they could get out of this mentality that the African is 'unteachable', and start trying to encourage their development, is beyond me*, he complained to his aunt.

Politics was turning out to be far more time-consuming than he had imagined. LegCo sessions took place in Lusaka for a few weeks at a time, two or three times a year. But in between he had to go and meet with his constituents, and as apparently the only one of the twenty-two LegCo members interested in bettering the lives of Africans, he found himself appointed to the Native Industrial Labour Advisory Board, various committees, and invited to meetings of provincial commissioners, all of which meant spending more and more time away from Shiwa. He supposed being away so much was going to put an additional strain on his faltering marriage. That was if Lorna ever came back. He wished she would, bemoaning to Ethel, *It's damned awkward having to explain her continued absence at government functions*. He didn't like the way people asked, 'And how is your young wife?' in what seemed to him a patronizing manner. Her latest letter, a scrawled sheet of blue air-mail written from an underground café in Brussels, said that she would be further delayed. *I wouldn't be surprised if she was taking something,* he confessed to Ethel, *what with all those musician types and students she mixes with.*

He blamed Audrey Richards, *that anthropologist woman with her clever talk and meddling ways*, for leading his wife astray, though he respected the Cambridge academic's intellect. She had returned to Shiwa in early 1933 and spent a year there, taking Lorna off on tour to villages along the Chambeshi river where she was compiling a census and study of nutrition. Lorna worked as her assistant, using her fluency in Bemba, taking the kitchen scales to weigh village babies while her own children were left with their nanny. As before the pair had got on extremely well, leaving Gore-Browne feeling excluded, and they had disappeared for weeks at a time, Lorna clearly enjoying being in the company of someone who wasn't a stickler for order and discipline. Richards wrote home of one of these trips: 'L and I started off on Wed. V deluxe with a bicycle boy each, two cooks, lots of kitchen boys and carriers etc. 15 miles the first day mostly with bikes. L arranged everything wonderfully . . . we arrived to find our tents up and a brand new kitchen and dining room.' Happy to be away from domestic problems and to be doing something useful, Lorna forgot about her illnesses and depression which kept her in bed so much at Shiwa, joined in dancing with the local women, Richards describing her as 'bold as a lion and very popular', and took her to see fish-spearing. One village they came to on the river was centred round a prophet named Mulinga. Richards wrote, 'He prophesies in bed by singing aloud from 3am to 5am (the same tune all the time). No one knows what the prophecy is, it's a hidden mystery.'

In between these trips Richards stayed at Shiwa House,

which had acquired a third storey and a cloistered courtyard since her previous visit, prompting her to write, 'it grows and grows'. Seeing Lorna's latest scheme, an experimental garden with different soils and seeds, she wrote, 'Lorna overworks incessantly and has a craze about getting fat so eats only oranges though she cooks exquisite meals for her husband and visitors.' Not warming to Gore-Browne, she added, 'I don't know what the Colonel will do with all his energy when the house is finished . . . the best way to give him pleasure is to compliment it,' adding, 'It's very beautiful though of course quite unsuited to its environment.'

Departing Shiwa at the end of January 1934, she wrote, 'I don't much like leaving L alone. She's quite alright some days but anaemic and tired as she can't eat anything without getting the stoppages.' Having had her eyes opened to another kind of life, Lorna was easily persuaded to follow her friend out to Cambridge the next month, ostensibly for treatment for her digestive problems. 'She means to stay 18 months so as to get quite right and means to have a fling!' wrote Richards, adding, 'She intends to study agriculture, music, German and medicine and all the things she meant to do before she married.'

Gore-Browne was not at all happy with the idea, though he hadn't tried to stop her. Lorna was supposed to be doing a course on agriculture and nutrition which she had said would be useful at Shiwa, but he complained to Ethel, *From what I can make of it, it is nothing but wining and dining.* He added, *I never meant to trap her at Shiwa, but I can't help feeling a woman's place is with her husband and children.* Eventually in January 1935, after she had been away almost a year, he had gone to England to bring Lorna back, but as the months went by, it seemed as though she just didn't want him around. Once she had even passed him, cycling along a cobbled Cambridge street, looking for all the world like a student with her long scarf, jumper, long woollen skirt and intellectual air, and affected not to see him. A balding fifty-something husband with a monocle, a loud voice, and an eminent war record was clearly an embarrassment around all her new young friends and suitors.

Now, after a two-year absence, she was finally supposed to be on her way back, but by a most circuitous route. Originally she had been due to arrive before he came down to Lusaka for the current session. But this last missive from Brussels, which had come before he left Shiwa, meant he had no idea what date she was turning up, and would, he wrote in his diary, *mess up my whole schedule*. The death of King George meant staying longer than he had intended in Lusaka for the parade and memorial service at the English church. Then it would be up to Broken Hill for the usual round of meetings with his constituents and the unions where he would *listen a lot and try not to say anything stupid*, before he could finally go back home.

Gore-Browne left Broken Hill in one of his black moods. He hated the Great Northern Hotel, which he described as *a squalid place*, and thought the town itself had little to offer beyond the discovery there by miners in 1921 of a skeleton which was said by scientists to be the oldest man. *Broken Hill makes me feel like lying down and dying myself*, he wrote to Ethel, complaining of *the refusal of most whites to understand how much their own futures were tied up with that of the black man*. When he was well on the road, he realized he had left his false teeth behind at the hotel.

But, as always, his humour improved *en route* to Shiwa. He had picked up a new car, a red Ford V8, from Proctors at Broken Hill, and commented in his diary, *My word what a nice car to drive*. The journey up the Great North Road through the changing scenery of thorny *miombo* scrub and sandy soil, to lush green-blue hills which rolled away either side of him towards the Luapula river on one side and the Luangwa on the other, made him feel *like a boy getting back from school for the holidays.* Although the red clay road was sticky from the rains and full of corrugations and potholes, the V-shaped engine *hummed along* and *the miles just slipped away.*

As usual they stopped the night at Kabwe, setting off early the next day. *One is supposed to keep to 40mph for the first 300 miles but it was tempting to let the engine go faster, particularly as we met no other traffic at all en route except for one Thatchers & Hobson lorry coming the other way.* The red truck almost pushed them off as there was little room for passing on the single-track highway. Only five or six lorries passed along the road a week and perhaps as many cars, and it was so rare to see another vehicle that if one did, one usually pulled over and made tea.

The last part of the road was very overgrown but he managed never to slip below 30 m.p.h. even on the Mwateshi Pass, or Danger Hill as Lorna liked to call it, which had once been the entry point of elephants into the Shiwa valley; he had used their trails to align the road for the section he had been in charge of building. His driving companion was Pinam, one of the older servants who had grown up at Shiwa, and who kept up a running commentary, pointing things out like, 'Oh look there, *bwana*, the remains of a store house built by the *bwana* who wasn't Livingstone.' Recounting the journey to Ethel, Gore-Browne wrote, *I might have known things were going too well.* Just at the top of the hill, only eight miles from the house, where the landscape opens up, he slowed to admire the first sight of the lake as he always did, the blue hill turning dusky in the mauve and gold sunset. As he reduced speed, the engine overheated, forcing them to a halt in clouds of steam. Pinam opened up and found the radiator solid with grass.

Night falls quickly in the bush and by the time Pinam had repaired the car, it was pitch black. To Gore-Browne's annoyance, when they reached the end of the estate drive, the house was dark and unwelcoming, the only light the ghostly reflection of the moon on the windows. He had hoped Lorna would have arrived back while he was away and be there to greet him, but the house looked completely deserted, with no sign even of Inga Carlsson, the nanny, or the two children. He had to shout to raise a servant, and old Kakumbi eventually ambled up, bearing a Tilley lamp. Learning from him that 'Mama Gory is not come back', he took the lamp and wandered wearily up to his study. A mountain of mail was piled on his desk, as well as a couple of brown paper parcels – one from Brooklands of soap and a boxed set of *Marriage of Figaro* records Ethel had promised him, and the other the book, *Naked and Unashamed*, that he had ordered for Joe Savill's thirty-fifth birthday. There was a letter with an American postmark in his brother's hand – Robert and Margaret were spending most of their time in Hollywood where they were in with the rich set. Near the top, he found one of Lorna's scrawled missives, this time with a Lisbon postmark. He slit it open with his paper knife to read that she was 'delayed' again and would be coming on something called the 'WAMERU', but with no details of what that was or when it would arrive. *A great disappointment*, he wrote in his diary. He had been looking forward to having someone to talk to about politics and the frustrations of LegCo. Instead he had only the large black and white photograph of her that he had had framed and placed on his study wall, next to one of the large Brooklands tapestries. Taken just after Mark's birth,

Lorna was sitting in one of the arched windows, the lake visible in the distance, legs straight out in front of her and crossed at the ankles, hair tucked behind her ears and dark eyes staring into the camera inscrutably. It was hard to say from the photo whether she had loved him even then and Gore-Browne suddenly felt very lonely.

Wondering what had happened to the children, he walked along the dark corridor lined with the leopardskins little Angela was so frightened of, fearing they would get up from the floor and go stalking at night. Finding their bedroom and schoolroom empty, he knocked at the door of the governess and was surprised to hear snuffling as she took an age to answer. Finally the door opened and Inga appeared, her face puffy and red. Apologizing for having left the girls over for the night at the Macminns, who had built a house on the estate, she handed over a letter from Leslie, her intended back in England – she had been working at Shiwa to save money towards starting a home. *Poor Inga, it was one of the rottenest letters I've ever read*, Gore-Browne wrote in his diary, *saying he'd become engaged to 'a sweet girl' and therefore Inga would not hear from him so often. There are some unbelievable swine in this world.*

Leaving Inga alone to her tears, things got worse as the evening progressed. There was no bath water because the dam had apparently leaked, leaving the pipe to the house dry. Running his finger along the furniture, Gore-Browne noticed a thick layer of red dust. *Inga's early enthusiasm for housekeeping appears to have waned and as usual the boys unsupervised get worse and worse*, he wrote. *I walked round seeing what work was needed and each time the atrocities were worse. What a curse this whole business is!* Supper was cold and when he went to bed there was no wick for his Super Aladdin lamp and no boy to be found, which meant he couldn't finish the biography of Haig he had been reading. Standing in his long nightshirt by the four-poster bed, in the puddle of light from the yellow moon, he decided it might be just as well. *The book is pretty uninspiring*, he wrote in his diary the next day, *though I can't get away from the idea that perhaps the subject was too.*

The next morning, after the drumbeat for the morning muster parade, Gore-Browne arranged for the house flag to fly at half-mast to mourn the King's death, and told the workers there would be a special memorial service in the chapel on Sunday which all would be expected to attend. Eliam, his secretary, had not turned up for work, so he decided to leave answering the mail, usually his first task, and went for a walk to see how the estate was doing and let Shiwa work its usual enchantment.

I wouldn't swap this for all the flowers and neo-Georgian grandeur of Government House, he wrote to Ethel, though he noticed that the lawn was so long and overgrown with weeds that *it looks like a meadow rather than a garden.* Heading towards the orchards to look for Mulemfwe, he thought *how serene the place looks and quietly prosperous with its limegroves and cattle, oxen ploughing and men working on the slopes of the blue lake. I wish L was here to see it.* Over at the orchards he checked on the huts being built for the baboon-scarers whom he had employed in an attempt to stop the monkeys stealing the oranges. The huts were almost ready but he was irritated to see an alarming number of lime windfalls going rotten, which meant he would have to get another gang on picking, and some of the leaves on the lime trees were yellowing badly. He hoped they weren't going to get some disease just as everything was starting to go well, and decided he would ask Unwin Moffat, the country's Agriculture Secretary, up for a look.

His head *capitao* was nowhere to be found so he wandered back to the estate store, thinking Peter might be there checking supplies. To his fury, he found someone had stolen the paraffin for powering the Electrolux refrigerator they had recently acquired. Telling himself to be above such things, he ran into 'Dr' Petro Kamuchimba who had replaced Aaron in the dispensary, a small man with a stupid wide grin which he found intensely irritating. Gore-Browne had heard there had been several *kabokosi** cases on the estate and questioned him about it. *I asked him what quinine he was giving*, Gore-Browne later noted in his diary. *He said 'none there isn't any'. So I hit him and sacked him. He's certainly a danger to the people he deals with and with a poss. epidemic of kabokosi, one can't risk having him here. I've stuck him for many years.*

It was a strange dichotomy that for all Gore-Browne's eloquent speeches in LegCo about equality and partnership, he saw no contradiction in beating workers on the estate with the large black stick which he always carried for the purpose, or even banging their heads against trees. But though his temper was quick to lose and so fierce that house-boys would cower under tables, warning each other 'the forest is on fire', it was also quick to subside. Paramount Chief Chitimukulu, who became a close friend of Gore-Browne in the late 1940s, having worked on the estate as a young boy, recalls, 'One day I was at Shiwa and saw Gore-Browne hover over a man kicking him right and left and screaming like a madman. But one thing we liked him for was that after being angry like that, you could say, "If you'd had a spear you would have speared that animal," and he would then laugh.'

Gore-Browne's mood soon improved when he entered the still-room and saw all the activity under way. To his delight,

*Smallpox.

Sam showed him that they had already distilled four and a half drums of lime oil – four times as much as the same time the previous year, and estimated that they would reach seventeen drums – about 630lb of oil. If the price went as high as Thomas Durrans, his analyst in London, was saying then the estate might finally start to make decent money.

Next door at the blacksmith's forge there was a loud sound of hammering. Two men were bent over the anvil, shaping iron bars to copy a scroll-topped garden gate he had had sent out from Brooklands so that he could put one on the entrance to each path and driveway. Impressed by their handiwork, he wrote to Ethel, *To think, before I came here these men had never seen an anvil or an iron bar, yet now they are making a gate any English blacksmith could be proud of.*

In the workshop alongside, the carpenters were also busy, chiselling and planing, the air sweet with the smell of woodchips. Under Joe Savill's instruction they had become far more elaborate in their carving, fashioning sophisticated items quite unlike the heavy-handed objects they had turned out in the early years. Examining the new 'Elizabethan' hanging cupboard they were varnishing, he made a note in his book to ask Ethel to send out the latest Heals catalogue to see if there was a sofa they could copy, then stopped over at the brickyard to ask the builders to extend the garage for the new V8, as he wanted the Mercedes to remain under cover. Only the Ford truck would be in the open air.

After lunch of cold venison and home-made mayonnaise alone at the house, Inga still moping in her room, he walked over to the aerodrome with his dog Kim. *I wish a big plane would land*, he wrote to Ethel, *it seems such a good hard surface.* But it was a long time since anything, even a single-engined plane, had as much as flown over. From the landing-strip he went over to check on the animals. Muleni, the chicken-boy, said lions had been round again and killed eight chickens so he arranged to lay out some poisoned meat, then went and gave salt to the oxen. Passing the cattle shed with its pungent smell of trodden earth and animal excreta reminded him of a time three years earlier, returning from a road-building trip to find his wife inoculating the cattle against sleeping-sickness. *What a sight*, he wrote at the time, *just her and the two cattleboys, the boys throwing the animal on the ground while her slight little figure hunted for the jugular and plunged in the needle*. She had been on safari with Audrey Richards at the time, and had walked sixteen miles through the forest back to Shiwa to do the inoculations, then once she had finished, turned round and gone straight back rather than spend the night with him, apparently fearing *domestic calamities*. She had managed to inject all sixty cows, then one of the boys had put an infected beast back into the herd, which meant she had had to return and do the whole operation all over again, much to her distress, saying she was worried *whether the black people would ever learn*.

As Gore-Browne wandered back up to the house, wondering when Lorna would come back, it started raining, *a thin English rain which just about suited my mood*. Inga had emerged from her room so he sent her with Pinam in the Mercedes to fetch the girls from Mpandala, the Macminns' house, where Mrs Macminn was teaching them to read. He went into the schoolroom and sat at the piano, the first time he had played it for more than two years, and without thinking found himself fingering the notes of 'Sonata Pathétique'. Cries of 'Papa, Papa!' disturbed his playing, and the two little girls in striped overalls came running in, fair-haired pigtails flying, one with red ribbons and one blue, both with the violet eyes of their mother, and Angela's Ridgeback puppy Daniel jumping round their ankles. Detaching himself, Gore-Browne gestured to Inga to take them away and clean them up, then bring them to the library for tea.

He loved his girls, though he generally found it hard to show any outward affection and still longed for a son. The eldest, six-year-old Mark/Lorna was more serious, while pretty little Angela – Angelica as Lorna referred to her – was naughtier and, he told Ethel, *bright as a button for a child not yet four*. He would like to spoil them, just as he would like to have spoilt their mother if she had let him, but sometimes he found their little faces *too painful a reminder*. Although the local women all made a tremendous fuss of them, it must have been hard for the girls, their mother being away so much, and they were scared of their fierce-tempered father who would beat them if he caught them taking a short cut through his study, which was supposed to be out of bounds.

He went over to the library, where a fire had been lit, and picked up an old copy of *The Times*, which was full of the King's illness and speculation about the Prince of Wales and Mrs Simpson, the American woman. Seeing it was already quarter to four, he rang the bell for tea then searched along the shelves of his classics for a story to read the children. He favoured *Ivanhoe*, but they didn't seem to appreciate Sir Walter Scott, *not in the way a boy would do*, and he tried to remember what else he had enjoyed as a child. His eyes lit on Kipling's *Just So Stories*.

As the clock chimed four, Reuben entered with the tea-things and laid them out on the table – hot buttered toast, small crustless sandwiches, glasses of milk for the children, a silver pot of Darjeeling for him along with a china cup and saucer and a silver jug of hot water. There was also a plate of oddly flat-looking cakes, and he asked the servant what had happened to them.

'Oh, *bwana*, George says the cakes were afraid because

bwana was angry about the stolen paraffin, and they refused to rise.'

'Indeed,' replied Gore-Browne. *One has to laugh at the excuses the servants make rather than take responsibility for anything*, he wrote to Ethel.

Eventually the girls arrived, faces scrubbed and shining, hair brushed, and neatly clad in white cotton dresses that Ethel had sent out. He ticked them off for being late, but Mark explained there had been no hot water for their baths so they had had to wait for buckets. Telling them to take their milk, and sit by him on the cushions, he opened the book at *The Cat That Walked by Himself*.

The moment Lorna got out of the car in which Gore-Browne had picked her up from the train, tired from the long rainy journey with her husband droning on about politics, and saw the initials L and S over the door, her heart sank. 'I knew when I saw the house again that I couldn't spend the rest of my life in that house,' she told one of her grandchildren years later. 'I felt as if I was entering a prison.'

She had thought she was ready to return, that her old black moods, which today would have been recognized as post-natal depression, were over. She believed she had got her yearning for independence and adventure out of her system, and could use some of what she had learnt at Cambridge to experiment and make a success of Shiwa, even if her marriage was not what she had imagined. But as soon as she entered the house, that old feeling of oppression returned and by the second day she had lost all desire to eat.

Ever since her last pregnancy in 1932 when she had given birth to a stillborn son, she had found it hard to look at her husband, feeling his eyes on hers accusingly for her failure to give him the thing he most longed for, and was convinced he had gone into politics as a distraction and an excuse to get away from her. He claimed it didn't matter, but everyone at the house knew he had even gone to a witch-doctor, Mulenga Chimuntu of Chimuntu village on the Mashinga river, and asked for medicine for a son to be born to his wife, which to Lorna had been the last straw.

L not well. Only three days into his wife's return to Shiwa, after more than two years away, and already Gore-Browne was having to write that familiar line in his diary. It seemed every time Lorna came back to the house, she was ill again. *I hope she recovers for her* [28th] *birthday next week*, he wrote to his aunt, *and for chief Nkula's visit* – his first in state since succeeding his brother as local Bemba chief the previous year. He wondered what the new chief wanted – he was being *suspiciously diplomatic* so far, even deploring taking *mulasa* money, the hand-out Gore-Browne was used to giving to keep on the right side of local chiefs.

A wire had arrived from the Governor's office with the dates of the next round of Constitutional negotiations, which meant he would have to return earlier than expected to Lusaka. He went up to the loggia where Lorna was sleeping and sat by the side of her bed just as they used to in the early years on Sundays when they would talk of their dreams and get up late. She opened her eyes, clear as the lake, and looked at him sadly, and he took her hand, noting how soft it had become after a couple of years away from farmwork. He knew she hated him being in politics, disliking all the pomposity and conventionality of it, but he told her of the summons, and of the rumours that the Governor was planning to appoint a LegCo member charged with looking after Native Interests.

'Won't you be glad if you are this person?' she asked him.

Gore-Browne wasn't sure. *Sometimes one fears one is just a voice crying in the wilderness*, he had written to her when she was in England. 'Perhaps I should be concentrating more on Shiwa, on getting this place running, providing more work here, going through with your idea of setting up a proper school and hospital.'

'Oh, Shiwa!' she had replied. 'Shiwa is just an experiment.' He had wondered what she meant by that, and would have been even more confused had he read her thesis at Cambridge which concluded, 'It is unlikely that white races can ever become sufficiently acclimatized to the Tropics to form communities omnipotent over nature.'

Gore-Browne worried that if he was appointed to the new post he would be away from the estate just as the essential oils looked as if they might take off, and hated the idea of leaving his mentally fragile wife alone. But it seemed every time she saw him she was ill again. The doctors in England said that the adhesions caused by the Caesareans had cleared up, and that the stomach pains she complained of were a nervous problem. *Knowing that makes it no easier*, he wrote to Ethel.

For all his stiff upper lip and inability to talk of emotions, Gore-Browne was a sensitive man. In a locked drawer in the dark lacquer desk in his study he kept all the letters Lorna had ever written to him, tied in a dark blue ribbon that she had used for her hair before cutting it into the short masculine bob she now favoured. Mostly written on scraps torn from exercise books, they were a mass of loops and unconnected thoughts, half-finished ideas flying across the page. He thought of their first year at Shiwa together as good times, remembering Lorna telling him she could live anywhere with him from Kensington to Timbuktu, but even the early notes, dated November 1931 when he was off overseeing the building of the bridge over the Mansya river, hinted at problems and recalled terrible fights.

> Dear Man
>
> I am so sad at making you sad; now I will try to please you not please myself . . . Mark is crooning and it is all very quiet and peaceful except for those awful loathsome flies . . .

> Dear Man
>
> I don't want you to be unhappy because in this short life of which we don't know the meaning we really might as well be happy as its just as easy as being sad . . .

By contrast, those sent from her trips with Audrey Richards in 1933 sounded full of life, writing of checking the diets of the women, playing campfire games with villagers in the evening, dancing and singing. In some she asked his advice on the best way to shoot a duck or a hartebeest, in another she laughed about the supper falling through the bottom of the pot. But she was aware of his concerns that they were drifting apart.

> Dearest Man
>
> . . . will you know that though I write exclusively about our affairs yet you are fully in my mind, so do no longer fear that you have a callous wife with no love in her heart . . . it is just that this is all strange and exciting . . . it is more new and enthralling than one could have thought.

Or the following week:

> Dear Good Man
>
> This is just to say that I have not forgotten you nor our Shiwa . . .

Our Shiwa. Sometimes Gore-Browne thought the place was the only thing holding them together, other times he felt it drove them apart. He recorded in his notebook that once, during an argument, she had said, 'Shiwa, Shiwa, Shiwa! That's all you really care about!' He felt she took the antics of the natives too much to heart, remembering how upset she'd been when, her last Christmas at Shiwa before going to Cambridge, she had suggested buying jumpers for the staff as presents rather than blankets as they always put them round their shoulders. They ordered blue sweaters from London, but knowing they didn't like change, he offered the servants a choice. Not a single one took a jumper. Those who were left with no choice put them on the ground as if they were rugs.

The sound of children's laughter from outside made him look up. Mark and Angela had cast off their shoes as usual, and were playing with some of the servant's children, showing them the red toy train he had bought in Selfridge's, and babbling away in Bemba as if it were the most natural thing in the world. *I hope sending them away to school, as we will have to eventually, won't change their wonderful innocence of the colour bar*, he wrote to Ethel. He might have felt that Lorna was lost to him, but he wrote, *If I can only leave a beautiful home for the girls and a better country for all my people at Shiwa, then it will all have been worth something.*

15

Shiwa Ngandu,
6 February 1940

Driving the V8 down the road from the house past the workshops and still-room to the new Shiwa hospital, Gore-Browne looked about the place contentedly. The bubu trees were starting to blossom, the earlier rains had cleared and he described the gardens of the new hospital to Ethel as *black with people, all dressed in their colourful finest.* Chief Nkula and three other chiefs from the surrounding districts and their retinues had turned up for the opening ceremony, as well as more than forty headmen from the local villages. Along the path stood the estate's *capitaos* in a soldierly line, wearing navy blue jerseys and shorts and black fez, the house-servants in their best scarlet and white uniforms, and a squad of honour of schoolboys from nearby Timba school (a part government, part missionary school which Gore-Browne had succeeded in getting open on the estate in 1938), all neatly turned out in scout uniform and waving Pathfinder flags. Knowing that none of the Africans had watches, and even if they had, their tendency to *completely disregard time*, he had sent Lorna over to the hospital much earlier to make sure everyone was in place by the appointed hour of a quarter to four, and he spotted her standing with a small gaggle of Europeans waiting at the entrance. The group included Dr Monica Hanford, his twenty-seven-year-old niece (daughter of his sister, Sapphire), who was to run the hospital, Joe Savill, his estate manager, Vera the flirtatious governess, *stylish as usual with her flaming red hair like fire in the sun*, holding little Angela by the hand (his eldest, Mark, having been sent off to Roedean boarding school in Johannesburg), the old Macminns, and Fritz and Friedel, the Jewish refugee couple from Berlin who had recently arrived to work at Shiwa. *The festive atmosphere reminded one of Ascot*, he later noted in his diary. It was hard to remember that back home there was a war on.

Lorna came down to the car to greet their special guests from the government – Dr John Haslam, the Director of Medical Services, and Walter Fairly, the Director of Public Works. As they walked through the crowds, the people cheered, sang and chanted at the tops of their voices. When the small party had reached the steps of the main building and taken their seats on the terrace, the little African schoolboys sang a specially written song of welcome.

Once they had finished, Gore-Browne waved his arms to hush the crowd and introduced Dr Haslam, who made a short speech through the megaphone, first thanking the Macminns for their pioneer medical work in the area for the last twenty-five years, and praising Monica, before expressing his delight at the completion of the hospital project. He then spoke to the Africans through an interpreter, reminding them of the importance of agriculture to produce plentiful food to keep healthy. He asked the chiefs and headmen to ensure their people made full use of the hospital, and not wait to bring in the sick until they were too ill to be cured. Finally he cut the ribbon, saying, 'It is with great pleasure that I declare this hospital open,' amid cheers and loud clapping. Speaking both in English and in Bemba, Gore-Browne thanked everyone for coming and reminded them that the hospital was for all, Africans and Europeans alike. Macminn offered a prayer, his frail voice faltering a little. The old missionary had almost finished his life work of translating the Bible into Bemba, and

Gore-Browne knew the couple were thinking of going back to Scotland. He would be sorry to lose them. The crowd then sang 'Nkosi Sikeleli Africa' – 'God Bless Africa', in a great rousing wall of sound, their voices a rich range of natural harmonies. They ended proceedings with 'God Save the King', under the schoolmaster's direction.

'Refreshments will be served at Shiwa House in the Great Hall,' announced Gore-Browne. News of food spurred a great move of people up the hill towards the house. He had slaughtered three oxen, ordered the cooks to make huge vats of tea and masses of cakes and sandwiches, and hoped it would be enough. *It looked like the feeding of the five thousand*, he wrote to Ethel, *still the weather held and it all seems to have gone off alright. Rather a good show in fact.*

The estate was looking glorious, clean and fresh after the rains which had turned the bush from bare and brown to vivid green, and coaxed out flowers in the garden of every shape and colour – red hot pokers, pink gladioli, tall mauve orchids and montbretias in yellowish orange. The only cloud was his frustration at being so far from the war, and desperate worry about those he loved back home, Ethel most of all. They had recently acquired a wireless in the library at Shiwa, and he listened to the latest on the BBC every morning and evening. *Reading between the lines one can piece together what is going on*, he wrote in his diary, *but that still doesn't explain how events actually affect one's own nearest and dearest.*

But he was pleased with the hospital – *However small it might be in the scheme of things, one feels glad to have something concrete accomplished*, he told Ethel, and thought it well worth the £1,500 he had spent on it and bringing out Monica from England. The hospital had been Lorna's idea, and he had even agreed to a carved wooden plaque in the outpatients' hall, dedicating the hospital to the memory of her father, Professor Edwin Monck Goldman, his old rival for the affections of her mother, making him realize how strangely life could turn out. The main building, one storey in pink brick with red tiles, all produced on the estate, consisted of a consulting room, operating theatre, treatment room, outpatients' hall, two surgical wards and a dispensary full of glass Winchester bottles labelled Flu Mixture, Fever Mixture, Stomach Mixture and Headache Mixture. *It all looks so square and solid*, he wrote proudly, *one hopes it is something that will last*. The hospital had room for thirty patients, mostly in separate brick-built huts in the grounds as many of the Bemba believed that sharing a wall with another couple would bring bad luck to them, and of course when one person was ill, the entire family had to move into hospital too. He planned to get his men to plant some of the thousands of lemon trees that Lorna had ordered and never planted, in gardens round the huts.

All they had to do now was to persuade people to use the hospital. Since Monica had arrived at Shiwa the previous year, she had been doing a valiant job, already making a reputation for herself by saving some lives and effecting cures that villagers thought were miraculous, like the case of the woman who had complained that her husband kept waking up in the night thinking she was a lion because she snored so heavily. Monica had easily solved that one by removing the polyps in the woman's nose. Other cases had been more complicated – a child bitten by a puff-adder who could not be saved and whose bloodcurdling cries could be heard all over the compound when she had amputated his gangrenous leg, and the lad whose foot had almost been blown off by a muzzle-loading gun. *He was a nice lad*, Gore-Browne wrote, *the son of an old headman I used to go elephant hunting with in the early days*.

It was no easy task, and *Monica certainly has guts*, he wrote. The Bemba people were highly suspicious of Western medicine, preferring to use their own traditional plant concoctions, but she had gone round the villages with her stethoscope trying to win their trust, even injecting herself to persuade them to succumb to inoculations. The hospital had little equipment, beyond an operating table, a microscope and Tilley lamps to operate under by night. Her only assistants were an illiterate boy, and Manasseh, an orderly who had taken medical exams in Lusaka but failed them. The £200 a year grant Gore-Browne had wrested from the government paid for little more than bandages, aspirin, quinine, iron tonic and laxative pills known as 'Livingstone Rousers'. They had no penicillin and used chloroform for anaesthetic, Monica often roping in Lorna, Mrs Macminn, or even house-guests to administer it as she wielded the knife.

Unfortunately, Monica and Lorna did not get on at all, somewhat ironically, considering the hospital had been his wife's pet project. The two young women clashed from the start to Gore-Browne's dismay – he liked his sister's clever and vivacious daughter and had thought she would be good company for his melancholic wife. But Lorna complained that Monica was bossy and officious, always meddling in everyone else's business, called her 'La Hanford' and constantly bemoaned the fact that she was still living in one of the downstairs rooms of the main house, rather than moving out into one of the guest-houses as they had intended. For Monica's part, she later recalled, 'I had little patience for someone who spent so much time languishing in bed with no real medical reason – *malade imaginaire*.' Gore-Browne wrote to Ethel, *Lorna's life continues to be one of extremes, alternating between such energy, working 26 hours a day, and complete knockout, but I don't know what I can do about it and have long ceased interfering.*

He went to look for his wife among the guests in the crowded hall, and instead ran into John Haslam, holding a cup of tea and a plate of sandwiches and congratulating him on the hospital, as well as remarking that he couldn't imagine any of their colleagues from Lusaka opening up their homes to the natives in this way. Gore-Browne told him, 'I've always felt that healing the sick was one of the things that no one can argue about whatever one's religion, race or outlook.' He knew that other members of the Legislative Council were horrified at stories that he often had Africans in his house and even at his dinner-table. 'But,' he added, 'perhaps if the world gets sufficiently troubled it will be better to be dead!'

Longing to be back in uniform and part of the action, Gore-Browne had told the Governor of his desire to go to Regimental Headquarters in Nairobi and perhaps take up a command. Instead, to his disappointment, he had been appointed Commissioner for Civil Defence, which meant travelling round the country, choosing local committees, making people aware of the possible dangers and selecting locations as air-raid shelters in what he described to Ethel as *a million to one event of bombs being dropped on Lusaka or Livingstone.* He personally thought it most unlikely that the Germans would attack British colonies in East and Central Africa as some feared, or that the Italians would manage to push south from Somalia. Much as he admired Italian architecture, as a race he thought them *far too lily-livered to be effective fighters.*

But he rallied to the task, even though he had no shortage of other work. At the start of the war, he and Roy Welensky had been invited on to the Executive Council, the closest thing Northern Rhodesia had to a cabinet, as well as retaining his old job representing native interests on LegCo, where he had been elected leader of the Unofficials, the members who were not civil servants. He had become something of a confidant to the new Governor, Sir John Maybin, a confirmed bachelor and workaholic, introspective and well-read, whom he greatly respected. Whenever he was in Lusaka for Council meetings, he stayed in Government House, telling Ethel, *the comfort of which makes visits to the dreadful capital far more pleasant*, and accompanied the Governor for long walks in the evenings, during which they talked of *every subject under the sun.* Sometimes they travelled together, Gore-Browne enjoying the luxury of the Governor's private railway carriage, which was something he had decided he would most like to have, hating crowding and pushing as he did.

All in all he found he spent less than half his time at Shiwa. Much of his days were wasted in simply getting from one place to another, as the roads were in *a pitiable state*, being unmetalled and not at all able to cope with hundreds of troop convoys, mainly from South Africa going north to Nairobi, from where some would be shipped to fight in Europe and some in Somalia. *These days one is lucky if one can average 23 miles per hour with all the traffic*, he wrote. Air was much faster, but what air services there were in Northern Rhodesia had been reduced, and he found the turbulence frequently made him sick. Still, he thought that at the age of fifty-seven he was lucky to have so much to occupy himself. *One cannot complain*, he wrote to Ethel. *I can think of others my age rotting away and howling and moaning in inactivity.*

It was good to have something to take his mind off what had been a troubled few years. First, in August 1936, Ethel had written to say she had sold Brooklands. He had known it was coming – the estate was far too big to manage on her own now she was in her seventies, but it didn't ease the pain.

Knowing he would never again sleep in his room, ride in the grounds or sit with Ethel by the fire in the library seemed like losing part of himself. The main house had been bought by Vickers, the aircraft manufacturers, and the racetrack sold to another company, and Ethel had moved out to Caenshill, a large handsome house on the estate, retaining just the stables and a small area of land, and auctioning much of the furniture.

The following year came the shock news of the death of his friend John Peacock, the former District Commissioner of Chinsali who had moved to Broken Hill. *Poor old Peacock's car spun out of control after the brakes failed, and turned over and pinned him down in a ditch, and he was found drowned in 31 inches of water*, he wrote to Ethel. At least he was later shown to have died instantaneously – the doctor certified his neck had been broken. Everyone was talking about the Bemba curse claiming another victim, and Gore-Browne couldn't help remembering how Peacock had used to toast surviving another year on the anniversary of entering the sacred burial grove, and had almost died a couple of years earlier canoeing on the river when a sudden rain started, capsizing him and his wife. He was sad to lose a friend at whose house he had felt a welcome visitor – *there are few enough good people in the country* – and he felt terribly sad for Peacock's wife, Pat, who had gone back to England to her parents, Sir Edward and Lady Crowe. They had buried her husband at Shiwa, in a grave on the small hill by the side of the house, which Gore-Browne made sure was kept well tended and often visited himself, finding it a quiet place to sit and reflect, and thinking of it as Peacock's Hill. Sir Edward had written to him that he was glad his son-in-law was buried where he was remembered because he had seen so many sad neglected cemeteries in far-off corners of the world.

Worse was to come. Later that year, to his initial disbelief and then *utter sadness*, they had discovered that some of their most trusted house-servants had been stealing from them, taking his large ring of keys while he was in the bath every evening before dinner and helping themselves to his wine cellar, as well as watering down his casks of vintage Delaforce port, getting drunk and selling some of it in the village. This was far more serious than the ticket fraud which they had often had to deal with, where workers claimed to have worked more days or forged the daily tickets he or Joe issued and signed. Even more upsetting, the theft involved people like Chikwanda, his faithful *capitao*, a retired servant for whom he had just built a house, and Kakumbi, whom he had taken with him to England all those years before. They were discovered when the dam behind the house, from which the water was pumped, got blocked and turned out to be full of empty bottles which had been thrown there. Gore-Browne called in Detective Philip Chilumba from Kasama, who had found seventeen of his servants involved. He sent the culprits to the *boma* at Chinsali, where they had been tried and locked up, but he must have felt terribly betrayed. Chitimukulu, who was working at the *boma* at the time as a clerk, said he was 'terribly sad. He valued trust above everything and when he liked a person it was for life, whatever the colour of their skin.' He had been trying to do his best for them at Shiwa, providing work for over 1,000 natives, funding scholarships for their children and opening up a social club. On the national stage, he had slaved away to improve their lot, campaigning single-handedly for schools and dispensaries, and to get the hut tax made fairer so that rural Africans were not forced to leave their villages to earn money to pay it, and had secured exemptions for the old and infirm. The one thing that had always kept him going through the long discussions in Lusaka was having Shiwa to come back to, and after the ring of thieves was uncovered, he confessed to Ethel, *now that too seems flawed*.

His problems with Lorna had not helped matters. His wife was so unpredictable that one minute she was all sweetness and light, *in sparkling form*, charming the pants off the guests at the dinner-table, and the next so completely unreasonable as to be *almost evil*, screaming at him and making schoolgirl jokes in front of important people like the Governor. The rare times they were together, he never knew which version of his wife he was going to find, or what had brought a certain mood on. Sir Douglas Hall, who knew the couple well as his wife Rachel had been Lorna's best friend at Sherborne and he was District Commissioner of Mpika from 1939–41, says of Lorna, 'she was beautiful, eccentric and trouble, there was a wicked streak in her. I wouldn't have been at all surprised if she had asked me to run off with her'. One former visitor recalls how during a house-party of eminent guests, Lorna had come down to dinner dressed as Anne Boleyn. Accompanied by two small boys dressed in red velvet and swinging enormous fans, she had curtsied to the stunned visitors and taken her place at one end of the table as if it were the most natural thing in the world. Another time he had come back to find she had given their piano away to some Australian fellow. She had moved up to the tower room and took to her bed most of the time he was there, or kept him awake by playing her violin up there to the accompaniment of howling hyenas until sometimes he felt like smashing the infernal instrument. Then, when he was away, she wrote pleading letters to him as if he were the great love of her life.

Only the previous June when he was away building a dispensary at Chitambo's village, she had written one of her rambling letters saying that she wished she was going with him to Europe. 'I got a doctor's order to go to bed again before dinner so I was able to play the gramophone all evening,' she wrote. 'Your birthday present has come and I hope you like it as much as I do. I think it belongs to Beethoven's maturity but I like it because it is not at all full of trouble unresolved.'

Telling him not to get 'too tired and depressed', she continued:

> I'm afraid I have rather made out lately that I am discontented and want parties and young men but this is not the case seeing that I have never liked parties and am not young myself [she was just thirty-one]. I certainly enjoy it when we get nice folk here and I would like to do the Banguelu thing [she wanted to build a dispensary for the fishing community on an island she was fond of on the lake] but do not want to press it and you must know by now that I am more than content with our life so long as you keep well. In fact my only complaint is that our life is mostly too full of lovely things and it is so hard to choose and keep a mean. I am feeling much better again and not so infernally tired but the betterness is at the expense of doing a full day's work.

She ended by asking him to get '15lbs of white paint for the boat, 15lbs of green and a touch of blue or yellow for decoration.'

Although their finances had improved, their arguments over money had worsened. The neroli and lime oil were selling at a good price, and total estate income for the oils now stood at £20,000, most of which had come in the last few years, but expenses had also risen enormously with the war affecting cost of shipping, leaving a yearly profit of about £1,400 (£1,000 on the neroli and £400 on the lime). Although they were just about able to make ends meet, any sharp drop in dividends on his capital would be disastrous. Gore-Browne was trying to cut back the estate's activities to the core – to concentrate just on essential oils, which Boake Roberts, the buyers in London, said they still wanted, for scenting soap and eau-de-Cologne, on the hospital, and on the ordinary maintenance of roads, buildings and bridges which would quickly fall apart if left neglected. This, he estimated, could cut expenditure in half – in a way he thought the war could be a *Blessing-in-Disguise* by getting them out of the bad habits they had fallen into.

It's not that Lorna isn't willing to save, he complained to Ethel, *but that she keeps wasting money*. Recently, when she was ill again with mouth abscesses, she had insisted on going to Johannesburg by rail, second-class, to economize, rather than by air, but then she had come back laden with *all sorts of things she didn't want and would probably never look at again*. She insisted on taking things on, then never did them, so they just got left, like the lemon trees for example, which were a complete waste of money. *Her head is always full of so many schemes, ideas she's picked up in Cambridge or from visitors*, he added, *yet she never sees anything through to completion*. He had noticed that she had now got Mulemfwe and his men planting strange clumps of grasses by the lake, which she said was an experiment to find a better grass for pasture. He thought she was too slack with the staff – he had come back this trip to find that a leopard had killed eight sheep in the kraal, which he thought could have been avoided if Pemba Moto, the night-watchman, had been doing his job properly. He confessed to Ethel, *I get rather scared sometimes when I think about what will happen when I'm dead.*

Sometimes he thought the only person he could really rely on was his manservant Henry Mulenga, nephew of his clerk James Mwanza. Henry had joined the staff in 1931 at the age of twenty-one with his brother Kalaka as a house-boy, after Gore-Browne had come across him in Salisbury, working for the police to pay his hut tax, and overheard him speaking Bemba. Discovering he was the son of the headman of Chisoso village, not far from Shiwa, he took him back and had him trained as a carpenter. Though he was illiterate, Henry had a certain noble bearing, though not of royal blood as Gore-Browne was to tell people, and he had taken a shine to him, trained him as a driver, bought him some smart clothes, given him his old bookmaker's coat and a cap and the old Shiwa guest-houses to live in, thinking of him almost as part of the family, though Lorna had little time for him. Now, when he travelled, Henry always accompanied him which, he told Ethel, *makes an enormous difference.* Not only was he a good companion, interested in everything, but if he arrived somewhere late at night and exhausted after a long journey, he could always rely on Henry to magic up a hot toddy or cocoa and a full English breakfast in the morning. Henry had been invaluable going round with him during his last series of meetings on the Copperbelt, and he thought he could educate him into something. He wrote far more about Henry in his diary and letters than his children, and after taking him on a plane the other day from Lusaka to Broken Hill, had noted that he had overheard Henry telling someone afterwards, 'One looks out of the window and sees nothing but cotton-wool.'

Lorna rarely got up to see her husband off any more when he left for his war work or political meetings. Setting off with Henry at the wheel in his chauffeur's cap and uniform, and a flask of coffee at the ready, Gore-Browne liked to get on the road before the first pink streaks of dawn had crossed the sky, though he suspected that with his wife's insomnia she was only feigning sleep when he looked in to say goodbye.

Stewart Gore-Browne's beloved aunt Ethel and her husband, Hugh Locke King, at their estate, Brooklands, in Weybridge, Surrey.

Gore-Browne as a boy.

The opening of Brooklands motor racing track, 1907. The first car in the procession was driven by Ethel Locke King, one of the first women in Britain to drive.

Stewart Gore-Browne at the wheel of a Piccard Pictet after a race at Brooklands in 1909. His father, Frank, is on the near right, in the cloth cap. In a race in 1911 Stewart Gore-Browne beat Malcolm Campbell into second place.

Captain Steel, one of Gore-Browne's senior officers on the Anglo-Belgian Border Commission, 1911–14. A second officer, Captain Everett, was eaten by a lion.

Officers from the Commission studying maps to plot the border between Northern Rhodesia and the Belgian Congo.

Wooden beacons were constructed on high points to mark the border.

Above Stewart Gore-Browne's servant Kakumbi up a tree.

Chikwanda, a messenger for the Commission and Gore-Browne's first foreman at Shiwa Ngandu.

Below Bulaya, Gore-Browne's cook, sitting on the first rhino ever shot by Gore-Browne on the shore of Shiwa Ngandu lake on Good Friday 1914. Bulaya and Kakumbi both accompanied Gore-Browne to England in 1914 to be 'trained in English manners'.

Gore-Browne's first house at Shiwa Ngandu, 1914.

Getting to Shiwa from the nearest railway station was a three-week journey involving marching across crocodile-infested swamps and canoeing along the Luapula and Chambeshi rivers.

Left Building a cattle shed at Shiwa.

Below left Stewart Gore-Browne made his own bricks, using clay from the river bed and following instructions from an Army building manual. For many years he was the biggest employer in north-eastern Rhodesia, employing hundreds of people.

Below In the early years the shores of the lake were full of game such as these reedbuck, providing the main source of food.

An aerial view of Shiwa House in 1931. The tower and chapel were added later.

Detail of the arch over the gatehouse. The rhino was Gore-Browne's own personal symbol, for his fierce temper, and the date 1920 marks when he started building after returning from fighting in the First World War.

Stewart Gore-Browne's first love, Lorna Bosworth Smith.

Stewart Gore-Browne's wedding to Lorna Goldman, orphaned daughter of Lorna Bosworth Smith. The ceremony took place at St George's Church, Hanover Square, London, on 23 July 1927.

Lorna (centre) on the steps at Brooklands with Gore-Browne's second cousin Lord Portsmouth.

Lorna in Venice on her honeymoon.

Stewart Gore-Browne in full military uniform in London for the Coronation of King George VI in 1937.

Stewart Gore-Browne's return to Shiwa with his new wife in October 1927. The servants always turned out on parade to welcome him back from trips.

Above Gore-Browne's favourite room in the house was the library.

Below The kitchen, where five-course gourmet meals were turned out.

Only favoured guests were taken to bathe in the hot springs.

Top left Lorna and a leopard trap. Leopards were a constant problem, killing chickens and terrorizing villagers.

Top right Lorna supervising marmalade production, one of a series of schemes to make money and keep busy.

Above Lorna and her daughters, Mark (Lorna mark III) and Angela, visiting Ethel Locke King at Brooklands.

Right The Gore-Brownes' children, Lorna/ Mark and Angela, at Shiwa. The two girls were brought up by governesses and sent to boarding school in Johannesburg.

The estate buildings. Behind is the distillery, where essential oils were produced from orange blossom and lime juice.

Kalaka, Stewart Gore-Browne's chief hunter, bringing in geese from the lake for Christmas dinner.

Gore-Browne writing letters by candlelight. He wrote to his aunt Ethel almost every day.

The front gardens at Shiwa included rose gardens, a walled ladies' garden, a tennis court and a swimming pool.

In 1932, the first Imperial Airways African mailplane made a forced landing at Shiwa – the first plane ever to land there. Lorna and Mark are standing in front with Air Marshal Sir Vyell Vyvyan, director of Imperial Airways, and his wife, Lady Frances.

Left Lorna alone in 1933 at Cambridge University, where she went to study nutrition and agriculture.

Below left Henry Mulenga, Stewart Gore-Browne's faithful batman, seeing snow for the first time on a trip to Europe in 1950.

Below Lorna in a canoe on the lake at Shiwa. She managed the estate on her own for much of the late 1930s and early 1940s while her husband was in politics.

Above Stewart Gore-

Above Gore-Browne watching his daughter Lorna marrying Major John Harvey at Shiwa, August 1951. The occasion was reported in the newspapers as the biggest party in Africa.

Browne's daughter Lorna throwing earth into his coffin at his funeral in 1967. Kenneth Kaunda, the first President of Zambia and a former protégé of Gore-Browne, looks on. Gore-Browne remains the only white man in Zambia to have received a state funeral and a chief's burial.

Right Gore-Browne's grave overlooks the lake.

Above The gatehouse at Shiwa. A drive lined by cypress trees leads up to the house.

Right Stewart Gore-Brown in later years.

With Gore-Browne away so much, Lorna and Joe Savill ran Shiwa during the war years. Even though they had cut down the estate's activities to the minimum, there was still a lot of work, Lorna noting in the estate book that they had eleven donkeys, 398 cattle, 207 sheep and seventeen goats, and she complained that she felt tired all the time. 'I feel ill inefficient and despondent to keep going round a place this size single-handed,' she wrote in the estate book. 'The temptation is not to go at all.' They had some help from the Jewish refugee couple – the Freudenthals, or Freedendales as they wished to be known – whom Gore-Browne had hired on a trial basis for £10 a month plus board, and whom Angela insisted on referring to as Mr and Mrs Jew. They had come from a well-to-do background, the family owning a steel foundry and a house in Cologne, near where Gore-Browne had been based in the Rhine Occupation Force. The husband, Fritzi, had owned an electrical shop in Berlin, and his young wife Friedel was principal buyer for a dress store, hardly ideal qualifications for farm life. Fritzi's shop had been ransacked by the Nazis and he had been put in a concentration camp, where he had witnessed terrible scenes of torture and cruelty which he found hard to talk about. Eventually an Aryan business friend had paid a 1,000 Mark bribe to get him out, and the couple had fled to Africa, winding up at Shiwa. Fritzi had taken charge of the estate accounts, which he had already reorganized with card files, and Friedel was helping with the housekeeping and giving German lessons to Angela.

Lorna found them both rather irritating, particularly Friedel, whom she described in a letter to her brother's wife, Stella, as 'so much the little woman', but she couldn't deny they were useful. The hospital had created more work, Monica forever dragging her in to administer chloroform, or 'go on wild goose chases to villages where screaming women are in labour for days'. And they had more house-guests than ever, with lots of troops passing through on their way up north. Her husband had told her to cut down on entertaining but she did not see how they could turn these young men away, knowing they were off to fight and might never return. One night, just a few days before Gore-Browne's return for the hospital opening, she had been going to bed early, exhausted, when glancing out of the window she saw a line of headlights coming along the drive. It had turned out to be an advance party from South Africa, thirty-two hungry young men led by a Colonel Cotton. George, the cook, was ill with what he called 'caterpillars', so she and Friedel had had to make bread and provide them supper. Afterwards she put on records and danced with them, finally getting to bed around 1 a.m. Then she had had to be up again before 5 a.m. to arrange morning cocoa and a hearty breakfast to set them on their way, managing to wangle a case of Army issue bully beef tins in return for the hospitality. She feared the estate was heading for a food shortage after the heavy rains of the previous year had destroyed so many crops, which meant there was little in store, and so much labour had been taken off to work on government projects such as road-building. They had ordered some bags of meal to distribute among staff, and she had been out on several shooting expeditions, mostly wildfowl – she had never really got the hang of hunting game. This year the lake seemed particularly full of pygmy geese, lapwing geese, yellow-bill ducks and a new kind the Bantu called Bumbio. 'This is a country rich in ducks and devils,' she had once told her husband.

Shiwa's isolation meant Lorna had long ago got used to making do. She had recently broken her front tooth again, the Hollywood crown that had been expensively done in London the previous summer, and was keeping it in place with chewing-gum and plaster of Paris as there was no chance of leaving the estate for a while. 'Oh, the bliss of being 2,000 miles from the nearest dentist able to do that sort of thing,' she wrote to her brother's wife, Stella. Still, she supposed she shouldn't really complain about life at Shiwa – at least they were safe, unlike those back home. Having the wireless had made an enormous difference, as it meant they could follow developments in the war and that the radio operator from Mpika could radio them with any important telegrams, although they could usually only hear every other word. Every morning, after dressing in her overalls, she would go down to the library and listen to the radio, not always sure what the news meant. One morning she switched it on to hear that Finland had made peace with Russia 'on very hard terms'. Outside rain was starting to spatter heavily on the windows, putting paid to her plan to go and check on the new mosses she had been experimenting with. Instead, she sat at her husband's typewriter and wrote a letter to Stella, suggesting she send her children Nicholas and Clare to the safety of Shiwa for the duration of the war.

Shiwa Ngandu
Mpika 28 January 1940

My dear Stella

Here at Shiwa life goes on the same so far, but we are preparing for not being able to have all we had, when present stores are exhausted. There is a lot to do which does not get done with Stewart away so much and the man Joe and I do the best we can.

My main difficulty is to get round to the places that all need watching at once. Although petrol is not yet rationed here, the price is high and roads bad, and it isn't always one's fault if one smashes something, and spare parts are naturally hard to come by. This is a hollow in the middle of mountains but the hollow itself is cut into by hills and rivers and rocks, so you can picture that lands and cattle feeding grounds are scattered. And now is the rainy season and it's damn nicer for Filimon the herd to stay indoors than to take his cows to where they can get something to eat, unless he knows I might be coming to look him up – and there are 7 or 8 different herds to watch.

At the moment we're planting out 1,000 lime trees from the nursery (the people call it the 'lime school') where the seedlings were put last year. And as soon as they are out, one has to see that they aren't washed away in a storm or scorched by a contrastingly strong sun – each of which contingencies comes without notice.

Then something goes wrong with the dairy and all the butter goes rancid and one finds the chap has been cleaning his teeth with the cream and that there has been a little untimely excretion into the water supply and everyone goes sick in relays . . .

She continued her account of life at Shiwa then stopped abruptly with the words: 'this all sounds so provincial . . . the war goes on and one knows little'. Whatever happened, she vowed she wouldn't let it spoil what they were trying to do at Shiwa, 'whatever that is'. At least they didn't have to worry about the safety of their own children. Eleven-year-old Lorna was in Johannesburg at Roedean, where she was becoming 'a proper little Rand Queen', while Angela was still at Shiwa in the capable care of Vera the governess. They had created a small school for children of some of the local far-flung colonial officers, all of whom paid keep which was a handy boost to the estate income.

'Sometimes I think Stewart has it the better being away', she wrote to Stella, despite all his complaints about the Copperbelt and the bureaucrats of Lusaka. She was, she admitted, often tempted just to close the door behind her and leave the place, to be free from the strange hold Shiwa seemed to exert. In fact Gore-Browne had suggested that she go to Lusaka and use her talents with music and languages to work as a teacher or something while the war was on, 'to free a man to go to fight' as he had put it, but she knew the place needed her.

The Rutland Hotel, Ndola, May 29 1940

My dear Ethel

Day after day I have wanted to sit down and write to you and I just haven't had the heart because I haven't known what to say. You will believe that there is not a moment of the day when one is not thinking of you, either consciously or in the back of one's mind when one is trying to attend to other things. It's no use trying to put in words what one feels and the shame of being all this way away from you in days like these, knowing the Germans are virtually at the doorstep in Boulogne. At the moment we've very little real news that means anything – we've just heard that the Belgian army has laid down its arms with all that implies . . .

Oh my dear, I would fain be with you.

Gore-Browne was writing the letter late at night in his hotel room, after another strenuous day shuttling between the Copperbelt town of Ndola and mining settlements of Nkana, Luanshya and Mufulira, where for the previous week he had been hearing evidence for a Commission of Inquiry on recent unrest. There had been strikes by white workers in two of the mines in March over pay and conditions, resulting in pay rises which inflamed already tense relations with African mineworkers, who earned in a month about the same as the whites received in a day and got none of their benefits. The public beating of the wife of a black miner after an argument about rations sparked further discontent, culminating in ugly riots in which police opened fire, killing thirteen Africans and injuring many more. Copper was vital to the war effort and Northern Rhodesia was the Empire's main producer, so the mines had to be kept operating seven days a week, and Gore-Browne had been called in urgently by the Governor to mediate. Summoning up all his courage, with faithful Henry by his side as bodyguard and interpreter, he had braved thousands of angry black miners brandishing spears and broken bottles, all backed by the menacing thump of tribal drums, to enter the compound of the ringleaders on the third day of rioting. Many were Bemba, and seeing 'Chipembele' they had agreed to speak, but it had taken all his persuasive powers to get them to down arms and return to work, having wrangled them a few concessions and got the Governor's blessing to promise an official British government inquiry into conditions. *I thank the Lord for my gift of getting on with people*, he wrote to Ethel.

Now the Commission was under way, and, along with Sir John Forster who had come out from England to head it, and Thomas Sandford, the Secretary for Native Interests, he had been meeting managers and workers, trying to get them to work together, and going underground to see conditions in the mines. Visiting native compounds, known as the 'locations', he was shocked by the squalid shacks, describing them in his diary as *so different to the neat bungalows with the square green lawns of the white workers*. European employees had their own club with swimming-pool, tennis courts and golf course, and during the rainy season their residential area was full of purple bougainvillaea, red flame trees, hibiscus and white frangipani.

Gore-Browne hated the Copperbelt, finding it *a queer uneasy place*, perhaps because of its mixed population dominated by South Africans. Ndola, which he remembered from before the copper boom as a one street place consisting of six corrugated iron huts, was *a pleasant enough town* with its neat white bungalows and avenues of mahogany trees, trunks painted white to prevent them being eaten by the white ants which devoured everything in the area, though it was hardly the 'new Johannesburg' everyone had predicted when the extent of the copper mines had first been realized. The road to Nkana, following an old Arab slave trail, was lined with beautiful thick teak forest. Mine shafts and derricks dominated the skyline, and there was something about the place that created mutual mistrust and suspicion between all the people – black and white, workers and officials, management and government. Gore-Browne was convinced that the situation would never be properly resolved until African workers were put on an equal footing with their white colleagues, a heretical suggestion for the times, and told Ethel, *the whole experience has left me feeling rather Bolshevik – the pettiness and narrow-mindedness of the managers (who deal in millions of pounds) is quite unbelievable. The General Manager of Roan and Mufulira mines for example refused to allow the Trade Unions a phone merely out of spite.*

But it all seemed very trivial to him compared to what Ethel was facing back in England. She was almost seventy-six now, but as usual *a tower of strength*, opening her house to friends and relations seeking to move out of London, and providing shelter in her stables for refugees. He tried not to keep thinking about her, constantly reminding himself how important copper was for the war effort. Frustrated not to be back in uniform himself, he sympathized with mineworkers who were restive because they were not allowed to join up, copper being considered an essential industry. Ironically the increase in copper production for the war, and the rise in price, was making Northern Rhodesia suddenly wealthy. The income of the Protectorate was almost three-quarters made up of copper revenue, and in the ten years since 1930 had increased fourfold. The new prosperity meant hardly anyone talked any more of Gore-Browne's old bugbear – Amalgamation with Southern Rhodesia. The government was able to spend more money on development and infrastructure, and he himself had secured some lucrative public works contracts for Joe Savill and his artisans to boost Shiwa's income. At his suggestion the Executive Council had agreed to donate £200,000 – ten per cent of the country's income – to the home government for the war effort. They had also sent a battalion to the concentration of troops on the Kenyan border.

Such efforts seemed meaningless to him when he thought about German bombs raining down on England. In a postscript to his letter to Ethel, he added: *One rages impotently as one thinks of all the world having to put up with this and says surely between us all we could have avoided it. I agree where you say 'what is to come after?' That's what I despair about. I'm confident we'll defeat the Germans but what then . . . ?*

Once the Inquiry Commission had finished, Gore-Browne was due in Lusaka for the next LegCo session, where he expected to be attacked by his great adversary Leopold Moore, whom he had ousted as leader of the Unofficial members. The main point of contention within the Council remained attitudes towards natives. Hardliners such as Moore were jealous over Gore-Browne's closeness to the Governor, and disliked the way he used his position as leader of the Unofficials to promote the interests of Africans, to push for their participation on various boards and for free and compulsory education for all blacks so that they could prepare for eventual home rule – something the other members would not even countenance.

In the days when he 'kept to his corner' in Shiwa, he had had little awareness of what the colour bar really meant, but in urban areas like the Copperbelt it was much more obvious, not just in terms of wage discrimination but also in a justice system whereby a black man could be jailed for six years for throwing a stone at a white car or stealing an orange, whereas a white man who had beaten his African servant almost to death got off with a £20 fine. Convinced it was wrong, he complained to Ethel, *We have not hit on the right form of government for colonies with a small white population and a large black one.* Sometimes he felt so despondent that he thought about resigning, but was dissuaded by Welensky who had taken his position as member for the Northern Province when he was appointed Member for Native Interests, and had become his closest and most unlikely ally. Welensky kept telling him how much the others were guided by him and reminded him that a new legislature would be elected the following year which might change everything. Sitting on the verandah of No. 24 Central Avenue, Broken Hill, Welensky's four-roomed tin-roofed railway cottage with no hot water and an outside toilet, the two men often talked late into the night, bemoaning the other LegCo members, and listening to music, though Welensky's tastes were rather too catholic for Gore-Browne, the younger man enjoying everything from opera to ragtime. During one such session, Gore-Browne told him, 'What we really need is a leader like Churchill, combining a flash of genius with the power to lead.'

Despite all his work and distractions, Shiwa was never

far from his thoughts. One evening, during a break in the Commission's deliberations, he had dinner with his niece Monica, who had come up for a few days' rest and to try to beg some equipment from dashing Dr Charles Fisher at the mining hospital, whom Gore-Browne described to Ethel as *he who all mothers in town have their eye on for their daughters*, and who was the son of Walter Fisher, a renowned missionary who had come out to Africa in the latter part of the nineteenth century and set up stations in Angola and Northern Rhodesia, one of which Gore-Browne had visited in 1913 during his border work and met the then eight-year-old Charles. The Shiwa hospital was apparently prospering as a result of Chief Mukwikile and the tapeworm. Monica told her uncle that one morning one of the chief's court counsellors had appeared at her surgery, bearing a scrap of newspaper with a segment of tapeworm wrapped up in it. She didn't have the right medicine but her book of remedies suggested a mix of castor oil and chloroform. It sounded dangerous, but to her relief was highly effective, the tapeworm passing straight out of the chief's system. She put the worm, many yards of it, in formalin in a jamjar and placed it on a shelf in the dispensary. Soon everyone had heard the story and villagers were coming from all over to gape at it, and to be treated themselves.

Monica also had good news about the estate, confirming that they were expecting a big orange blossom harvest. Gore-Browne was delighted, as he had read that neroli oil was fetching the extremely high price of 57s 6d per ounce. *In one morning we could pick and distil £80 worth!* he wrote excitedly in his diary. However, she told him that Joe had returned from building a government dispensary north of Chinsali very depressed, talking about the war the whole time and sounding as though he might leave. Mrs Vicars Harris, a Brazilian divorcee whom Lorna had befriended and whom Gore-

Browne detested, was apparently staying at Shiwa again, his wife trying to matchmake her with Dr Campbell, a scheme which Gore-Browne wrote in his diary *I don't much like the sound of.* The last bit of bad news was that his old dog Kim, which had gone missing just before he left for the Copperbelt, had still not turned up and was presumably dead. *I sometimes wonder why one bothers having dogs in this country*, he moaned.

It was well after midnight when he finished transferring his account of the day's events to his diary from the little black notebook he always carried to note down interesting comments, much to the discomfort of their speakers. As he always did before retiring, he rang the bell for Henry. *I have never known such a wonderful bodyservant*, he had written to his aunt, constantly amused at the way when things went wrong, Henry would solemnly insist that they had been 'bewitched'. Lying in the lumpy hotel bed, missing the chimes of the grandfather clock and the bush sounds of Shiwa, and too tired to sleep, he kept himself company with his memories. He was very glad he had been to England the previous summer, as who knew when or if there would be another opportunity, and often pictured himself sitting on the terrace with Ethel at Caenshill, the Sunday before war was declared, sipping a glass of port, talking about everything and nothing, and watching the stars slowly disappear beneath the pine trees.

16

Lusaka, 2 February 1946

The door burst open and the crowded hut was flooded with light. Three white policemen entered the room and swung their torches strobe-like on the whitewashed mud walls and raffia-thatched ceiling, freeze-framing startled black faces mid-conversation. An old blind man in a chalk and crimson striped jacket and black porkpie hat whose crooning concertina had been barely audible above the chatter kept on for a few moments longer, until somebody nudged him.

'Well, well, well, looks like someone's been 'aving a party,' said one of the policemen, a stocky figure with a florid complexion, tapping his truncheon against his khaki trousers. His two colleagues, taller, thinner and younger, waved their torches around the hut. Forty pairs of frightened eyes stared into the bright flashlight, sweat glistening on black temples, lips moving slightly. The warm air was heavy with hops, and thick with flies, bugs and beetles, attracted in by the light.

'Can you lads smell something in here?' asked the stocky policeman, clearly the most senior. 'Something bad . . . something black?'

His colleagues pretended to sniff the air vigorously. A dull thud echoed in the nervous silence as someone dropped their cup on the mud floor.

'I can definitely smell something rotten, sarge,' ventured the youngest of the three, his face pockmarked by acne.

'Then let's get rid of it!' bawled the sergeant, raising his stick and advancing towards the cowering figures, smashing through clouds of insects. 'Get out of here, you stinking kaffirs!' he shouted, bringing his stick down with a sharp whack on someone's shoulder.

At the back of the crowd where he had been seated out of sight, watching the scene in disgust, Gore-Browne stood, drawing himself up to his full six feet to tower over the Africans. He had been brought to the African beer club in a maize field on the outskirts of Lusaka by his manservant Henry and his latest protégé, Harry Nkumbula, a bright young African whom he had come across at a teacher training college during his travels round the country and had arranged to send to the prestigious Makerere College in Uganda. Harry was staying in Gore-Browne's rented house in Lusaka, doing some typing for him in his remaining few days before setting off for college, and had suggested the evening excursion as a change from Gore-Browne's usual round of sundowners and dinners with colonial officers.

Many of the people in the bar were Bemba, and after the initial surprise of Harry's friends at seeing a white man walk in, the word went round, 'It's Chipembele.' Several Africans offered to buy Gore-Browne a beer to thank him for his work on behalf of their people, for 'speaking so beautifully', and he had been enjoying the evening. But the arrival of the British police made him feel *physically sick*, he later recounted to Ethel. He had seen police brutality before in clashes with miners but it was the first time he had been involved in anything so unprovoked, and as he stood up, he commanded the police to stop.

'What 'ave we 'ere then . . . a gentleman?' The sergeant halted in his stride for only a moment then contorted his face into an ugly leer. 'Bit of a kaffir lover are we?'

But Gore-Browne was a well-known figure in Lusaka, his

picture often appearing in the newspaper, and after some urgent whispering from one of his colleagues, the officer suddenly realized whom he was talking to. Apologizing profusely, the sergeant couldn't resist a surly aside, 'in a nigger bar!'

Telling him that there was absolutely no need for such brutality or offensive language, Gore-Browne pointed out that it was no longer illegal for natives to sell beer, a law having been passed in LegCo the previous year. The sergeant retorted that the bar had no licence, was paying no taxes, and was selling illegally brewed 'kaffir beer', but Gore-Browne had lost his patience. *I told him these people here have worked all day for a few pence*, he wrote to Ethel. *Their wives work and their children work. They probably haven't eaten meat since Christmas. While you are stuffing your fat faces with beer and chicken and slurping your whisky sodas, they are surviving on one bowl of watery porridge. And you begrudge them one bowl of millet beer you wouldn't even let your dog drink!*

Later, walking back across rain-softened fields under a sky brilliant with stars, Henry told him to forget what he had seen, but Harry seemed profoundly affected, saying that he was 'both proud and ashamed'. Gore-Browne noted in his diary Harry's comment: *Tonight is the first time that I have ever seen a white man defend one of us against one of his own. My shame is that we cannot stand up for ourselves. But one day we shall have all the fine white words at our command and then you will be proud of us.* Gore-Browne nodded thoughtfully, wondering if he had gone too far this time. His little speech to the police would no doubt be reported back and seized upon by his enemies. He had been knighted in the previous January's New Year's Honours list for his work on LegCo, following in the steps of his father and grandfather before him, and though he was fiercely proud of the recognition of his work, the title had made some of the Council's other members even more resentful and eager for any opportunity to bring him down a peg.

But, as he told Ethel, *seeing the colour bar enforced, particularly by uncouth whites of no breeding, so infuriates me.* In the last LegCo session he had outraged the hardliners by saying he saw no reason for discrimination against Africans in shops and post offices, many of which still did not allow them in, making them stand in the road at holes in the wall, even in the cold or rain; in buses and trains where they were packed in *like cattle*; railway stations where they always had to wait until the last white had been served, often missing their train as a result; and the general manner in which they were *treated as potential criminals* and called 'boy' whatever their age. He hated going to the bank in Lusaka and seeing *a piteous crowd* of twenty or thirty Africans waiting, waiting, often a whole day, until any European who had dropped in had been attended to, served tea, families discussed, etc. He did not think it right that a man should be prohibited from doing skilled work because he had a black skin. Worst of all, he could *see no excuse for not extending common courtesies – if an African is in my house at teatime, I would naturally ask him to tea*, and he always invited his house-servants to have a glass of port or wine after dinner. *It is*, he told Ethel, *a simple question of manners.*

Gore-Browne took his job seriously as representative for Native Interests in LegCo, travelling tirelessly around Northern Rhodesia to gather opinion from as many of the country's 1.5 million Africans as he could reach, then 'hammering on about it' in Executive Council, 'like a broken record' as some of the others complained. He had bought an Austin Vanette, fitting it up with a bed, mosquito net and curtains so that he could sleep in it at night anywhere on the road rather more comfortably than the makeshift huts they used to erect in his early days in Africa. He and Henry must have made an odd sight as they set off for what the other Council members referred to as 'bundu-bashing', bumping across tracks and rivers to the farthest reaches of the country, Henry ever-smiling in his chauffeur's cap and uniform and Gore-Browne barking instructions to him such as 'Sound the horn!' or 'Put your foot down!' On arrival in towns and villages, they would hold meetings with chiefs and workers, miners and schoolteachers, long-drawn-out discussions with tribal elders which would have tested the patience of most men. Henry would interpret if the language was not Bemba and Gore-Browne was often introduced as 'our beloved Chipembele', his fierce-tempered reputation apparently preceding him. The previous year the pair had travelled more than 8,000 miles, holding eighty-four meetings, and these encounters made him more and more aware of growing black political consciousness. At one recent meeting on the Copperbelt, an African had stood up and said: 'We Africans do not want £60 a month for our work and we realize that Europeans must be better paid but we do feel it is an injustice that a man who has worked perhaps ten or fifteen years underground should be receiving £4 or £5 a month whereas a European who comes fresh to the work from South Africa or England starts at £40 a month.'

Listening to such views, which he recorded in his notebook, and having seen with what valour and dedication the 15,000-strong Northern Rhodesian regiment had fought for their colonial masters in the war, serving in Europe, Somalia and Burma, killing Italians and Japanese, Gore-Browne was convinced of the need for them to have more say in the political process in their own homeland. Meeting him again at that time, Chitimukulu was surprised how much his attitude had changed: 'He was a very kind man who understood the African and worked happily with the African and gave me accommodation in that big house as if it were the most normal thing in the world. I began to think of him as a white native.'

Gore-Browne persuaded the Governor to allow the setting up of Provincial Councils, bringing together chiefs and educated Africans with colonial officers in the form of Provincial and District Commissioners to give them a forum in which to make their views known, and these had quickly become open in their criticism of government policies and the colour bar. To him, these were just a start, but his colleagues seemed frightened to go further, the landslide election of a Labour government in August 1945 having heightened fears of white settlers who regarded Labour as anti-white. Even his great friend Welensky was *refusing to see the way the wind is blowing* and the two men started to drift apart, Welensky spurning Gore-Browne's pleas to accompany him on one of his tours to see the situation for himself.

The more uphill he felt the struggle, the more outspoken he became in government debates. In the last LegCo session, he had deliberately shocked the assembled members by saying, 'I cannot believe that it is impossible to find some means to enable white people to stay on in this country and prosper, and at the same time to deny the black man no advance of which he himself is capable . . . that is my confession of faith and I would be prepared to devote my whole life to achieve that end.' Never one for self-doubt, Gore-Browne was convinced his views were right. He realized too that if Africans were going to make their participation in politics more effective, they would need education. He had personally arranged and funded bursaries for some promising young men such as Harry Nkumbula, and persuaded the Education Department to set up a three-man scholarship committee to send bright students to university in London. However, as most Africans had only had the most cursory mission education, it was hard to find potential candidates. He had his eye on a nattily dressed twenty-one-year-old teacher from Chinsali who as a boy had been a frequent visitor to the Shiwa estate, as he had grown up on Lubwa Mission and his elder brother was a teacher at Timba school. From the Bemba tribe, and currently teaching on the Copperbelt, he had interpreted for Gore-Browne at several meetings with miners and his name was Kenneth Kaunda.

Referring presciently to Harry Nkumbula and Kenneth Kaunda, Gore-Browne wrote in his diary, *These are the shoulders on which the future of the country will depend, though they don't realize it themselves.* Watching Harry spread his few belongings on the bed to pack for college in a small battered case, *with all the excitement of a young man going up to Oxford*, he was quite sure things would change in their lifetime, though probably not in his.

Harry's train was on time, and after seeing him off, Gore-Browne returned alone to the house which he had been renting in Lusaka. He had taken his own place after the sudden death of the last Governor, his good friend Sir John Maybin, a bachelor with whom he used to stay whenever Council was in session. The new Governor, Sir John Waddington, had also invited him to stay at Government House, and Gore-Browne wrote to Ethel, *He is an Oxford man and perfectly decent but he has his family with him and it is not the same.* It was a Sunday so he went to morning service at St John's, the British church, turning down several invitations for lunch at the club, noting in his diary, *not in the mood for that kind of polite company.* Henry was ill with fever and had gone to bed, and Belle, the Great Dane which he had recently acquired, was on heat and he had locked her up in a room out of harm's way where she was whining softly. Although he liked solitude, sometimes as he got older the days seemed to drag when he was alone. For a while he worked on a paper he was writing for the Fabian Society in London, but felt uninspired so went through his mail, as usual mostly begging letters. He wrote a £20 cheque for Mutale, *an enterprising young fellow* who had come to him wanting a loan to set up a chicken farm, and then a reply to Hastings Banda, the outspoken doctor in Harrow whom Ethel had introduced him to at Brooklands, where she often entertained young Africans. Banda had written recently from London to say he was planning to go back to Nyasaland to practise, and no doubt get involved in politics. Gore-Browne had introduced him to Welensky and tried to get him a position in Northern Rhodesia to lead a campaign against venereal disease, but the administration would not agree to pay him a European salary.

Starting a letter to his aunt, he took out his pocket watch to check the time, writing, *the hands seem to hardly move*. He had arranged to go and see Lorna that afternoon to discuss arrangements about money and where their daughters would stay during their Easter vacation. The couple had been officially separated over a year, but had had little to do with each other since the first half of the war. The breaking point had really come in 1942 when Lorna had gone off on her own, canoeing 100 miles to Lake Bangweulu, to a hut she had built on an island in the middle of a swamp. Ostensibly there to buy fish from the swamp-dwellers to supplement food at Shiwa, and to oversee the building of a dispensary, she had stayed months in her hut, painting one room red and one room blue, planted an orange tree and some pineapple plants and written of setting up home there with only her violin and radio for company. On finally returning to Shiwa, she had immediately gone to Johannesburg where she had taken some biology courses at Witwatersrand University near the girls' school, which was where Lorna Katharine, their eldest, was hoping to study.

Gore-Browne had been so busy with his war work, supervising camps for Polish refugees who had come to Northern Rhodesia in their thousands, as well as all his political obligations, that he had had little chance to do anything about his wayward young wife, and had fooled himself that once the war ended everything would be all right. But when Lorna had finally returned the previous year, it had not been to Shiwa but to Lusaka and a job as a technician in the government pathology laboratory.

In a way it was worse for Gore-Browne having her around. As an attractive high-spirited woman in her thirties in a town with a large proportion of lonely bachelors and glamorous army officers, she was much in demand, and he hardly ever saw her alone. The white community was small and close-knit and everyone knew everybody else's business, and there were many stories about Lorna and her admirers, particularly *a certain pianist fellow* named Gordon Watson. Once he had gone to the cinema and seen his wife on the arm of a handsome young army captain, eyes shining as she laughed up at her companion in a way they had never shone for him. Much as it hurt, Gore-Browne thought there was little he could do. Lorna was thirty-seven and looked years younger, and he was almost sixty-three – an old man with his black bowler hat and walking stick for his arthritic knee, the result of an encounter with a lion when he was on the Border Commission years earlier. He had suggested that she went back to England, presumably thinking it would be easier if he did not have to see her at all, but she reacted angrily, sending him a note in which she said, 'I wish I was dead or at least some sort of oblivion', and comparing her situation to what he had experienced during the Great War in the Retreat from Mons when he could not stop for sleep.

Gore-Browne dressed smartly to go and meet his estranged wife. He was always careful with his appearance, favouring light tropical suits from Gieves, often with coloured cravats and matching handkerchiefs, and splashing on eau-de-Cologne that the girls bought him for Christmas, and like most white men in Lusaka at that time, wore a dinner-jacket in the evening even to go to the cinema. He wished he still had some hair – without it his Gore-Browne nose was more prominent than ever, but his blue eyes had lost none of their piercing intensity.

He planned to take Lorna to the bioscope to see *A Song to Remember*, the new film about Frédéric Chopin and his affair with George Sand. He had read in *The Times* that the film had been a smash hit in London, and had already seen it twice in Salisbury, where he had spent the previous week attending the Central African Congress. He thought Lorna would enjoy it with her passion for music.

The afternoon did not start well, Lorna arriving at their agreed meeting place *28 minutes late*, according to his diary, and they missed the newsreel. But she was enthusiastic about the film and sat rapt throughout the whole two hours, Gore-Browne watching her and finding her more attractive than ever as she followed the action on screen, the magical fingers of José Iturbi flying across the ivory keys for the 'Polonaise in A flat'. All her old illnesses seemed to have gone since she had left Shiwa, and he noticed she was no longer wearing his ring.

Afterwards Lorna refused his invitation for a nightcap at the Gymkhana Club, which was probably just as well as everybody would stare and speculate. Instead he walked her formally back to her lodgings, an awkward silence hanging between them after swapping views on the film and the quality of Iturbi's piano-playing, which Gore-Browne found *a little flamboyant* for his tastes. In the past the couple would have talked about their dreams and he would have told her about the strange one he kept having in which he was building Brooklands with Nunk, but he decided that might not be appropriate. However, they did need to resolve some issues and tentatively he tried to broach the subject of the estate. As she stood there, regarding him wearily, he was reminded of their first encounter all those years before at the church at Bingham's Melcombe when she was just a schoolgirl and had looked at him as if he were a boring old uncle. He had told Ethel that the last time he had tried to talk to Lorna about Shiwa she had almost spat at him, telling him that was all he cared about and adding, 'That stupid red earth in which nothing grows . . . I'm surprised you don't sleep with it under your pillow.' The comment had stung, because whatever his wife had felt about him, he had always believed she shared his passion for the estate.

Standing outside her doorway, he pressed on, telling her that the citrus was doing well, the servants were starting to learn, and proposing they both go back to Shiwa. He even offered to give up his political work, suggesting she give up *her ridiculous job* and join him. 'We could row on the lake, walk in the hills, bathe in the hot springs, build more schools for the villagers and one day have our grandchildren around us.' But it was far too late for all that. Having finally realized that Shiwa had been built for Ethel, and boyhood memories of her own mother, Lorna would never get over the fact that he had 'married the wrong Lorna' as she put it, and in years to come refused to talk about the Shiwa years even to her own children. 'I remember terrible scenes as a child,' says their daughter Angela. 'The problem was it was always his dream not hers.'

Bitter that she had sacrificed so much of her youth to his 'stupid fantasies' of creating a miniature idealized England in the middle of tropical Africa, Lorna made one parting shot. 'Africa will always defeat you in the end!' she told him. Then, without so much as a goodnight, she walked in and slammed the door.

Gore-Browne arrived at Shiwa in the moonlight, the lake *like molten silver*, and the air fragrant with honeysuckle mingled with woodsmoke from the chimneys of the staff houses. As always the place seemed to give him new energy, and though he slept badly, disturbed by a plague of bees in the chimney of his dressing-room, he felt refreshed when he got up the next morning for the 6 a.m. drum. There was plenty to do. Mark, or Lorna Katharine as he was supposed to call her, and Angela were due to arrive in Mpika, from where Henry would pick them up in the Chevrolet, and they were expecting several guests for Easter, including Baronet Sir Alfred Beit (from the same family as the late Alfred Beit who had been Cecil Rhodes's financial adviser and right-hand man), one of the Beit Trustees and a director of Rhodesia Railways, and his wife Clementine, daughter of the Hon. Clement Bertram Ogilvy Mitford.

With Lorna no longer there, Joe Savill having left to work for the Public Works department, and Gore-Browne so busy with all his war work and the Polish refugee camps, Shiwa had been rather left to its own devices. Fritzi had been running the place along with Laurie Crawford, a manager he had hired from England, and they had been doing a good job, making about £6,000 a year profit for the last five years, the longest period in the black since he had built the place, which was rather fortunate what with the girls' school fees and travel to pay. There had been some improvements too – Shiwa had been fitted out with modern sanitation, the first flush pulled by Lady Bledisloe when she and her husband stayed at the house, looking dismayed when Gore-Browne told her, 'I intend to put up a plaque to commemorate the event.' Fritzi had used his electrical expertise to fit the house with electric lighting, run off a waterwheel and dynamo, and he was working on installing power for the lime presses. But Gore-Browne moaned to Ethel, *It's not the same as having someone from the family here who really cares for the place.* Now that the girls were older, particularly Lorna Katharine who was almost seventeen, they had started taking charge of housekeeping during school holidays and acting as his hostess at dinners.

His own prestige locally had shot up with rumours spread by senior chief Nkula that the Royal Family had fled Buckingham Palace during the air-raids on London and taken refuge at Shiwa. He was not about to contradict the chief, who claimed he had personally seen King George and Queen Elizabeth in the Shiwa kitchens waiting for a kettle to boil for a cup of tea.

Gore-Browne spent the first morning back ensuring the guest-rooms were ready, then walking round the estate, an excited Belle by his side, discussing plans with Crawford and Fritzi and getting reports from all the *capitaos* who lined up as always with the Timba schoolteachers and children to greet him. Conditions for the workers had improved with a new housing compound to replace the slum the previous lot had fallen into, a proper welfare centre with dancehall, beerhall, tea-room and small library, as well as a savings bank. Some of the staff had applied to him to be allowed to produce *chipumu* and *katata* beer themselves to sell and share out the profits on a kind of cooperative basis, which he thought was a good idea, and he had requested a licence from Rowland Hudson, the Secretary for Native Affairs.

The girls turned up at lunchtime, accompanied by Vera, having left their mother at Mpika where she would stay with friends, and the Beits' plane touched down on the airstrip in the afternoon. Gore-Browne relished having some new and important visitors to show around, and lapped up their astonishment as he drove them up the drive from the aerodrome, past the smooth terraced lawns on which Cleo the crested crane was holding court, showing off her orange headfeathers, and the walled rose gardens styled on the Tudor Ladies' Garden at Bingham's Melcombe and dotted with ornate garden benches crafted by his own blacksmiths.

Looking spick in their uniforms, Henry's brother Kalaka and Spider, two of the house-servants, came out to collect the trunks, and Reuben the butler held open the front door for the guests. The Beits passed through the doorway with rhino heads either side and into the hallway where stood a marble bust of Julius Caesar displaying a proudly Roman nose. Gore-Browne liked to tell guests how a visiting White Father had on seeing it, said 'A very good likeness of you if I may say so, Sir Stewart.' Reuben showed them to a set of rooms leading off the courtyard, where Lady Clementine marvelled at the walls decorated with framed Gustave Doré dream sequences, the colourfully embroidered counterpanes on the beds, and the silver bowl of roses on the dressing-table. Gore-Browne was delighted when she said she felt every inch that she was in an English country home.

That night, sherry was served in small glasses along with cheese straws on the library terrace against the backdrop of the changing colours of a fiery sunset, the men all dressed in dinner-jackets and black bow-ties. Gore-Browne had arranged a big dinner and the courtyard and terraces were lit by flaming torches which, he wrote, *I fancy makes it all look very eighteenth century.* The table in the main dining-hall was resplendent with all the best silver and crystal on white linen, sparkling in the candlelight. In the centre stood a vast Victorian centrepiece which had been presented to his grandfather Sir Thomas Gore-Browne while Governor of New Zealand. Four tiers high, it was floridly decorated with leaves, fruits and animals, a warrior on top with one hand stretching upwards as if towards the chandelier hanging from the high-beamed ceiling above. Gilt-framed hunting scenes and large *sitatunga* horns graced the walls, the latter forming strange shadows in the half light of the log fire burning in the huge stone grate.

Footmen showed the guests to their seats according to the seating plan drawn up by Gore-Browne, Beit declaring, 'One would never think one was in the middle of the bush!' Later, describing the evening to Ethel, Gore-Browne wrote, *Lady Beit said 'to think that only 30 years ago this place must have been prowling with lions' and I told her it still is. Naughty Angela terrified her by saying that sometimes the lions pass right in front of the windows and stare in at the dinner table.*

Apart from his daughters and the Beits, the other guests were Vera and her beau Pete, Fritzi and Friedel, Dr Phillips, the Australian doctor from the hospital, and Richard Hall, the editor of the Central African Post, and his wife, Carol. Eyebrows were raised among the outside guests when Henry slipped in and took his place at the table, looking ill at ease, stiff in the unaccustomed jacket and tie, one of Gore-Browne's old ones which had been altered for his slighter frame but was still too long in the arms. Africans were regular guests at Gore-Browne's table, unlike anywhere else in Northern Rhodesia, where white contact with blacks was usually conducted in a series of imperatives such as 'Bring tea!' and 'Wash up!' Seeing the Beits' and Halls' astonishment, he quickly opened champagne, telling them that Henry had just heard that his wife had given birth to their first son. His servant beamed shyly as everyone offered congratulations, and the ice was broken.

It was a lively dinner. Nothing made Gore-Browne happier than compliments to the house, and he could be the perfect host, telling stories and charming the ladies, though guests were always rather taken aback at his insistence on the waiters serving clockwise round the table, rather than ladies first. (Angela recalls one dinner where the Archbishop of Central Africa was present and told the waiter to serve the ladies before him. Her father called the waiter over and told him not to serve the offending prelate, and the archbishop sat through dinner with an empty plate.)

His eldest daughter, Lorna Katharine, was playing hostess, *looking quite the lady in her grown up clothes*, and he told Ethel, *I was proud of her fine manners*. Angela had everyone *in hoots of laughter* with her irreverent impressions of South Africans she had come across on the train back from school. George, the head cook, had done them proud with a wonderful meal of hartebeest cutlets in an orange glaze followed by saddle of beef with madeira sauce, french beans and duchess potatoes. Far more food was produced at Shiwa than in the past, and Gore-Browne told his guests that they were even sending food parcels back to relatives in England to supplement their ration books. Henry was still awkward at table, fumbling his cutlery, and he tried to bring him into conversation, almost as one would a shy young child, getting him to talk about the animals they had seen on a recent motor trip north to Tanganyika.

'There were birds that don't fly even when I chase them in the car,' he said, leaving Gore-Browne to explain that he meant ostriches. 'And giraffe like what you see at bioscope.' The other guests looked at him uncomprehendingly.

'He means slow-moving,' said Gore-Browne, suggesting they adjourn to the library for port and to listen to his newly acquired recording of *Figaro*.

The following day was Easter Sunday, and began as most Sundays with a hearty breakfast of eggs, bacon, fresh orange juice, coffee, newly baked bread and fish from the lake, caught by the one-legged fisherman (he had lost his other through polio). There was no marmalade served, Gore-Browne detesting what he called *that terrible American custom of eating toast with jam for breakfast rather than tea.* Well fortified, the party followed him to the chapel at the side of the house for Easter Service. Built in the 1930s, it was a lofty building with a black and white tiled floor, whitewashed walls, a golden candelabra hanging from the high ceiling, an old gold altarpiece decorated with paintings of the Madonna and child, above which hung a large wooden crucifix, and carved wooden angels in each corner. Clearly influenced by his travels in Italy and Portugal, it looked like a Catholic church but was multi-denominational and services had been taken by everyone from Scottish Methodists to German White Fathers, Gore-Browne always maintaining, *I don't attach much importance to labels where religion is concerned.*

Coloured sunlight streamed through the two stained-glass windows, which rather than religious scenes depicted his own personal symbols. Divided into three sections, the first contained the *chipembele* or rhinoceros, an elephant to represent Africa, and the motto 'Forget Not I Mean Well'. The top part of the second window was the Gore-Browne family coat of arms, which consisted of a green falcon over the 'Suivez Raison' motto, just as on the cupboard in the library. Beneath that was the crossed sword and keys of the Bishop of Winchester to commemorate his uncle, and at the bottom the red dog which was the family arms of Lorna's family, the Bosworth Smiths.

Leading his guests to the leather-cushioned family pews at the front, Gore-Browne looked around with satisfaction at the bowl of white flowers on the altar table, and at all the workers in their Sunday best on the packed wooden benches behind them, women on one side, men on the other. He gave a nod to the Reverend Isaac Mfula, who had come over from Lubwa Mission, the Macminns' old place, to begin the service. *The sermon was on the Resurrection of the body*, Gore-Browne later grumbled in his diary, *but I was mollified by the final hymn The Lord's My Shepherd, sung with great gusto and gospel style harmonies by the Bantu.*

Afterwards, he blew the whistle for the start of the traditional Easter Egg Hunt for the children in Shiwa gardens, modelled on the old Brooklands ones of his childhood but with real eggs, pencils and packets of sweets because chocolate would have melted. He and his eldest daughter, Lorna Katharine, then walked up Peacock Hill to lay flowers on his old friend's grave, before joining the others who were scrambling up Nachipala or Bareback Hill, the granite outcrop behind the house where Livingstone's dog was supposed to be buried. At the top, after a ninety-minute hike, they signed the book kept inside the stone pillar he had erected, then sat under acacia trees and admired the views of the lake shining far below, while tucking into a picnic lunch served by Spider and Kalaka of cold duck and mayonnaise, fresh bread, estate cheese, cold sausage, guava fruit and a bottle of fine claret.

That afternoon, Gore-Browne took Alfred Beit on a tour of the limes, taking the opportunity *en route* to complain about the treatment of Africans on Rhodesian Railways, *packed in like cattle*, and the appalling condition of their workers' houses, one of his favourite bugbears. Driving over to the orchards and nursery, he showed the network of irrigation channels, then back to the still-room, explaining how they extracted the oil to sell to soap and perfume manufacturers in Europe, and recounting some of the problems they had experienced in getting the operation going. He drove him over to Kasakalabwe to see where they were making tiles for a new kitchen roof, mixing the clay with kaolin to make a lighter colour. After stopping to see the milking of the cattle, a crossbreed of local Angoni and red South Devon, he showed him the hospital, noting in his diary, *irritated to see the place even dirtier than usual.*

When they got back to the house, the others had returned from their boating on the lake with Angela, who he assumed had terrified them with tales of man-eating crocodiles and mysterious spirits, and were putting together a tennis party. Dr Phillips asked him to join in, but Gore-Browne excused himself, saying he was too old and that tennis was never really his sport. Instead he sat for a while watching, drinking some of the fresh lemonade that Reuben had brought out, and smiling at how the local children never seemed to tire of acting as ballboys, fighting to be first to reach the yellow balls.

That night there was to be a dance in the beerhall for Lorna's seventeenth birthday which was the next day, and the girls were in *a state of high excitement.* As the evening chill settled, they abandoned the tennis to go and change, emerging late for dinner, wearing what, Gore-Browne wrote to Ethel, *I assumed must be the latest fashions in Johannesburg.* Dinner was a much less elaborate affair than the previous night, though there was champagne in Lorna's honour, and after eating, the whole party went down to the beerhall on the edge of the servants' compound. It was hot and crowded inside, people whirling around to drums, chanting and instruments made from bottle caps strung from tree branches. Lorna had begged permission to bring the old gramophone down, which he had agreed as long as he was there to supervise, after which they would have to make their own music or rely on the wireless. Soon the place was buzzing with a strange combination of traditional Bemba songs and bop records which the girls had brought back from South Africa.

After what he judged to be a decent amount of time, having greeted most of those present and made sure Vera would keep an eye on the girls, Gore-Browne boxed up the gramophone and went back to the house. In his study he poured a glass of port from the decanter and flicked through the large pile of mail. Among it was a stiff envelope bearing a gold-edged invitation card to the Buckingham Palace Garden Party in June, as well as the usual scrawled blue sheets complaining of colour bar incidents.

> Dear Gore-Browne, Sir
>
> I am writing to you about the problem of shopping in Rhodesian shops. Recently I witnessed with my own eyes and ears a case in this township when a certain European lady, wife of a high-up officer, found many Africans buying at a sale in a shop situated on so called European site. This lady said to the trader 'You are going to lose your license because you are selling European goods to these stinkin kaffirs and what not'. All the Africans kept quiet in the usual way, and walked out one after one, greatly disappointed . . .

Gore-Browne received hundreds of such letters and at the end of the last LegCo session had made his most outspoken speech to date on ending the colour bar, proposing that post offices, banks and railway stations employ African clerks, that Africans be allowed to form trade unions, and that the other LegCo members set an example by inviting Africans to take tea with them, a suggestion which had been greeted by a shocked intake of breath. 'We English are not cruel by nature,' he had said. 'All I would ask, as I have half a dozen times before, is the recognition of our common humanity with the African.' There had been a hostile silence around the panelled room, as he ended by reminding them of the Northern Rhodesians' role in the war, and appealing to the Governor who presided over the sessions, 'I would ask whether those men back from Burma who marched past you, Sir, the other day, I would ask whether they are stinking kaffirs?'

As he wrote in letter after letter to Ethel, he felt more and more that he should resign from the Council but feared that would leave nobody to stand up for the Africans. One evening when having dinner alone with Henry in his study, as he often did when there were no guests, he had asked him if he ever wondered what would happen to Africa. Henry's brow creased into a puzzled expression, and Gore-Browne rephrased the question, asking him what he thought about the future of Africa, after all political meetings they had attended together. *Africa will always be there, bwana*, Henry had replied. *Like the sleeping lion.*

He missed Henry when he was away at his wife Elizabeth's village, and was pleased when there was a soft knock on the door and he opened it to see his servant hovering at the door. Gore-Browne had given him a week off for the traditional celebrations for the birth of his son, and was surprised to see him back so quickly. *He looked dejected and I asked him what was wrong*, Gore-Browne later wrote to his aunt, *and he said solemnly 'the news was incorrect, bwana. It is a daughter'*. Telling him not to worry, Gore-Browne poured him a glass of port, then, to cheer him up, asked him if he would like to go with him on his trip to England for the Victory Parade. Henry was very excited, saying, 'I would like to meet the Queen and visit the fine buildings in your photographs and see how is the bush in your country.' *Then his face fell*, Gore-Browne recounted to his aunt. *I asked him what was wrong and he said, 'But now I have a daughter. I must make more children to have a son.'*

While Henry was turning down the covers and laying out his nightshirt on the Chipembele bed, so-called because Gore-Browne had recently got his carpenters to carve four rhinos, one on the top of each of the four posts, he added a final note to the day's events in his diary:

I had a feeling as if we were all on a comfortable raft in some unknown sea and that while some were dancing to jazz music, others were crowding silently to the edge staring into the fog ahead. Staring anxiously too for in that mist there might be fearful as well as wonderful things.

17

Croydon aerodrome,
4 October 1948

The swing doors opened and an elderly woman with piercing blue eyes swept ceremoniously into the main booking-hall of Croydon airport, trailing two porters laden with trunks and hatboxes, and sniffing the familiar aroma of cedar polish which struck everyone who entered the building. Hanging round the Imperial Airways check-in counter, waiting for her to arrive, was a reporter from the *Daily Mail*, who stepped forward briskly as he heard the steward say the name 'Dame Ethel Locke King' and welcome her. Air travel was still a relative novelty, and the headline on his story the next day would be '6,000-Miles Air Trip at 80. Woman's Jaunt to Africa'. Ethel was eighty-two, though she told the reporter she was 'rising eighty' and it was 'no business of his'. But she stopped by the pillar lined with clocks showing the different time in all major airports in the world, rearranged her mink stole and large pink hat for his photographer, and agreed to answer a few questions.

She was, she told him, 'a regular flyer', having flown several times to Egypt with Alan Muntz, and had made her first trip in 1910 with Monsieur Paulham on one of his trials for the first London to Manchester flight for which he won the prize offered by the *Daily Mail*. 'Today I am going to visit my nephew Stewart who lives near Mpika in Northern Rhodesia and I am looking forward to my trip very much,' she added.

'That's a long flight,' said the reporter, noting in his story that she would only arrive in Mpika ten days later.

'I think air travel is the quickest and most sensible way of travelling,' replied Ethel.

'But Africa – aren't you afraid of the wild beasts?'

'Young man, I've never been scared of anything in my life! Now, I think you've got enough.'

Lusaka, 12 October 1948

The Executive Council session dragged on interminably, the wooden chairs uncomfortable and the slow whirr of the ceiling fan doing little to relieve the pre-rains heat. *Lunacy*, Gore-Browne noted in his diary, fiddling with his bristly white moustache as he listened to *the usual prosy speeches* about such crucial matters as the water being wasted in Central Offices due to automatic flushing of the urinals at night. At lunchtime a secretary passed him a telephone message from Henry to say that he had been told the *Bonanza* was in and had gone down to the aerodrome but it was a false alarm and Ethel's plane had not yet arrived.

Finally, at four, the session ended and Gore-Browne shot off home before any of the other members could trap him in conversation. At the house Henry was still waiting for news of the plane, so Gore-Browne busied himself with the day's mail. There had been a stream of angry letters from Africans since January, when he had made a speech in LegCo advocating 'responsible government' – his plan for home rule by minority white settlers. The proposals had provoked a storm of black protest, Africans all over the country condemning them before even knowing what they were. To them, his plan was a way of entrenching white domination and a backdoor to Amalgamation with racist Southern Rhodesia with its pass laws and land restrictions, and which clearly wanted to get its hands on the north's mineral wealth. In fact he had intended the exact opposite. As he constantly moaned to Welensky, who had taken over from him as leader of the Unofficials on LegCo and shared his loathing of civil servants, under the present set-up the Unofficials had no real power, despite being elected and having a majority. *I thought if we could get the place out of the hands of the colonial government, we could really make it tick*, he had written to Ethel, as well as safeguard it from Amalgamation and ensure black representation in any future set-up, but the Africans hadn't appreciated that.

The Bantu is all up in fire and smoke over my plan, he admitted. What angered them most was that the plan had been announced without consulting them, and all subsequent attempts to explain the proposals in numerous meetings were hopeless because their minds were already made up. The newspapers were full of letters accusing him of favouring a *Baas and boy* policy. Some even charged him with wanting to take them back to the time when the country was run by Rhodes's British South Africa Company and Africans were not allowed to wear shoes in the *boma* and had to carry officials in *machilas*, canvas hammocks on poles. Ironically white settlers were also critical of the plan, not liking the share of power it included for blacks and asking how only 20,000 Europeans could govern almost 1.8 million mostly primitive natives without support from Whitehall. But most hurtful of all was the outraged cable from his protégé Harry Nkumbula at the London School of Economics, where he was studying on a bursary arranged by Gore-Browne. It seemed as though that one speech had lost him all the influence in the African community that he had spent so many years accumulating.

In July, the newly created African Representative Council (ARC) voted unanimously against Gore-Browne's proposals and he offered his resignation as LegCo member for Native Interests. He had handed over leadership of the Unofficial members of LegCo to Welensky in 1946, feeling he couldn't reconcile their support for Amalgamation with his role representing African interests. After the outrage over his speech, he felt he should step down altogether and retreat to Shiwa. But the ARC passed a motion of confidence in him, excusing 'his mistake', and he had been renominated by the Governor to the new LegCo which took office in September and which, for the first time, included two Africans, Nelson Nabumanga and the Reverend Henry Kasokolo, elected by the ARC.

He still wasn't sure he had done the right thing. He had received a few letters congratulating him on his renomination and promising support, including, surprisingly, one from the Northern Rhodesian African Congress, a new nationalist party. But most were like that from Nelson Mwija in Kitwe which read, 'We thought you were our father but you have stabbed us in our backs while we were sleeping in your trust . . .'

The controversy had even made the British press, prompting a letter of commiseration from Lorna, who had moved to London and was renting a flat in Notting Hill. 'It all made me think of the first time I was deeply hurt by the Bantu – that time when we bought them nice sweaters for the cold and they put them on the ground saying they wanted blankets – and later bought the sweaters! But then I had made the fundamental error of thinking I knew what was good for them . . .' She went on, 'I do know how very unhappy you must have felt after all the trouble you have taken for them . . . what puzzles me is their attitude, because you must, before having presented the scheme to the Colonial Office and the other non-officials, have discussed it in essence with the blacks . . .' In fact he had not, thinking he already knew them well enough to know what would be good for them. Had Lorna known that, perhaps she would not have felt so strongly that he should not resign. Her letter had ended: 'I so much fear you'll go because you are hurt, and please, please stay Dear because you are much too valuable to them even if they are Beastly sometimes.'

The phone rang, announcing that the *Bonanza* was due to arrive in twenty minutes, and Gore-Browne put his papers to one side and followed his manservant out to the Vanette. *Henry looking v smart*, he noted in his diary, seeing he was wearing the blue serge suit he had ordered for him at Hogg, his London tailors, as well as a pale blue shirt from John Jones, his shirtmaker in Bruton Street, and a red and yellow striped tie which he had bought him in Austin Reed. 'It's for Mama Locke King,' Henry told him, pointing out that he was wearing the tiepin which Ethel had bought him in Winchester.

Henry had accompanied Gore-Browne to England the previous year, and stayed several weeks at Ethel's house, Caenshill, where he had become a great favourite, helping wait at table and playing guitar to her, in return for which she indulged his weakness for chocolate in expeditions to the local Woolworths in Weybridge. Gore-Browne had had to attend several meetings at the Colonial Office to discuss the future of Northern Rhodesia, but in between they had taken Henry to St Paul's Cathedral where he had been terrified by the Whispering Gallery; to Livingstone's grave in Westminster Abbey; shopping, as Gore-Browne loved to buy him new clothes; and on the London Underground where he was terrified of the moving staircases, refusing to jump on. One of his favourite trips was to Hampton Court where Henry had got lost in the maze, been impressed by the great vine, and *being a good Bemba*, used to blood feuds between aspiring chiefs, *quite took the point that Henry VIII thought that Cardinal Wolsey might be after his throne and that when the Cardinal gave him the palace that didn't prevent the king from ordering his execution.*

To further Henry's education, they had taken him to *Les Sylphides* and *Tosca* at Covent Garden, and to a Chopin recital by Gertrude Peppercorn at the Albert Hall. They had heard the bells ringing for the twenty-first birthday of Princess Elizabeth, and had even gone to see the King, Queen and Princesses arriving back from South Africa, when Henry was quite convinced the Queen had waved at him with a white-gloved hand. One weekend the three of them had stayed at Winchester to celebrate Gore-Browne's sixty-fourth birthday, and they had shown Henry the cathedral with the tomb of Ethel's uncle and Gore-Browne's great uncle, the Bishop of Winchester, and driven him to Bingham's Melcombe so that he could see one of the inspirations for Shiwa. Ethel had then taken them to Southampton and he and Henry had returned to Africa by flying boat, stopping at the Gold Coast to meet politicians there and visit the castles where slaves used to be held packed in dungeons prior to shipping them to the Americas.

Travelling with Henry is a joy, wrote Gore-Browne. His driver had never before been beyond Tanganyika, and was interested in everything, being particularly intrigued by the sea, and was *quite a hit* on the flying boat with his guitar. On their return to Shiwa, Henry went back to his wife's village laden with presents, later telling Gore-Browne, 'I have told all my family and village about the Queen waving at us and how is the sea and all the beautiful things, and how cunning is man.'

Gore-Browne recalled the trip as they stood by the landing-strip of Lusaka airport, waiting for Ethel's plane to arrive. Henry saw it first. A small silver speck just visible in the light blue sky, gradually becoming discernible as a plane, the noise of its propellers filling the air until they could hear nothing else. The pilot made a smooth landing, the plane came to a halt, steps were lowered and passengers began to disembark. *Heard ELK's voice, then she appeared, v white but alive*, Gore-Browne later wrote in his diary. Waving her large handbag in greeting, Ethel stepped stiffly on to the ground and he went forward to embrace her, too full of emotion to speak, until an officious immigration officer appeared to check her papers. Finally the paperwork was completed and her trunks and hatboxes unloaded from the plane and on to the heads of various porters, and with he and Henry each holding one of Ethel's elbows, they set off for tea and ginger biscuits in the garden.

The flight up to Shiwa was bumpy and uncomfortable, the small Beechcraft pitching from side to side as it passed through clouds of smoke from the fires of Africans burning their fields to fertilize them ready for planting millet. *It is worth the discomfort to step onto Shiwa soil just two hours and 25 minutes after taking off, rather than the two long days it takes by road*, Gore-Browne wrote in his diary, adding that even his airsickness could be tolerated *for the chance to see Shiwa by air, all laid out like a grand country estate with the jacaranda in a blaze of violet glory*. They came into land by the small brick hut he jokingly called the Terminal Building, the wheels bumping several times on the hard ground before righting, scattering cattle grazing on the landing-strip.

Several servants came forward to help him and Ethel out and take the luggage as well as to offer the pilot some coffee from a Thermos. Laurie, his manager, appeared with the Chevrolet to drive them up to the house. As they approached, they saw the house servants and *capitaos* all lined up in uniform on the front lawn in a welcome parade, and a small group of children began to sing and dance, and he noticed how lovely the gardens were looking, filled with roses, petunias, white bougainvillaea and the colours of late spring. The house too was looking good, everything having been cleaned and polished for the recent visit of the new Governor, Sir Gilbert Rennie, and his wife – 'the dour little Scot' or 'wee Gibbie' as Gore-Browne and Welensky referred to him. The only sad thing was the absence of his dog Belle to jump up and bark excitedly in greeting. She had died in August while he was away in England with Welensky for meetings at the Colonial Office. *I'll never forget the last time I saw her*, he wrote to Welensky, *when I drove away from Shiwa in July as she lay crying on the gravel under the bu-bu tree, broken-hearted at knowing she was being left behind.*

He introduced Ethel to all the servants and led her to her rooms, Lorna's old rooms with the arched windows overlooking the lake. After leaving her for a while to freshen up, they met for lunch which had been set out according to his instructions in the small dining-room upstairs. Duck in orange sauce (one of two shot by his hunter Kalaka, one of Henry's brothers, the day before, along with four geese), followed by strawberries from the estate and ice-cream, and washed down by chilled Veuve Cliquot. Afterwards they walked to the library, along the corridor decorated with swords and spears and the photograph he had had done of himself when he went to London for the King's Coronation, in full military regalia with a chestful of medals. Drinking Turkish coffee poured from a silver pot, Ethel studied his book collection, much of which had come from Brooklands, commenting on his juxtaposition of the works of Voltaire, the Great Sceptic, next to those of Bossuet, the philosopher of Louis XIV, and admiring the gold lettering over the mantelpiece reading 'Ille Terrarum Mihi Super Omnes Angulus Ridet' the quotation from Horace which he had recently got his carpenters to engrave. Tactfully, she did not point out till later in her stay that it should have been Praeter Omnes, though in years to come Gore-Browne would test visitors with it.

The following weeks were among the happiest in his life. Ethel was often described by people as biting and sarcastic, but on this trip she had clearly decided to behave. Gore-Browne revelled in showing the place off to her, Henry driving them round in the V8. They went to the lime and orange orchards where he bemoaned the increasing difficulty in finding casual labour for picking blossom, to the nursery to see the seedlings, to the dairy which had recently been rebuilt after white ants had devoured the roof timbers, and to see the pigs and cattle in their new twelve-foot high thorn stockades to protect them from lions. They drove to Kasakalabwe to see the clay being mixed and flattened into tiles by women wrapped in colourful cloth, Gore-Browne explaining the process and complaining that there was always some building on the estate that needed re-roofing. They visited Timba school, where Ethel presented some English books and sets of coloured pencils which made the children's eyes light up in wonder, and one class put on a show for her, banging drums. Despite Ethel's advanced years, she seemed as energetic as ever, the only cloud being an occasional memory lapse, such as when he showed her the hospital and she seemed surprised to learn of its existence, though recovering quickly to make some suggestions based on her experience running Brooklands as a hospital in the Great War.

In the cool green light of late afternoon, after the four o'clock drum had been beaten to mark the end of the day's work, they walked in the gardens watching small children jumping in the hosewater of the garden-boy spraying the roses. Sometimes they sat quietly, happy in each other's company, watching the goldfish in the pool and listening to the soft 'chit, chit' of the swallow-tailed bee-eaters in the trees, almost as if they were competing to show off for her. It seemed to him, as he had often written to her, *the loveliest spot on earth.* Sometimes they wandered round the staff compound, seeing the small brick houses with smoke puffing from their chimneys, runny-nosed black children playing on the doorsteps with toy cars and trucks cleverly made from wire and bottle-caps, as their mothers ground finger-millet on large stones to make flour. He strolled with her in the avenue of blue gum trees, passing the estate office and the clocktower, the two Indian stores, the tailor's shop, post office and welfare centre, all with newly painted signs. The savings bank had been closed down after money went missing, but some of the staff had accounts at the post office. 'It's like a proper English village,' Ethel told him, adding that she had never expected it to be so neat and civilized.

One day he drove her to the Katete river to see the first arched bridge he had built. Workers were busy renovating it, ready for the coming rains. Seeing her nephew lose his temper with Paulos, one of the old *capitaos*, for being 'too slapdash' in overseeing the cleaning of the weed, Ethel asked him shrewdly if he was still hurt by the black reaction to his self-government proposals. He had written to her:

They just didn't understand that I only wanted what was best for them. If they had let us settlers run things and we had joined up with Nyasaland and Southern Rhodesia on a federal basis with a proper Constitution with safeguards, it would have protected them from Amalgamation or worse . . . look at South Africa now with this Malan fellow and his Afrikaner cronies fencing the Bantu off into townships . . .

She had replied, 'Maybe they've grown up. They don't want someone telling them what's best for them. And that's a credit to you with all your work trying to educate them . . .'

Gore-Browne realized the world was changing. India, Ceylon and Burma were already independent, and his trip to the Gold Coast had shown him Africa was also moving that way. But what hurt him so much was that the Africans wouldn't listen to him, and could think that he *of all people*, who had always fought for their rights in LegCo, would be *trying to sell them down the river*. They even seemed to think his plan meant he was trying to take their land, an irony after he had spent the previous few years fighting in LegCo to have Native Land recognized. He wondered if he would ever regain their trust.

Maybe Ethel was right, and it was time to let go. She had suggested he turn his attentions back to Shiwa, pointing out that he was always complaining in his letters that things kept going awry on the estate because of his absence. But though it pained him to say so, Gore-Browne felt even that had lost its magic. He had recently written to his friend Welensky:

When I first came here I wasn't so different to the other white settlers in some ways. I imagined living a patriarchal kind of life in some quiet part of the country, surrounded by contented happy-go-lucky Africans and enjoying a certain amount of big-game shooting and entertaining, an attractive wife by my side and a son to take over from me. That's all lost now.

That evening he took her to the still-room to see the presses running, producing eucalyptus oil. Production of neroli had almost stopped because it was too expensive to find labour for picking the orange blossoms, for the return they would get. The lime was no longer doing well, the trees producing less fruit, and the price had collapsed since producers in France and Bulgaria had come back on line after the war. Lime oil was now 20 shillings per ounce – less than half what it had been a few years earlier, and little more than it cost to produce. Shiwa's annual income from oil exports had plummeted, from £6,000 during 1941–6 to just £264 the previous year, and his total income was once again less than his outgoings by the time he had paid for school fees for Angela, university fees for Lorna Katharine, who was studying at Johannesburg's Witwatersrand University, and updating equipment such as buying tractors to replace oxen for ploughing. Once again he was dependent on Ethel and her chequebook, though she never complained.

Several times during her stay he took her out on the lake in the new canoe, *Venus* having long since rotted away. One day Kapianga and Spider paddled them down the Mansya, among the herons and papyrus. Aunt and nephew sat on the cushioned chairs which had been fixed down to the boat, under a canvas canopy to protect them from the sun, and watched a floating log near some rocks transform itself into a crocodile and slide away. They stopped at Mwenge for sandwiches and a bottle of claret on the bank, and dozed for a while under the shade of an acacia tree. Kapianga produced a napkin of small sweet strawberries which reminded them of those eaten years before in the Café de la Madeleine in Paris during one of their motor trips. But a tiresome plague of horseflies nipping at their skin forced them to leave, and they set off back, the wind against them making the rowing hard work for the two boys.

Listening to the rhythm of the oars splashing back and forth made Gore-Browne remember boat outings with Lorna in the early days when they would discuss their dreams of the night before, and he used to think he was so lucky. They had been happy at the beginning, he thought, but he had lost all hope of a reconciliation. Lorna still wrote to him occasionally, usually to let him know of concerts by Gordon Watson to be broadcast on the BBC. He thought she had a rather sordid life which seemed to revolve around gin parties and strange musical soirées. There was still rationing in England and he sent her sugar. Visiting her to try to arrange a place to study at Cambridge, Angela had recently written to him, 'Life isn't very easy whenever one is in England. I wonder what Spider would think if he could see Ma scrubbing kitchen floors and cleaning the stove.' When he was in England with Henry, Lorna had turned up at Caenshill on a motorbike and stayed the night, but he wrote in his diary afterwards, *I was at a loss to understand what she wanted*. Not him, anyway.

One day, so that Ethel could see some of the surrounding countryside, Gore-Browne asked Henry to drive them up the Great North Road to Chinsali and Lubwa Mission, pointing out the beehive huts of the natives, made of red and brown mud and thatched with grass, so different from the brick houses of Shiwa. On the way back the car broke down, its carburettor coughing and failing. As night was already falling, they decided to sleep in the nearby *boma* shelter and Henry built a good fire and managed to get hold of some eggs and beer from local villagers. Wrapped in tartan blankets from the car, they sat by the fire, listening to the whoops and howls of the bush, and telling stories. Ethel claimed to be enjoying the *adventure*, and feigned disappointment when Laurie turned up in the truck looking for them, having been alarmed by their absence.

During those weeks they hosted several dinner parties, inviting the District Commissioners from Chinsali and Mpika, Dr Brown, the new lady doctor from the hospital and Henry's parents, who had come to pay their respects to Ethel and were celebrating the birth of another child for Henry, a daughter again, this time by his second wife, Zilika. One night the servants held a dance in 'Mama Locke-King's honour' at the beerhall, but they didn't stay long, as Gore-Browne was suffering from a painful boil on his foot and Ethel got tired if she stayed too long on her feet. She never complained and her wit was as acerbic as ever, though she continued to have odd memory lapses, one morning suddenly asking, 'Where's Lorna? I haven't seen her around,' to Gore-Browne's alarm. Her pigeon-blue eyes were still bright and alert, if a little rheumy, and her skin remarkably smooth, though her hair was thin and snow-white. Her ankles were as slim as he remembered from the days when he used to massage them on the chaise-longue at Brooklands, but her calves were criss-crossed with swollen knotted veins and Gore-Browne could see sometimes they were paining her. It was hard for him to realize that she was an elderly lady – in his mind's eye she would always be the vivacious young aunt with the luxuriant strawberry hair and laughing eyes whom he had so idolized.

Some evenings he took her to films at the cinema that he had rigged up for staff in the welfare centre with a projector which he had brought back from his last trip to England, much to their excitement. His programme began with information films on Britain which he borrowed from the British Council, on subjects such as 'English Gardens', 'How to Build a Bicycle', and scenes of London, the Africans fascinated by the red double-decker buses and by the King, Queen and Princesses, and shocked by the sight of whites doing manual work. Their favourite was the races at Ascot, which made them scream with laughter. After an interval for changing spools, during which they could buy beer and soda, the noisy crowd packed back into the hall for the main feature, usually a cowboy film as they loved all the shooting, horses and action, and would boo noisily at the villains and shout for the hero. The first few times Gore-Browne had shown a film there had been a near riot, as the natives all wanted to find the *little men in the box who were doing the talking*, and they still didn't really believe there was no one there, desperately searching for John Wayne behind the screen. There was an outcry when, having been killed in one film, John Wayne reappeared in another, people all shouting that it was *cheating*.

But what Gore-Browne most enjoyed were the evenings alone together on the terrace, sitting under the moon with a glass of port and a cigar, or a mug of cocoa, listening to Chopin's piano sonatas or Mozart's operas on the gramophone, or the frogs in the lake and the wind rustling the eucalyptus trees. Ethel told him about the new long-playing records which everyone was talking about back home, and sometimes he read to her from her favourite books, Walter Scott's *Bride of Lammermoor* or Robert Louis Stevenson's *Master of Ballantrae*. When she nodded off, he read some of the books she had brought out for him – *The Last Days of Hitler*, or General Fuller on the Second World War.

One evening when the moon was particularly full and yellow, the perfume of magnolia filling the air, Gore-Browne tried to persuade his aunt to stay on at Shiwa till Christmas, but she refused, claiming responsibilities back home. *Oh these partings at either end!* he wrote bitterly in his diary. *What is the point?* The previous year he had spent Christmas Day alone, watching the Timba schoolchildren perform a nativity play, dressed as Herod, angels and sheep, followed by the usual dancing by the lepers from the hospital, accompanied by a wheezing concertina. He was not looking forward to being alone again. *This year I won't even stay up to hear the drums usher in New Year*, he wrote. Convinced that with Ethel by his side Shiwa would have been the most glittering place in all Africa, he had never understood why she had refused to come and live with him at Shiwa. It was she, after all, who had insisted it would have been *ruin* for him to marry the first Lorna, *not entirely because of your 'career' perhaps more by what they call our woman's intuition.*

Beginning to doubt whether Ethel had ever really shared his fantasies and cared in the way that he had, and wondering whether she had after all loved Hugh, he had written to her, asking, '*Don't you ever think of what might have been?*' She had replied, *What might have been is a land that no wise soul should step into. All that Greek history at Harrow should have taught you the gods don't always let us have things as we would want.*

Despite the lingering sadness Gore-Browne felt over things lost and his impending separation from Ethel, he wrote in his diary, *The days are as idyllic as I have known.* But the rains were late coming, the skies sullen and the air so hot that venturing outside was like facing the blast of an oven. And suddenly everything started to go wrong. A leopard got into the pantry just before dinner and devoured the meat for the week which the hunters had brought and which was waiting to go into the coldstore. *Annoyed with carpenter Petros who is dawdling over fitting of doors to keep leopards out of kitchen*, Gore-Browne wrote angrily in the estate book. Paulos's nephew was bitten by a puff-adder and died. There was the first case of leprosy on the estate for years. Henry's new daughter Mandalena died, and he went off to the funeral. Then one day, as Gore-Browne was sitting in the estate office trying to make sense of the figures, Laurie walked in looking downcast and told him there was something wrong with the lime trees. They had arranged more irrigation because the trees were looking dry, but however much water they got to them, the leaves still kept turning yellow and dying. It was obviously some form of disease. Gore-Browne looked at him in dismay. The lime trees were the only thing that had ever made any profit for the estate. *The Lord hates primary producers*, he wrote wearily to Welensky. *I pray they're wrong. I'm too old to start all over again.*

18

Shiwa Ngandu,
9 January 1953

Gore-Browne took the telegram from Michael Mukungule, the post office clerk, and opened it with shaking hands. It was from Luanshya on the Copperbelt, where his eldest daughter Lorna had been living with her husband Major John Harvey since their marriage at Shiwa eighteen months earlier. 'A DAUGHTER NOON TODAY STOP BOTH VERY WELL STOP IT IS A G-B STOP LOVE JOHN STOP.'

His first grandchild. After all his years of struggle to create Shiwa, there would now be another generation to inherit the place. He was disappointed that the baby was not a boy – he had had a dream the previous week that it would be. And, as he told Ethel, he would have liked it to have been born at Shiwa. But he had handed the Shiwa hospital over to the government after the war, and there was currently no doctor. They were even threatening to close it – *a deliberate move to get at me by my political enemies in Lusaka*, he told Ethel, complaining that they had removed the doctor, nurse, seven of the nine orderlies and closed down eighty of the 100 beds despite the fact there were forty inpatients with TB. By contrast the mine hospital at Luanshya was well-staffed and equipped, and run by Charles Fisher, husband of his niece Monica. Lorna had already suffered one miscarriage and he had not wanted her to take risks.

He rang the bell for Henry to tell him the good news, and

opened three bottles of champagne for his household staff. Then he sent a message to the Reverend Simon Sampa, the local evangelist priest, asking him to conduct a thanksgiving service in the chapel on Sunday.

He wished his wife Lorna was there to share his joy. But they were divorced now and she was far away in her poky basement flat in north London. The divorce had been her idea – arriving back in England in 1950, he had found a letter waiting for him at Caenshill in her familiar multi-looped script, requesting it. *I suppose it makes sense to regularize things*, he commented in his diary. Having spoken to his lawyers in London, they had arranged for the matter to be finalized in Northern Rhodesia, and at 9.30 a.m. on Monday 11 September 1950 the case had opened at Ndola High Court with Henry and his old friend John Haslam acting as witnesses, and Richmond Smith as lawyers. By 10 a.m. Judge Palmer had issued the decree nisi on grounds of desertion. Afterwards, sitting alone in his room at the Rutland Hotel, Gore-Browne scratched the words *Pretty beastly* in his diary in black ink. Six months later he was surprised to receive a letter from Gordon Watson, the pianist, saying, 'Lorna has asked me to let you know that I have been obliged to break off our association . . . I hope you will believe I did everything in my power to avoid acting unkindly.'

The final split from Lorna was not the only way Gore-Browne's life had changed. In 1951 he had retired, resigning from LegCo and what he had taken to referring to as *Government by Frustration*. His political career had never really recovered from the outcry over his proposal for self-government for settlers. *I miscalculated my own power with the Africans*, he admitted to Welensky, though he still thought they trusted him more than any other white man. He could have stood for renomination, but he felt the Governor, Sir

Gilbert Rennie, wanted him out, and that even his friend Welensky thought him *no more use*. And he couldn't see how to reconcile representing native interests with the way LegCo was moving towards union with Southern Rhodesia. Nor did he wish to fight for self-rule for Africans as they were starting to demand, as he did not believe they were ready. On resigning he wrote to Rita Hinton, a friend at the *Economist*, *The day of Europeans representing Africans is over in countries like this. It's a pity, for one can do a lot for them they can't do themselves, but there it is.*

Ironically, within weeks of his resignation, putting an end to his punishing schedule of travelling round the country holding meetings, he had been taken ill and had landed up in the Luanshya mine hospital being operated on for a double hernia under the care of Monica and Charles. That had not solved the problem, and as soon as he was able, in May 1951, he had travelled to London with Henry and had his gallbladder removed. So big was the offending gallstone, *the size of a well-grown date*, that he kept it in a jar in his bathroom. With that removed, he felt years younger, and wrote to Welensky, *They've been very flattering about my constitution . . . I overheard the eminent surgeon saying to the matron 'he's a wonderful old man' which made me rather angry as you can imagine.* He enjoyed a long recuperation at Caenshill, being cosseted by Ethel and Henry as he lay in the Elizabethan four-poster bed, reading and looking out over the rhododendrons and azaleas, flowering against the dark background of pines.

He returned to Shiwa in August 1951 to preside over the wedding of Lorna Katharine to her fiancé John Harvey in a spectacular ceremony attended by prominent whites from all over the country, around 200 Shiwa workers, and local chiefs including Chitimukulu, the Bemba Paramount Chief, who presented the couple with a ceremonial bow and five arrows as *a suitable present for a soldier and soldier's bride*, and which Gore-Browne told Ethel *was worth far more than half a dozen cows*. The chapel was decorated with scarlet lilies and a new gallery had been built specially so that it could take more people. The 'Wedding March' was played on the gramophone as Lorna Katharine entered the church on her father's arm, wearing the lace veil worn by her great-grandmother Harriet at her wedding, fastened with a wreath of orange blossom from the estate, and a five-string pearl choker which Gore-Browne had given her as a wedding present. After the marriage rites and Benediction, the chapel resounded with the harmonies of the Timba school choir singing 'Ave Maria' and 'Sheep May Safely Graze', the service rounded off by Purcell's 'Trumpet Tune and Air' just as at Gore-Browne's own wedding.

In the lavish celebrations afterwards, more than 250 gallons of beer and 1,500 pounds of meat (a combination of slaughtered cattle and game bagged by Kalaka and his hunters) were consumed, as well as an iced three-tier wedding cake sent out from Fortnums. Later there was singing, dancing and boating on the lake, while a sports day was arranged for African staff including football, races, a tug-of-war, egg and spoon race and greasy pole event which had them falling about laughing as they had never seen such games. Many of the guests said it was the biggest ever party in Northern Rhodesia, and Lorna was described in the *Central African Post* as 'the bride of the year'.

Since the wedding, Gore-Browne had barely left Shiwa. Arriving back, he had written in his diary, had been *like one imagines arriving in heaven*. That first evening, watching the lake turn black in the fading light and shadow of the hills which his Afrikaner friend, the late General Jan Smuts, had once joked that Gore-Browne had 'annexed', he thought, *I have known that view for more than 30 years yet I felt just the same as when I first set eyes on it.*

Life at Shiwa carried on as always. Philemon beat the first morning drum at 5.30 a.m. and work started after the muster parade and flag-raising at 6 a.m., carrying on till 4 p.m. when Gore-Browne took tea in the library, eating lots of cream as advised by his doctors to put on weight. The postman came every Friday and took mail back every Tuesday. There were fewer letters now that he had given up politics, though he still corresponded every other day with Ethel, weekly with Welensky who kept him abreast of goings on at LegCo, and monthly with Hastings Banda, and he continued to receive numerous requests for charity donations and scribbled notes from people asking for help, usually to educate their children or help them set up small farms, as well as some thanking him for what he had done for them or giving reports on their children's school progress.

The estate had undergone some modernization. They now used mechanical sprayers instead of boys with hoses, tractors instead of oxen, and had dynamo-powered electric lights in the house. All these devices saved a lot of labour, but were always breaking down and cost so much to maintain that he had contracted a full-time mechanic, Monsieur Jasmin, from Mauritius, a swarthy French-speaking forty-one-year-old with eight children and an engaging smile. Sometimes when the motor broke down for the umpteenth time, plunging the house in darkness or holding up the lime-presses, he wrote in his diary, *How I long for the days of hoes, oxen and candles.*

But in many ways it was an enjoyable time. It was a relief no longer to have to go to hot, dusty Lusaka, which was looking more and more like one of those Wild West frontier towns in the cowboy movies he sometimes showed at Shiwa. He had shut up his house there, and only went to the capital a couple of times a year for committee meetings of the African War Memorial fund, which he chaired, his only remaining public office. The rest of the time he spent pottering about the estate, and saw that Ethel had been right – the place needed him. Already the grounds of the house were looking better – the previous year he had planted a row of poinsettia between the steps of the house and the estate office, more roses in the walled Ladies' Garden, sweet oranges on the terraces, and mahogany trees below the new tennis court. Sadly, he had discovered that some of the blue gum trees in the avenue below the house were diseased and he had had to get them chopped down.

In the house there always seemed to be more building to do, walls to whitewash or distemper, and repairs to carry out – ceilings falling down because of the rains and leaks in the roof or white ants eating the supports, and cracks in the walls caused by occasional earth tremors. The chapel had been renovated and a new altar put in for Lorna's wedding, but sometimes Gore-Browne wondered why he bothered – since the Reverend Macminn's departure they rarely had services apart from on special occasions such as Remembrance Sunday, Armistice Day, Easter and Christmas, though they had held a 'fine' memorial service for the death of King George VI, the previous February. They had filled the place with marigolds in black earthenware pots, and Henry had set up the gramophone on the gallery to play Mozart's *Requiem*. Later, just as they had for the death of George V, the elders had collected in the evening for their own mourning rites. Father Corbeil, one of the White Fathers from their mission at Chinsali, occasionally came down on his motorbike to say Mass and hear confessions, but even then they were lucky if they got a congregation of thirty, including the lepers from the hospital who always turned out.

Inside the house, his manager Laurie Crawford had rigged up a system of buzzers to replace the old hand-held bells so that he could ring for specific servants. Without his political work, Gore-Browne found he had more time for reading and was enjoying the works of Saki, Woodrow Wilson on America, which he thought sounded *a most queer place*, and the memoirs of the Duke of Windsor, which he did not really approve of, commenting in his diary, *It is strange that he doesn't seem to grasp that the king of England marrying an American woman who'd had two previous husbands just won't do*. But he wrote to Welensky, quoting Shakespeare, *forbear to judge for we are sinners all.*

To an outsider looking in on Shiwa, with Gore-Browne taking tea on the terrace, the Union Jack flying, the flame trees outside the loggia a mass of blossom and green hills all around, the place looked as if it shouldn't have a care in the world. Down below, African workers were drawing their weekly meat ration after the day's work and returning to small brick houses, woodsmoke puffing from the chimneys. But there was one very big cloud over what might otherwise have been a contented existence. Over at the lime orchards on which the estate depended, this time of year should have seen a mass of fruit being picked by chattering women. Instead there was hardly any fruit, the branches blackened and bare, and many of the 10,000 trees seemed to be dying, as did some of the 10,000 seedlings in the nursery. The distillery, which once would have been going round the clock, was quiet.

Not only had production plummeted but so had prices. Income from lime oil had dropped to just £800 the previous year, with outgoings of £8,000. This year they would be lucky if sales reached three figures. A stream of agricultural experts had been through to try to identify the problem, the last from the Ministry of Agriculture reporting that it was not caused by a disease as Gore-Browne had feared, but that the soil was poor, their 'cultivational methods at fault', and the trees suffering 'starvation and neglect'. They had recommended an annual expenditure of £3,000 on fertilizers, which made no economic sense. While relieved by their assurances that he would have his orchards to pass on to his grandchildren, Gore-Browne found it odd that after all these years of producing the same way without fertilizers, all six of the plantations – which were all of different ages – should suddenly, and simultaneously, stop bearing fruit. He wrote to Welensky:

There is a very great temptation for a man of nearly 70 to close down an enterprise that needs largely rebuilding . . . and to live out the remaining years of one's life in quietude and comfort in lovely surroundings, adequately cared for by agreeable servants. To be honest I don't know what stops one. Some sort of pride I suppose, some disinclination to admit what would in effect be failure . . .

On top of the lime problem, the rains had been bad this year, far below the usual fifteen inches they would usually have had by then, affecting all their foodcrops. For the first time in years, Gore-Browne had ordered the sacrifice of a goat and for white cloth to be placed on the shrines of local spirits in an attempt to appease them. He firmly believed that one should pay respect to the religion of the place where one lives. As he always told guests who poured scorn on the natives' witch-doctors and spirit worship, there was Peacock's grave on the hill to remind them of the perils of taking such matters lightly.

Even in a good year, the estate still did not manage to produce enough food for their needs, despite all the years of hard work and investment. They had continual problems with snakes killing chickens, and lions getting into the kraal and eating the sheep, though it was a long time since they had seen any leopards. Every so often a crocodile from the lake would attack one of the villagers and a hunting party would be sent out.

All the time everything was getting more expensive. Crawford had estimated that running costs would be £12,000 for the coming year, and Gore-Browne feared he might even have to get rid of his manager and run the place on maintenance level to get it back down to £7,000. He had not cut back on port, sherry, wine and champagne orders or lavish entertaining, but he had reduced his permanent labour force, which once stood at more than 800 people, to just over 100, which he thought was *really the absolute minimum* for an estate that size. Even so they were living on his capital, as well as cheques from Ethel, and *digging deeper all the time*. Every letter from the bank saw an increase in his overdraft, which now stood at more than £2,000.

At times he despaired of the future. Ethel, who was almost ninety, had written recently that she was *weary of life* and *wishing it were over and done with*, and he wrote to Welensky, *sometimes I can't help feeling the same*. But his aunt was still very active, accompanying him to concerts during his last trip to England two years earlier, once he had recovered from his gallbladder operation, and even managed the usual ritual of travelling to Winchester Cathedral for evensong before dropping him at Southampton for the boat, though she no longer drove herself, much to the relief of friends and relatives such as the Earl of Portsmouth, who described Ethel behind the wheel as 'fiendish and terrifying'. She still enjoyed her after-dinner port and her mind was as razor sharp as ever, apart from the odd memory lapses which were the only sign of her age along with her tendency to nod off while he was reading to her.

Gore-Browne's biggest hope, as he confessed to Ethel and Welensky, was that his daughter Lorna and her new husband would come to live at Shiwa and take over running the place. John Harvey had been working as a labour officer in Roan Antelope mine on the Copperbelt since leaving the British Military Mission in Saudi Arabia, where he had been stationed before marrying Lorna. He had hoped to enter the Colonial Service in Northern Rhodesia, but had been rejected, apparently for lack of education, though Gore-Browne feared it was because he was his father-in-law. He himself confessed to Welensky to having 'mixed feelings' about Harvey – *he's a jovial enough fellow*, with an Army background and he liked hunting, but he clearly did not consider him good enough to marry into the Gore-Browne family and feared he was marrying Lorna Katharine for her money. Harvey had been born in Rhodesia and brought up alone by his mother, who was now a teacher at Unity High School for Girls in Khartoum. But Gore-Browne did not like to pay attention to gossip, and thought it would be good to have some of his family around. His younger, and favourite, daughter, Angela, had stayed in London since graduating from Girton College, Cambridge, with a third in Agricultural Sciences the previous year, and seemed set on marrying Basil Bell, a hydrologist who had been her instructor when she took gliding lessons at university. Gore-Browne had offered the couple a place at Shiwa, but they had turned him down, Angela writing that they preferred to 'do their own thing'. Anyway Lorna had long been acting as housekeeper and hostess at Shiwa during holidays, and she knew how to run the place. *I marvel at how level-headed she is*, he wrote to Ethel, *so completely different to her mother, though sometimes looking uncomfortably like her*.

Harvey had first approached Gore-Browne with the suggestion of them moving in while he was in hospital having his gallbladder removed, and after thinking about it, he had written back, saying, *there's nothing I'd like better*. With his usual insistence on things being done properly, he had set out conditions – Harvey would run the administrative side, training Africans and trying to control spending, for which the couple would be paid £650 a year plus housing and farm produce, on top of the £350 Lorna already received from the £10,000 endowment he had settled on her at the time of her marriage, though eventually he hoped they would live on a share of the profits. They were to live in an annexe to be called the Harvey House, connected to the main house by a covered walkway, but with its own separate entrance and consisting of the old schoolroom, the guest-rooms referred to as the Prophet's Chamber, Kakoma and Mutambishiba, and a new kitchen outside the back door of the chapel which his workmen were currently measuring out. The adjoining door was to be kept locked: he didn't want them in the main house, writing to Harvey, *there's always a certain risk in living all mixed up together of getting on each other's nerves. I've seen plenty of that, and you must have seen it too*. Feeling that he was too old for upsets to his schedule, he had always liked everything precise, keeping a careful note in his diary of how long letters had taken to arrive from London and Lusaka each month, and whenever he was in England he always noted the times of trains he had caught to London each day.

He was hoping Lorna would take some of the weight off his shoulders caused by the endless visitors which Shiwa seemed to attract more than ever since the Great North Road had been tarmacked up from Lusaka and on into Tanganyika and Kenya. He enjoyed entertaining and was delighted to play host to invited guests like Lord and Lady Montagu of Beaulieu who had recently stayed, or Lady Nancy Astor who was due to visit in June. But he told Welensky, *I'm fed up with people I have never seen before, turning up and saying they are on their way to Nairobi and is there anywhere to stay, and then adding, 'I suppose you hardly see anyone here' as if they are doing me a favour bestowing their company.* It was not always easy providing food and lodging when the nearest shop was 120 miles away in Kasama. He particularly disliked civil servants, whom he referred to as *chimpanzees*, and had joked with Welensky about opening a guest-house, sending him a mock letterhead for the Wiliki-Brown Hotel which read:

Terms: Daily with bath £5.5.0
without £6.0.0
Special tariff for civil servants 25% increase
Prostitution a Speciality
Contraceptives supplied free
Gratuities welcomed
Service Optional

There were other things on his mind apart from the shortage of limes and excess of guests. *What most depresses me is the recent change in African attitudes and the way they seem to have lost all faith in the white man*, he complained to Welensky, who was becoming ever more prominent in the region's politics and had been knighted in the New Year's Honours list. Since Winston Churchill and the Tories had taken office in 1951, the British government had clearly been moving the Protectorate towards Federation with Southern Rhodesia and Nyasaland, regardless of unanimous African opposition and the outrage of leaders of the African National Congress such as his old protégés Kenneth Kaunda and Harry Nkumbula, the party's President.

Officially proposed in London in 1951, Federation had been

discussed in a series of conferences in Victoria Falls and London, and a draft Constitution prepared. Welensky, Sir Godfrey Huggins, former doctor and long-time Prime Minister of Southern Rhodesia, and the Governors of all three countries were currently in London with Oliver Lyttelton, the Colonial Secretary, putting the final touches to the matter and the creation of the new Federation was expected to be announced before the summer.

Gore-Browne was sympathetic to the Africans whose views were being ignored, particularly as they had seen their brothers in the Gold Coast and Sudan be granted self-rule. But he was still convinced that there was no way Africans could govern a country as industrialized as Northern Rhodesia, or be put in control of copper mines which might one day be crucial to victory in war – something not to be ignored with the Cold War reaching a height. However, *nationalism is in the air*, he wrote to Ethel, and he had already begun to see what effect that might have in his own remote little corner of the world:

It's amazing the change that has taken place in the last year or two . . . most incredible things happen now even in an out of the way place like Chinsali District and the situation needs careful handling . . . I still feel this place is as it always was and we've got a decent hardworking crowd. But I'm not such an ostrich as not to know that at any moment some rumour may sweep through the land and scatter every scrap of good feeling that exists here at present . . .

One such rumour was the so-called 'Poisoned Sugar Plot', a story that whites were poisoning Africans' sugar so that their women miscarried and men became impotent. The rumour had spread across the whole country, eventually even reaching Shiwa Ngandu. Crawford told Gore-Browne that he kept getting requests from villagers and Shiwa staff to sell them sugar and salt from the house stores, claiming that supplies in the shops had been contaminated. When Crawford suggested they buy from the trading stores in the village, they refused, saying, 'Oh no, their stock comes from the Europeans who are plotting to destroy us.' They also stopped buying tinned meat, claiming it was human flesh.

On the whole, however, he thought the Africans at Shiwa were still loyal and happy. Some of them had worked for him for more than thirty years, and just a couple of weeks earlier, after the Christmas morning service, a delegation had come to him in their best clothes and made a presentation of two candlesticks carved out of the wood of the very first tree he had planted at Shiwa, a blue gum which had grown to 142 feet high and which he had reluctantly had to fell because it was so big it was becoming a menace to the house. He had been touched by their address: 'When you look at these candlesticks on your table, *bwana*, we hope you will see them standing like the old trees used to stand. They were the first you planted at Shiwa. We hope you like them will stand for many years to come. Thank you.'

Later, after the usual distribution of blankets and brandy, he had given £5 and six 12-bore cartridges each to Walimposo and Chilufyu, his two old retainers in charge of building, noting in his diary that *ammunition is the thing they most value in the world.* The two men bowed and clapped their hands beaming, and Walimposo said earnestly, 'Don't die yet, Chipembele.'

Even so, listening to BBC reports on the wireless it was hard to ignore what was going on in Kenya, where white farmers were being murdered in their beds by once faithful retainers with pangas, part of the Mau Mau uprising, spreading terror through the White Highlands. Gore-Browne's new son-in-law Basil had got a job in Nairobi, which meant Angela would be moving there, much to his distress, and, fearing the trouble would spread south, he started signing off his letters to Welensky, promising to be in touch soon, *if I haven't been Mau mau-ed into another world.*

One night, when they were woken at midnight by what sounded like heavy rifle fire and women running screaming into the forest, he thought the Mau Mau really had arrived. Then he saw the blaze and shower of sparks coming from the bamboo thickets behind the house and heard someone sound the fire drum. The fire had been caused by a kitchen-boy pouring live ashes into a rubbish-pit just by the bamboos. Everyone ran out to help, even the lepers, some drunk, others climbing the bamboo and pouring on water, and by 2 a.m. it was under control. All those who had helped were rewarded with hot coffee and ginger biscuits in the old schoolroom.

Thoughts of the Mau Mau were far away six months later, on 3 July 1953, at the christening of Gore-Browne's first grandchild Penelope Jane at Shiwa. It was, he wrote to Ethel, *a beautiful crisp day, the lake clear sapphire, masses of blue morning glory spilling over the walls in front of the house and over the tower, and a few fluffy white clouds sailing in an otherwise blue sky.* It reminded him of an English spring, *a time of year which always gives me a feeling of mixed pleasure and sadness*, remembering long ago days at Rowners where he had proposed to Lorna, and even longer ago at Bingham's Melcombe, that precious spring with the first Lorna.

Ethel had not been able to come to the christening, finally having to accept she was too old for flying, and he had just received a worrying letter from his brother Robert to say she was ill, having had some kind of attack which left her weak and breathless. Once the celebrations were over, Gore-Browne planned to go to England to see her. *You would have loved the ceremony*, he wrote to her,

the shiny pink and white baby already with Gore-Browne features, in Grammy's lace Christening dress, and young Lorna, every bit the proud mother, very smart in a green silk suit and the gold pearldrop earrings which Lady Astor gave her when she was here, suddenly pulling them off at dinner, exclaiming, 'you're so pretty, you must have these!'

The chapel was filled with pink and white petunias for the occasion, the Timba school choir adding rich gospel harmonies to favourite hymns such as 'The Lord's My Shepherd', and the Reverend Simon Sampa leading prayers that the new child 'may grow up like a young straight tree'. Watching the women all dressed in bright-coloured wraps and headdresses, and all the old retainers bearing small gifts, Gore-Browne wrote to Welensky that *it seemed the picture of racial harmony*, adding that his second cousin Gerard, the Earl of Portsmouth, who had come over from his estate in Kenya to be the child's godfather, said it reminded him of *a gathering of tenants in the old days in England.*

But everyone was wondering how long it could last. In recent weeks Gore-Browne had heard some disturbing reports of unrest in the area, particularly in the wake of official celebrations for the coronation of young Queen Elizabeth in May. He told Welensky,

Things are pretty queer here. I wonder how much you get told and how much they gloss things over and bury your heads in the sand. At Chinsali, erstwhile home of peace and content, schoolchildren threw away their Coronation medals and stamped on them. The

man who helped the DC plant the Coronation tree was mobbed and had to be rescued and lodged in jail for his own safety and the children marched past the DC singing one of those 'seditious' songs twice . . .

There had been other incidents too. Apparently at the bidding of Nkumbula's Congress Party, carriers from the *boma* had refused to carry a White Father's loads as they usually did on his evangelizing round. Bad feeling between the races could not have been helped by a white Army captain, driving up to Nairobi, who had run over and killed a child in part of the district which was most anti-European and carried on without stopping.

Such incidents gave Gore-Browne grave misgivings about the future. The Churchill government was moving them relentlessly towards Federation – a referendum of whites in Southern Rhodesia in April had voted in favour and been endorsed by the legislatures of Northern Rhodesia and Nyasaland – and it was due to officially come into force in October. Harry Nkumbula had threatened non-cooperation by the Africans, but as Gore-Browne had written to Angela, Nkumbula was *no Gandhi*. His call in April for a general strike and two days of national prayer had been a failure, less than a third of the population stopping work. *I fear that rather than trying to work out a compromise, Nkumbula is suffering from the African lack of realism*, Gore-Browne wrote to Welensky, illustrating what he meant by recounting something that had happened twenty years earlier:

The two Smith brothers who were then living at Sundzu wanted an addition to their property of a few 100 acres. This included a native village and the headman was quite properly asked if he'd move, and offered a very large sum for those days of £100 in compensation. He replied no, nothing would make him move. But he would like the £100.

Welensky insisted that the problem was that the Africans didn't understand the concept of Federation, pointing out that at one of their protest marches people had held placards proclaiming 'Down with Ventilation'. In his letters to Gore-Browne, he claimed that the Africans would come round to Federation 'once it is put in place and they see how it reduces control of the Colonial Office and government by puppets where the strings are pulled 6,000 miles away'. Preferring to dwell on other matters, he asked Gore-Browne,

> Have you heard of the long playing gramophone records? I know you have a magnificent library but I think you should consider looking at these. The 10″ play for 15 minutes and the 12″ for over 20 minutes and they are turning out a fine selection of records now. You can buy a fairly simple attachment for about £14 which you can fit to an ordinary instrument because these records revolve at a third of the usual speed . . .

Gore-Browne, who had already started buying LPs, was more interested in discussing politics with his well-placed friend. He could see the economic and strategic logic behind the Churchill government's desire for Federation. Forming a union of the three territories to create an area ten times the size of England, with six and a half million Africans and about 200,000 whites (mostly from Southern Rhodesia), would reduce the British government's liability as the copper wealth of Northern Rhodesia could be used to fund the debt-laden south. It would also establish a British bastion in Central Africa as a bulwark against Malan's Afrikaner-controlled South Africa.

It was principally because the three territories treated natives so differently that he thought Federation was *heading for disaster*. Southern Rhodesia had been a self-governing colony since 1925, when Cecil Rhodes's British South Africa Company had relinquished control, and native policy there remained, in the words of its Prime Minister Sir Godfrey Huggins, addressing the Rhodesian Parliament, 'one of beneficent autocracy – the native is told what is good for him and has got to do it'. By contrast Northern Rhodesia had been a British protectorate since 1924 where native policy had officially been one of 'partnership' between the races, though in practice it was not clear what that meant, as a social and labour colour bar remained. Federation was supposed over time to create a multi-racial state, but from what Gore-Browne could make out, African representation within the new Parliament would be so limited as to be meaningless, and he was not surprised that leading Africans saw it as a device to maintain white supremacy.

Although Welensky's weekly letters kept Gore-Browne in touch with developments, he missed being in the middle of things, and their own meetings, where Welensky's half-moon eyebrows would slowly rise at some suggestion, and his white shirts strain and dampen with sweat under his ever-increasing bulk. The last time they had met in Lusaka, his friend was so huge that people were saying his wife Lizzie made all his shirts and pyjamas because no shop sold ones big enough. Gore-Browne admitted to Welensky, *Sometimes I feel I'd like to be in Council again for a couple of hours to give tongue on how Northern Rhodesia is run by civil servants.* He devoured Hansard and LegCo proceedings which he had sent to him, writing to Welensky, *Were we ever so futile or divided amongst ourselves as this present lot?* and he often had dreams that he had been called back to sit on LegCo. Much of his spare time was spent in his study furiously tapping away at the typewriter, filling his carved wooden Zanzibari chest with carbon copies of letters to newspapers and journals such as the *Manchester Guardian*, the *Economist*, and the *Bulawayo Chronicle*. Most were on the subject of Partition, his own plan which he had first discussed with Welensky in 1950, to divide Africa north of the Limpopo river into European and African self-governing territories. He attached small printed maps showing one European state consisting of Southern Rhodesia, the Copperbelt and the farming area along the railway line in Northern Rhodesia, and two African states, one comprising north-east Rhodesia and the Protectorate of Nyasaland, and the other made up of Barotseland, Bechuanaland and north-west Rhodesia less the Copperbelt and European farming areas. To compensate for the incredibly uneven wealth of these regions, a fixed percentage of revenue from taxation on profits in the industrial area of Northern Rhodesia would go towards development of the two African states.

The plan was strongly rejected by both whites and blacks, and Gore-Browne freely admitted this was not a solution, but thought it *the best we can do at this late stage*. Worried about reports of Ethel's illness, and angered at what he saw happening to the country he so loved, he tried to calm himself by listening in the evenings to Bach's Mass in C minor and Beethoven's Quartets, both of which he found very soothing. As he often wrote to Welensky, sometimes he wished for the end. *A quiet grave on the hills here is what I'd like best of anything, though Henry tells me off when I say such things.*

More and more Henry had become his main solace. He had taught him to read, and at the christening lunch for baby Penelope had been amused to hear him telling the Earl of Portsmouth about their latest trip to Europe, a conversation Portsmouth later recounted in his autobiography.

'What did you think of England, Henry?' Portsmouth had asked.

'Well, it teaches you the value of education, sir,' replied Henry.

'Why's that, Henry?'

'Well, sir, I would not have been at all OK if I had not been able to read the words "Gents" at Marble Arch!'

I miss Henry terribly, he wrote in his diary when his servant was away for the funeral of his cousin, a young schoolboy who had been killed while out on a buffalo shoot with his father, Alifeyo. The buffalo had been shot, but before dying suddenly turned on the boy, ripping out his stomach then smashing him against a tree. The villagers had decided to bury the buffalo carcass and boy together in a big ceremony.

Whenever Gore-Browne was unwell, Henry took charge of nursing, coming in to check on him and give him medicine during the night, sometimes even cooking his supper of hot soup or Bovril, and sleeping next door in his study. One night when all the household staff except for a small kitchen-boy were off sick with malaria or chest infections, Gore-Browne had suffered a slight stroke. Henry was away in his village fifteen miles away, sowing his 'gardens' with crops for the year, but somehow heard that his master was ill and alone, and cycled all the way to Shiwa on the new red bicycle Gore-Browne had bought him. He was at the house within a couple of hours. Gore-Browne wrote in his diary afterwards, *I have seldom been so glad to see someone as when Henry walked through the bedroom door.* The previous Christmas he had sent out cards featuring a photograph of Henry in a black overcoat and bowler hat standing in the snow looking bemused and holding a snowball, taken on a trip they had made through Europe in 1950. 'Henry was the only person in my father's life who remained completely faithful,' said his daughter Angela. 'First he took the place of his wife and then his children.'

It was in Henry's company that Gore-Browne had celebrated turning seventy in May, with a bottle of Lanson champagne and a glass of vintage port. And in July of the previous year they had drunk whisky and sodas to commemorate what would have been his silver wedding anniversary. Mostly they just sat on the terrace, a strange pair, the old bald white man with the monocle and bristly moustache, and the small middle-aged black man. Sometimes Henry brought his guitar and would strum softly on it as they talked. Just as Gore-Browne had years before with Lorna, they would discuss their dreams – Henry's usually involving large birds and Gore-Browne's often about building Brooklands with Nunk. Henry confided in him his problems with his adulterous wife Zilika and the Lozi postal clerk, whom he suspected might have fathered some of their children.

Often they reminisced about trips they had taken and discussed where they might go next. Their longest trip so far had been in 1950 when they had travelled by the SS *Imperio* from the port of Lobito in Angola to Lisbon, Gore-Browne in first class on a £111 ticket, and Henry in third class for £27. After a few days exploring Lisbon, they took the train to Oporto where they were met by Gore-Browne's old friend Victor Delaforce, who took them to Quinta da Foz de Temilobos, his family port estate on the Douro river. Henry had been astonished, Gore-Browne wrote to Angela, when he saw casks of port which he said were 'as big as Bemba houses'. Back in Oporto, Delaforce had shown them the Shiwa sample bottle, and arranged a banquet in Gore-Browne's honour at the Factory House with his old comrades from his time as liaison to the Portuguese Expeditionary Force in the First World War, producing a bottle of 1917 vintage.

Well supplied with port for the journey, they had then travelled by train through Spain to Paris, where they checked into the Hôtel Terminus for a few days before heading on to London for the State Opening of Parliament, for which occasion Gore-Browne had given Henry one of his old tail-coats. In Paris, Gore-Browne bought Henry *a chic Parisian hat*, walked with him in the Tuileries so he could show it off, and took him to see Napoleon's tomb after explaining who he was. On the last night they went to the Opéra to see *Samson and Delilah*, and Gore-Browne wrote to Angela, *as the Temple of Dagon crushed down on Delilah I couldn't resist whispering to Henry, 'you should tell Zilika that's what happens to people like her'*.

When they eventually returned to Shiwa, Henry regaled friends and family in his village of Chisoso with tales of what he had seen. Kalaka, his brother and Gore-Browne's chief hunter, recalls, 'Henry came with gifts of men's suits and Church shoes which were very strong and very special and lasted a long time. He told us stories of the good conditions in which people lived and also how you could see white people cleaning and labouring, which was very hard for us to believe.' Disappearing into his mud hut where he lives with his two surviving wives, several scrawny pigs and some of his thirteen children and their children, Kalaka brought out a yellowing exercise book with the name Henry Mulenga at the front and stuck with black and white photographs of Henry in front of the Colosseum in Rome, in London with a group of schoolboys and standing in the snow. Turning the pages, he recalled, 'Henry told us how cold it was and of something called snow – an ice which came from the sky and people could take and mould. We all said how good God is to put white men in those cold places because if we blacks happen to go there we can be frozen like hell.'

19

Shiwa Ngandu, 5 November 1960

It was the first day of the rains and Gore-Browne was sitting at his desk in the newly red-painted study, finishing his Christmas cards to send to England, which this year featured a picture of his three grandchildren playing on the lawn at Shiwa with those of Sondash, the Harveys' cook. His eyesight, which had always been poor, was getting weaker, and with 162 cards to write, he found it an onerous task. In his diary, he noted the list of presents ordered from the Army & Navy stores for the servants – sports coats for senior house servants such as Simoni, Sondash and Kasaka, as well as Kalaka and Brush his hunters; jerseys for cattle-herders such as Philemon and Moses; trousers, ties or shirts for the others, and some boxes of his favourite Cadbury's Dairy Milk chocolates for himself and Henry.

In the library along the corridor, preparations were under way for a party to celebrate the Shiwa cattle herd passing the thousand mark. Ten-shilling bonuses had been handed out to each of the four cattle *capitaos*, and there was to be champagne and Montmartre cocktails (Gore-Browne's favourite blend of gin, Cinzano and cointreau) for the Europeans and a few selected servants, followed by fireworks over the lake, provided the rains held off. Outside the study door, Gore-Browne could hear glasses rattling as servants padded past, trying hard to keep quiet. He was becoming increasingly crotchety in his old age and, apart from Henry who was always welcome, most of Shiwa's inhabitants knew better than to disturb the *bwana* while he was busy in his study. But occasionally the door would burst open and in would run Charles, the elder of his two grandsons and his pride and joy.

Gore-Browne still couldn't get over having a grandson – *Chipembele* 2 as he referred to Charles in his diaries or 'the little *bwana*' as the servants called him as he trotted about the place, fearless on top of his small grey donkey, chasing his elder sister on her tricycle, and chattering away in Bemba. Charles Stewart Harvey had been born by Caesarean at Luanshya hospital on 13 April 1955 and afterwards Gore-Browne had written to Roy Welensky, whose own first grandson, Shaun, had been born in 1953 to his daughter Joan: *I cannot tell you what it means to me but you'll be able to guess. The nice thing is the unfeigned delight of all the people here, they are just radiant . . . Roman Catholics, Free Church, Pagan priests and Chiefs had all prayed for a boy to be born . . .*

He often recounted the boy's escapades in letters to his friends such as Welensky, who was now Prime Minister of the Federation of Rhodesia and Nyasaland, or Victor Delaforce in Oporto from whom he ordered his port and sherry. *The port arrived safely and has now been bottled and is quite delicious*, he wrote in a typed note inside the Christmas card the previous year, adding,

You will be amused at this little tale of my elder grandson, now aged 4 years, and the cask of 'Royal Palace' on the top of which my head carpenter, a gentleman called Spider, an African of course, was sitting drilling the hole for the spigot. Spider and grandson Charles are the greatest friends and chatter away to each other in fluent vernacular. Charles said to Spider 'You've got beer in there'. 'No' answered Spider, 'it's paraffin'. Just at that moment the spigot was fixed and turned, and out gushed a lovely red stream. 'There' said Charles, 'just as I thought, it's lion's blood. I'm going to kill lots of lions when I'm grown up.'

He had declared a holiday the day the baby boy had arrived at Shiwa in the small plane with his parents Lorna Katharine and John, and there had been tremendous rejoicing on the estate. Chief Mukwikile had turned up to pay his respects to 'the new Sir Stewart', bringing a black sheep as a gift to Gore-Browne's amusement, though he realized its unusual colour made it a prized object in Africa. Gore-Browne had provided two hartebeest and unlimited beer for the servants, who partied till dawn, and he used his new cine camera to film the Harveys stepping out of the plane to be greeted by chanting and dancing with spears, and a parade of *capitaos* and house servants. He insisted afterwards on showing it to all subsequent visitors to Shiwa, telling them proudly how on first seeing baby Charles, young Penelope had asked, 'Where did they get him?'

At the christening that September, sprinkling holy water over the heir to Shiwa, the Reverend Simon Sampa preached, 'As the child Moses was spared to be a leader of people, so preserve this child, Oh Lord, that he may be a leader of the people and maintain his house in strength.' Gore-Browne later recounted to Welensky that *the chapel was a mass of scarlet lilies which had lain snug in the ground whilst the frost was on and were now in their full glory. It was packed from floor to gallery with our people and many from outside*, women on one side and men on the other as usual, and Abel Goram Yia, a Bemba chief, standing proudly in front as godfather. It was the first time it had been full for ages – most of the estate workers had stopped going to chapel, preferring the more emotional services of the followers of Alice Lenshina, a

Chinsali woman around whom a whole cult had developed since she had suddenly emerged the previous year claiming that Christ had spoken to her in a vision and put a Bible on her head.

After the service as the congregation filed out, the choir, which comprised the local schoolchildren, spontaneously broke into 'Once in Royal David's City' and everyone joined in. *I've seldom heard anything quite so moving, and it was a wonderful start off for the young man's career as a Christian*, Gore-Browne told Welensky. Tea and scones were served in the hall, as well as sherry with which the estate workers all drank the health of 'Charles *bwana golo* – the new Sir Stewart', followed by dancing *in a pagan fashion* by children from Timba school. Later that evening there was a champagne dinner for selected guests. The table was set with the family plate and decorated with white roses and white candles in silver candlesticks, and the guests in black tie and white tuxedos rose to toast both the Queen and the new Sir Stewart.

There was a double celebration that night as a cable arrived from Nairobi to say that Angela had given birth to her second daughter, Miranda. Gore-Browne noted in his diary that John Harvey told him that on hearing the news that it was another girl, Kasaka, one of the house servants, had said to him '*wa wina*' – 'you win'. Gore-Browne had made no secret of his longing for a grandson, and Angela had written to him from Middlesex hospital after the birth of her first child, Karen Oliva, in February 1954, saying, 'I'm pleased you like her and hope you are not too disappointed that she wasn't a boy. I was for the first 5 seconds and when the young doctor said to me "Look isn't she lovely", I said "she's like any other baby isn't she?" and he was most shocked.'

*

The joy of having a grandson, great as it was, could not compensate for the loss of the most important person in Gore-Browne's life, though he was glad that Ethel had been able to see baby Charles before she died. She had suffered a slight stroke in 1953 and he had flown to England, but she had recovered enough to attend a sculpture exhibition in London with him. However, her letters had become more rambling, her handwriting visibly weakening, and knowing that the time could not be far off, in 1956 he had paid for his daughter Lorna to take Charles and Penelope by plane to England. Disliking air travel, he had sailed there with Henry, arriving at Caenshill in July to find Ethel in a very frail state, though *still up and about and far more alert than most 92 year olds*. Then one Monday she had a fall and took to her bed, where her breathing became more and more laboured, though she still did not lose her caustic tongue, telling Lord Portsmouth, 'Gerard, I hope heaven will be a place where fools are not suffered gladly.' Gore-Browne sat with her every day, and on the Friday she told him to go, whispering, 'I have not many words left.' He knew then the end was not far off.

The following evening, Saturday 4 August 1956, he was having supper alone in Ethel's library listening to *Don Giovanni* on the wireless, broadcast from the Salzburg Festival, and remembering the time, back in June 1937, that he and Ethel had heard it at Glyndebourne. Henry, who had been helping Alice the maid get his aunt comfortable in bed, came in, looking solemn and said his aunt was 'very bad indeed'. Gore-Browne called Dr Hood, her local doctor and friend, who arrived and examined her, saying her heart was giving out and he doubted that she would last the night. He gave her a morphine injection, though she was already unconscious, and left. Gore-Browne sent Alice and Henry away, and sat alone in the armchair by the two-bar electric fire that they had had to persuade Ethel to install, caressing her fragile hand, the veins vivid blue under the paper-white skin and trying to hear her shallow breathing, which every so often would catch and he would think it was all over. At 12.55 a.m. there was a long sigh, and her breathing finally stopped. Closing her eyes with his palm, Gore-Browne laid his cheek against hers, a silent tear running down his face – the first he had shed since he was a boy. He knew that for Ethel to have survived, confined to her bed, would have been *purgatory* for her, but he was devastated, writing to Welensky, *It's hard to realize what the world will be like without her. She's been the best part of my life for almost as long as I can remember.*

He stayed on in the room all night, sitting holding the cold hand of the dead aunt whom he had loved more than anyone in the world, while the house slept on. As the grandfather clock in the downstairs hall ticked louder than ever, chiming the hours, he brushed her hair, once so deep red and luxuriant, now white and wispy thin, almost hearing her voice as he did so admonishing him for being sentimental. He would never know now what might have been if Ethel had gone out to Africa with him, as he so wanted, to be mistress of Shiwa. In his diary, he wrote only: *the night seemed very long and noisy with aeroplanes, trains and motors.*

The next morning he informed the household staff and his daughter Lorna of Ethel's death, and began the laborious process of going through her address book and writing to inform all the many people she had known, from government ministers to racing drivers, English lords to African students, bishops and admirals to Hastings Banda, who was back in Africa working as a doctor on the Gold Coast and preparing to return to Nyasaland and enter politics.

An obituary in *The Times* later that week described Dame Ethel as 'a supreme product of her upbringing and of her generation . . . with a gallantry, an appreciation of quality in all its forms, warmth and great generosity and a puckish sense of humour', and spoke of her 'fierce driving when well over 80 of her Ford V8'. A note added by the Earl of Portsmouth recalled her as 'a dear, astringent saint', and said 'she had a trenchant wit allied to a kindness and understanding that accepted but was never blind to faults in others, and a discriminating enjoyment of the good things in life, complex or simple'.

The funeral was a private affair at her graveside in Weybridge cemetery, where she was buried next to her husband in the Locke King section, having not wanted 'crowds of people howling and bawling', as she had put it. Afterwards Gore-Browne walked in the gardens of Caenshill, breathing air heavy with the fragrance of rhododendrons and remembering all the happy times he had shared with Ethel, both there and at Brooklands, and wondering what life would be without her. It was, he wrote in his diary, *as if the North Star had disappeared from the sky.*

There was a lot to do the following weeks, and though it saddened him to pack up the house, Gore-Browne found it a relief to be busy, going through Ethel's papers which included a trunk full of his own letters tied in ribboned bundles, right back to when he was an unhappy schoolboy at Harrow writing of his indignation at the Dreyfus affair and his dreams of one day owning a grand house. Following the detailed instructions she had left, helped as always by Henry, and surprisingly his ex-wife Lorna, who came down from her flat in north London to Weybridge, the bronze bust of John Locke was wrapped and sent off to the Bodleian library in Oxford, some petitpoint needlework by Lady King taken to the Victoria & Albert Museum, the sundial from the garden delivered to Weybridge Hospital, and various books on local history and paintings donated to Weybridge Museum. His sister Sapphire and brother Robert came over and selected a few objects, and some balldresses and jewellery were put aside for his daughter Lorna. As the principal beneficiary, he marked others to be shipped to Shiwa – Persian rugs, some paintings including one of his mother Helenor Shaw Stewart, the grandfather clock in a lacquer cabinet, the Lord King chandelier, the oak bed with the velvet canopy, his letters, and most of her large collection of books. Her DBE, in its velvet box, he put among his most treasured things, and the Ford Zephyr Mark I, which right up till her late eighties she had driven herself, her face creased in a frown of concentration, he traded in for a new red Mark II for £80, to take back to Shiwa. The remaining items of value were to be auctioned at Sotheby's and in a house auction, though he hated the idea of *strangers coming poking around* his aunt's things.

The rest of the furniture and ornaments were moved to Studley, an elegant house owned by Ethel in Elgin Road, Weybridge, which had been built by Peter Locke King in the mid-nineteenth century and was divided into three flats. Alice, the maid, moved there to look after the place. The following year, in May 1957, Caenshill was sold by auction for £35,000. Gore-Browne told Welensky, *I found it sad that what had once been a very big landed estate had come down to comparatively little in terms of property and land, just 12 and 1/2 acres*, various parts having been sold off or requisitioned at different times for building by the county council, including extending Weybridge cemetery. The house was bought by Vickers, the aircraft manufacturers which had already bought part of Brooklands, for use as a training centre, and the land purchased by developers who planned to build sixty cottages. When everything had been totalled, Ethel had left an estate of £110,645, on which £48,000 had to be paid in death duties. Gore-Browne was the main heir, but after various legacies and bequests to servants, there was not a great deal left of the once vast Locke King fortune. Still, there was more than enough to solve his immediate financial problems at Shiwa and buy a white Ford Zephyr estate wagon to ship back for the Harveys, as well as a small farm for Henry and his ever-growing family in his village of Chisoso, about fifteen miles from Shiwa, the other side of the Great North Road. Henry named it Caenshill in Ethel's honour, erecting a special painted sign.

The money was timely, as Shiwa had been devouring funds faster than ever with the collapse of the essential oils business. In 1954, when they had managed to distil only 21lb of lime oil compared to over 1,000lb back in the 1940s and income from lime oil had plummeted from its highpoint of £6,000 a year to less than £100, a group of horticultural experts had finally diagnosed the problem affecting the lime trees as a virus, which was what Gore-Browne had always suspected, firmly contradicting the report of the previous year which to his fury had blamed his cultivation methods. This group, from the Gold Coast, had found characteristic symptoms of the deadly *tristezia* virus in all six lime plantations as well as in the nursery, which meant that all 10,000 trees and seedlings were doomed. They thought the infection must have been brought into the estate years before in sweet orange seedlings he had purchased in South Africa, but lain dormant and then been carried by aphis fly.

There was no known cure for *tristezia*, and the diagnosis proved the final blow to Gore-Browne's attempts to create an essential oils industry at Shiwa. Initially the Gold Coast experts suggested sowing rough lemon stock and then budding limes on to them the following year and planting them out the year after that, which would have cost an estimated £14,000 and meant that at best he could only have gone back into oil production after seven years. But then they concluded that even that would not work and he would have to start completely anew or give up. *So that was that*, he wrote in his diary bitterly, *over thirty years of work and £50,000 all gone.*

Sadly, he closed down the distillery and abandoned the nursery, dismissing Ephraim who had tended the seedlings for seventeen years. He admitted in a letter to Welensky that he found it hard even to look at the plantations with their blackened withered trees because it made him so depressed. *It looks like one of the worst hit areas during the last days of the Depression. Once it was a hive of industry, so to speak, and prosperity. Now we are down to nothing . . .* Where in the old days there would have been 800 or more African workers going about the place singing and a dozen oxcarts, ploughs and wagons, the staff had shrunk to less than 100, equipped with half a dozen tractors and lorries.

In an attempt to find a new source of income, he and John Harvey turned the estate over to producing timber and raising cattle. Funded by Ethel's chequebook, and then, after her death, by Gore-Browne's inheritance, they had put together a large herd, 1,084 at the last count, mostly Angoni, Southern Rhodesian and Afrikander, not quite the plump-looking chocolate-box Guernseys he remembered from long-ago days at Brooklands. It had not been easy – neither he nor Harvey had much experience with cattle, having only ever kept a small herd for their own dairy needs, and Shiwa's remoteness made it difficult to get hold of breeding stock. They had had to learn about calving, dipping and inoculating, and had lost many cows to TB as well as having constant problems with them getting stuck in the mud or being dragged into the lake by crocodiles. The previous year, twenty cows had been eaten by lions, despite Harvey's occasionally successful hunting trips with his Afghan hound, and twenty-two were struck dead by lightning. Gore-Browne wasn't convinced that they would ever make money. Even if they sold 10 per cent of the herd each year at the going price of £27 a cow, the money would hardly pay for the herding, and though they had set up a butchery which was quite busy, selling meat and dairy products throughout Northern Province bringing in about £100 a week, their recent accounts had shown they needed to cut £6,000 from that year's expenditure if they were to be solvent.

Using Ethel's bequest, they had built a Stenner sawmill and brought in a 46-horse-power Massey Harris engine to run it, which was inaugurated by his daughter Lorna breaking a bottle of beer over it. Gore-Browne had then cut the first log and raised a toast in Spanish sherry to the prosperity of the estate. They had started producing logs from mahogany and toona, the beautiful red cigar boxwood, as well as the cypress and eucalyptus which he had planted as seedlings not long after first arriving at Shiwa. These were loaded into the trailer of a tractor which was driven by Henry, his dog Billy by his side, and sold to local storekeepers and the Lubwa Mission. So far, they had not got the big contracts he had hoped for from the government Public Works Department, which, he complained to Welensky, *seem to prefer importing expensive timber from Sweden and America*, despite all his lobbying efforts, and had suffered a setback when James Sampa, the head of the sawmill and a servant who had worked with Gore-Browne since joining the Border Commission as a young lad, had fallen out of a tree and died, his body discovered by his wife.

He didn't know if he would ever get the place firmly on its feet, but he told Welensky, *it's a good life and keeps me trim and fit*, apart from the occasional attack of pneumonia, lumbago or malaria. Out in the fields, they planted new crops such as coffee and chickpeas, Gore-Browne constantly telling Henry, *One is a fool to leave any stone unturned even if there's a lump of cowshit underneath.* After a long day around the estate, he was always glad of a hot bath and dinner, and sometimes, if his back was stiff, a massage from faithful Henry, who often stayed over in one of the old guest-houses which Gore-Browne had given him, rather than returning to his village. John Harvey was officially running the place, and though Harvey clearly found it hard living so much in his father-in-law's shadow and Gore-Browne sometimes clashed with his son-in-law and resented him making decisions and doing things differently from the way he would have chosen, he had to admit it was a relief to have the Harveys to hand the estate on to. Harvey was turning into an accomplished hunter, often catching lions and recently killing an elephant with just one shot in the brain to provide meat for the estate, a feat celebrated with much dancing and beer by the villagers and champagne by the family. Gore-Browne had written to Ethel before her death:

Lorna has grown into a wonderfully steady self-reliant person . . . and John is getting hold of things well, and when the time comes I'll have no qualms about leaving it in their hands. That is something so wonderful that I can't be too thankful to Providence or whoever arranges these things, and makes up for all the worries of dying lime trees, maddening government officials, cattle being bitten by snakes and bushfires destroying eucalyptus trees.

Having a grandson to eventually inherit the place made all his work worthwhile, and when Lorna gave birth to a second son, Thomas Mark, on 25 September 1957, he thought his joy could hold no bounds, writing in his diary, *it seems too good to be true.*

Despite Gore-Browne's initial worries and the growing number of children, they had managed to keep their two households apart. To maintain his privacy, he insisted that whenever any of the Harveys came into his part of the main house from their annexe, they go all the way outside and enter through the front door, rather than using the adjoining door, even if it was pouring with rain. He often took tea with the children in the library, them lying on the sofa while he played opera records on the wind-up gramophone, or read fairy stories like *Ali Baba and the Forty Thieves* or classic adventure stories like *Robinson Crusoe*, just as he had with his daughters. 'It was really difficult,' recalls Charles, 'because he read very stiffly and it was hard to keep still.'

Several times a week he, Lorna and John had meals together, particularly if he had important guests such as the Governor-General of Northern Rhodesia, Sir Evelyn Hone, and his wife, or the former Governor Sir John Waddington and Lady Waddington, when Lorna supervised the kitchen and they got out the family china and crystal, dressed in wing-collared shirts, white bow-ties and dinner-jackets and broke open the champagne like the old days, Gore-Browne telling tales of lion hunts while passing the port to the left and sometimes organizing games of Consequences in the library afterwards.

There was nowhere else like Shiwa Ngandu in Central Africa and visitors still turned up in their droves, keen to see the 'palace in the bush' with its arched terraces, rose gardens, wine cellars, magnificent library and crocodile lake, and be served five-course meals of guinea-fowl soufflé, saddle of hartebeest, jugged warthog or duiker stew, and fine wines by uniformed servants in pillbox hats, the men then retiring to the library for vintage port, cigars, and talk of politics. Christmas and Easter were occasions for monumental house-parties, and even members of Kenya's Happy Valley set like

Denys Finch Hatton ventured over. One visitor during these years, the writer John Heminway, later described how

> after dinner we were led through stone passages covered in tapestries and along a balcony which faced on to a courtyard lit by flickering torches. In the bedroom the covers of the bed were turned down and a kerosene lamp was hissing on the bedside table. The walls were covered with pen-and-ink scenes of the canals of Venice. In the morning I wandered through the gardens . . . From whatever angle I chose the house was impressive and bizarre. Even in England it would have been an extravaganza. The walls were indiscriminately covered with porches and gargoyles . . . The structure was covered with turrets, enclosed bridge-like corridors and iron latticework.

But though he was renowned as a gracious and generous host, a raconteur who sprinkled his stories with quotes from the classics, Gore-Browne liked most of all to dine alone in his study or bedroom with Henry, enjoying their favourite supper of scrambled eggs followed by peaches or strawberries, if the *sitatunga* hadn't got to the beds and eaten them, washed down by white wine and a glass of port. Afterwards Henry would read to him, wearing the glasses they had got from the optician in Weybridge just after Ethel's death. Sometimes they would listen to music on the new Decca long-playing gramophone he had bought in London, particularly enjoying *Elektra*, which they had gone to see with his friend Edward Montagu of Beaulieu at the Salzburg Festival in 1957, or Henry's favourite, Caruso. Other times they would discuss family problems such as Gore-Browne's worries over Angela, who had been divorced from Basil the previous year but seemed set on staying in Nairobi rather than coming to live at Shiwa as he would have liked. Henry would relate the antics of his own children, most of whom lived on the Caenshill farm with his two wives Elizabeth and Mary, the adulterous Zilika having finally run off with the postal clerk. He talked mostly about his young son Stewart by his third wife, Mary, the progress of James, his eldest, who was working in the copper mines, and Unity, his clever daughter whom Gore-Browne was funding through school in Broken Hill, and had recently fathered his tenth child at the age of forty-nine. Gore-Browne often used to recount these tales to his own friends and wrote with amusement to Victor Delaforce, *Before the birth, Elizabeth (who is Henry's senior wife and over 50), had been complaining of discomfort, so he said, 'well, you asked for it, and now you've got it'! What cads we men are!*

That May, Henry had driven Gore-Browne to Salisbury to visit Roy and Elizabeth Welensky, enjoying seeing the friend he had first known as an engine driver, now Prime Minister of a state larger than Britain, France, Holland and Germany combined, Huggins having finally retired in 1956. The main reason for his trip was to attend the various festivities surrounding the visit of the Queen Mother to open the Kariba dam by turning on the switch of the great generator, after which she would tour the Federation. In his diary, he noted that *the Queen Mother looked charming*. But the colour bar added a sour note, hotels in Southern Rhodesia refusing to give his manservant a room. *Henry slept in the car outside my bedroom window*, he wrote. Yet in Salisbury he ran into Lord Dalhousie who had succeeded Lord Llewellin as Governor-General and who invited both him and Henry for sundowners. *I wondered how Henry would manage*, he wrote, *but he was admirable. He said once again how it is always the greatest who know what true courtesy is.* One of the guests, *a lady from university*, told him that her driver had said Lorna (his ex-wife) was *the only European who really knew the Bemba*. After dinner the two men strolled round the streets of the capital, Henry recalling his days working for the police when the area consisted of fields of duiker.

Following the Queen Mother's retinue back up to the Copperbelt where he was due to be presented, Gore-Browne was delighted when, attending a trooping of the colour parade at the Scrivener Stadium in Ndola, dressed in uniform, his medals proudly displayed on his chest, he found himself in the front row just three seats along from the Queen Mother. Describing it as *another most wonderful day to be remembered for the rest of one's life*, he wrote, *The Queen Mother sent a Rifle Brigade equerry to tell me to put on my hat because the sun was so hot.*

Other than that trip, he rarely left the estate except for twice-yearly visits to Lusaka for meetings of the War Memorial Trustees and the Bursaries Committee to award scholarships for Africans to study in Britain, or to Chinsali to present the cups at the annual show, when he always wore his medals. The rest of the time when he was at Shiwa, he often wandered over to the hospital to give cigarettes to the lepers. There was always a motley collection of patients, which brought home the many perils of life in Africa and made him worry for the health of his grandchildren. On an average day, there would be several people suffering from malaria or TB, perhaps a child bitten by a puff-adder, a woman mauled by a lion, and accident victims like a boy who had fallen out of a tree, a young girl with a badly burnt hand, a man gored in the stomach by a buffalo, or a woman with a toe amputated after she had caught her foot in the spokes of her husband's bicycle.

Occasionally he went over to Timba school to talk to the children about England, or show them an information film from the British Council, then answer questions like 'How does a car go in a ship?' 'Why don't planes fall out of the sky?' 'How many churches are there in London?' 'Are there DCs in England?' and 'Where do the buffalo live?'

When he had nothing else to do, Gore-Browne walked slowly up Peacock Hill, enjoying the view over the acacia trees to the blue waters, or round the lake itself, never tiring of its ever-changing colours and watching the ducks and geese, which they rarely shot now, as there were so few left. Occasionally Henry would accompany him, if he was not away at his farm planting mealies, though his manservant never quite understood the concept of going for a walk just for the sake of it, with no destination, and would always suggest he drive the car. Sometimes a flock of flamingos would fly over, a cloud of pink long-legged ladies, and occasionally the big grey bulk of a hippo would rise to the surface and open its mouth in a huge pink-tongued yawn. John Harvey had bought a boat with an outboard motor to take the children out, but apart from very rare trips such as when Ethel had come to visit back in 1948, Gore-Browne had not gone on the lake since Lorna left.

By the late 1950s, Gore-Browne felt that with his son-in-law managing the estate, even handing out the pay packets the last Friday of the month, and the sawmill and cattle operations up and running, if not actually making a profit, the time was right for him to return to full-time politics. Despite Shiwa's isolation, he had kept in touch with events through the BBC news on the wireless, subscriptions to various newspapers (even if they did come two weeks late), and by reading the debates of the Federal Parliament as well as his regular letters from Welensky, which now came stamped 'Confidential'. Although Welensky was extremely busy, he kept up his correspondence with the man who had in many ways been his mentor, once even sneaking out of the budget debate to dictate a letter to Gore-Browne, explaining, *Many of the pearls of wisdom that were dropping from the lips of my friends and colleagues were wasted on me.* In between a running discussion of health problems (both men suffered from piles) and the merits of pets – Welensky's dog Springer was the son of the late Belle, Gore-Browne's beloved Ridgeback – they wrote frankly of the political situation and managed to maintain their friendship despite their increasingly divergent views. Apart from his late aunt, Welensky was probably the only person who could have got away with writing, 'You do talk some rot, Stewart!'

As Gore-Browne had predicted, Federation had been a disaster. Even in the first years, when he was still prepared to hope for the best, he had confided to Welensky that he was worried about all his past work, building bridges between white and black, being thrown away. *I don't feel as you suggest that the Black Man has not got on far enough. It's rather I think that we've not got any nearer to the right solution of the racial problem . . .* he had written. In 1955 he had swallowed his pride and indicated to the Governor his availability as a Northern Rhodesian nominee to the Parliament, but had been snubbed, not even receiving a reply.

By 1956, most Africans realized that Federation was never going to give them any say in the running of their country and that they had been cheated by the white man. Whatever racial good feeling had been left soon dissipated. The Congress Party, led by its President, Harry Nkumbula, and Secretary General, Kenneth Kaunda, organized a series of boycotts of white-owned stores, work stoppages, skirmishes with police and threatened worse unless Federation was replaced by a 'one man one vote Constitution'.

The action rattled even the calm atmosphere of Shiwa. The usual rituals continued where white and black would get together to drink *nsupa*, the maize beer brewed by the Africans at the start of the harvest and offered to the spirits, or to watch the stirring of the Christmas cake by Lorna and the three grandchildren. But in between, there were gang raids on the stores, a hut was mysteriously set fire to, and Gore-Browne joked somewhat drily with visitors about waking up to find their throats slashed. One evening he was listening to a belligerent speech by Welensky on the wireless, insisting that the Federation could not be allowed to 'play hostage to people like Kaunda who think in terms of Mau Mau terrorism', when he heard rifle shots just outside the house and thought the end had come. It turned out to be Harvey, who, returning from going round the fields, had come across three lions by the Shiwa House signboard. He shot two, the third escaping and eating the favourite dog of Moses, one of the cattle-herders, which the villagers, always eager to blame things on witchcraft, later said was because of *buloshi*, a curse by Moses' senior wife.

Placards demanding 'FREEDOM' appeared on the trees around the house and the walls of the Welfare Club, yet, to Gore-Browne's amusement, films showing the Trooping of the Colour at Buckingham Palace were as popular as ever among the natives when the mobile cinema, Lever's Daylight Cinema or Sunlight Soap, came to Shiwa.

In nearby Chinsali, the Coronation tree in front of the *boma* kept being cut down, forcing the local colonial officers to plant new ones; there were clashes with police over attempts to close down Alice Lenshina's churches; and a District Officer had his face slapped by an African. One day, driving through Serenje on his way down to Lusaka, Gore-Browne had a stone thrown at his car.

He could understand the Africans' frustration. He himself was intensely irritated that whenever he went to Lusaka and checked into the Ridgeway Hotel, Henry had to eat in the kitchen, not being allowed in the restaurant, and that on train trips through the Federation they could not sit together in the dining-car, while on motor tours Henry often had to sleep in the car, hotels refusing to give him a room.

For a while he toyed with joining the Capricorn African Society of Colonel David Stirling, in which his niece Monica and her husband Charles Fisher (who had become a LegCo member in 1945) were very active. Stirling was a heroic figure who had set up the SAS during the Second World War in his early twenties and had led his unit to fame in the North African desert campaigns before being taken prisoner, escaping, then being captured again. He established the Capricorn Society under the SAS motto of 'Who Dares Wins', with the aim of bringing together what he termed 'responsible and forward thinking' whites and blacks in a common front against all forms of extremism and racial nationalism. Gore-Browne stayed with the Fishers in their Luanshya home several times in the mid-1950s and attended meetings with Stirling, even introducing him to Kaunda. But though he admired Stirling's courage, he told Monica he was 'not taken in by his charisma and do-gooding', and believed it 'all too utopian'. He also thought the movement 'too much of a personality cult around Stirling', which Monica interpreted as envy of Stirling's status and heroic field record as Gore-Browne had always been behind the lines.

Besides, the Congress Party was becoming more militant, and for the first time he was convinced that Africans could and should run the country. Believing that if there was a place for the white man in the future of Northern Rhodesia it lay in assisting blacks, in the late 1950s he started to form his own links with the nationalist movement, the leaders of which were almost all his former protégés. His decision was motivated partly by a wish to secure the future of his estate and descendants, but also because of his admiration for Kaunda, whom he had known for years, Kaunda having grown up at the nearby Lubwa Mission.

In the summer of 1957 Gore-Browne and Kaunda were both in England at the same time, and the unlikely friendship flourished between the fiery young black nationalist who wore his heart on his sleeve, never afraid to weep in public, and the crusty white aristocrat with his monocle and firm belief in the stiff upper lip. Kaunda was there, along with Nkumbula, as a guest of the Labour Party, studying party politics, and Gore-Browne for the sale of Caenshill and the Golden Jubilee of the Brooklands racetrack. They met frequently, Gore-Browne entertaining both Kaunda and Nkumbula to dinner at the Studley flat in Weybridge. Occasionally he took Kaunda to dine at the Army & Navy Club in Pall Mall and had him back for the night, where they would talk politics for hours, Kaunda then sleeping on a sofa in the dining-room.

Gore-Browne admired Kaunda's eloquence, particularly in the face of a hostile audience, and his vivid imagery – insisting that joining with the white man was like 'trying to share a small stool with someone with a big backside'. Kaunda was an extremely determined man and Gore-Browne found himself almost believing the apocryphal tale that he had once outstared a lion on the road to Isoka. He told Welensky that he could see that Nkumbula and Kaunda were drifting apart. Kaunda was losing patience both with Nkumbula's inclination to deal with rather than oust white control, and with his taste for high-living in London using party funds, not least his fondness for the bottle, which was anathema to Kaunda, the teetotalling vegetarian son of a preacher. Gore-Browne was not surprised when, after a trip to India to meet Gandhi, Kaunda returned in October 1958 to break away from Nkumbula and establish his own Zambia Africa National Congress (ZANC), with himself as President and a largely Bemba membership.

Meanwhile in neighbouring Nyasaland, the other unhappy partner of the Federation, Dr Hastings Banda had finally returned and was running a campaign of civil disobedience, having written to Gore-Browne of his intention to lead a secession movement (as well as establish a coffee plantation, which he never got round to). In March 1959, after clashes with the police in which thirty-eight people were killed, Banda was locked up.

Kaunda soon followed him to jail, along with fifty other leading ZANC members, after urging Africans to boycott the March 1959 elections, which were so complicated that they were known as 'the slide-rule elections' and in which Africans would be allowed to vote for only a minority of seats. Publicly vowing he would not rest till he had removed the Union Jack from Northern Rhodesia, Kaunda was jailed for nine months, a situation he had prepared himself for by giving up his beloved cups of tea, knowing he would be deprived of tea in prison. Just before Kaunda's arrest, Gore-Browne, who had no intention of removing the Union Jack from his own terrace at Shiwa and still had no qualms about beating his servants if they disobeyed, dined with Kaunda at Lusaka's Ridgeway Hotel, shocking the rest of the white community by so publicly socializing with the man they called the Black Mamba. Dick Hobson, who had arrived in Lusaka in 1954 to be Federal Information Officer, recalls the shock this caused: 'We ate with whites, danced with whites, drank with whites and lived this life in the middle of Africa with very little to do with Africans. Even Kees department store only had white shop assistants.'

Kaunda wrote to Gore-Browne several times from detainees' camp in Kabompo, asking to be remembered to 'the entire family of Shiwa Ngandu', and when he emerged from jail in 1960, his credibility among Africans had risen enormously. By contrast, Nkumbula, whose Congress Party had participated in the white-run elections of the previous year, was seen as having sold out and took more and more to the bottle. Kaunda quickly seized advantage of his own enhanced popularity by merging his ZANC with breakaway groups from Nkumbula's Congress to form the United National Independence Party (UNIP), with the avowed aim of destroying the Federation and creating a black government. This time there was to be no compromise.

It was not just the rhetoric that was becoming more militant. In March, a crowd of 2,000 had held up the Governor, Sir Evelyn Hone, and Iain Macleod, the new Conservative Colonial Secretary, at Lusaka airport and broken the windows of fifteen cars in their convoy. Two months later, in Ndola, a mob of angry people returning from a banned UNIP meeting set fire to a car containing a white woman, Mrs Barton (whose husband used to service the Shiwa tractors), and her two young daughters. Mrs Burton was burnt to death and the girls suffered severe burns, causing outrage in the white community. When riots broke out in Salisbury and Bulawayo in July, they were brutally put down by Welensky's police.

Internationally it was clear that colonies were becoming unfashionable. French President General Charles de Gaulle had cut free all twelve French colonies in Africa. All indications were that the Conservative government in Britain was realizing that there was now no stopping what Prime Minister Harold Macmillan called 'the wind of change blowing through Africa'* in a speech in Cape Town that February. Ghana – the former Gold Coast – had already been granted independence, as had Nigeria, and it was evident that independence

*Address by Harold Macmillan to South African Parliament in Cape Town, 3 February 1960.

was round the corner in Britain's other colonies. But *it has to be done properly*, Gore-Browne wrote in his diary, listening every night to the wireless reports of fighting in the neighbouring country of former Belgian Congo. Independence had been declared there in July with no preparation, and rebels from the Force Publique had gone on the rampage, burning, killing and looting, sending Europeans fleeing. In Gore-Browne's view, white men would be needed after independence, for their technical and administrative expertise if nothing else.

Although most white settlers in Rhodesia were bitterly opposed to black independence and Welensky was even threatening to declare a Republic, Gore-Browne was quite convinced change was coming. He gave funds to UNIP and Kaunda personally, cheques of £50 or £100 at a time, and made Kaunda and his wife Betty welcome at Shiwa, giving them the best guest-rooms. He offered shelter to Kaunda's mother, Helen, when her life was thought to be at risk, and had several of the party leaders to his house for secret meetings, even paying for their bus fares to get there. He allowed UNIP meetings on his estate in the Welfare Club dancehall, where he was impressed with the discipline of the 400 or so Africans who gathered singing and chanting 'Freedom'. He wrote in his diary, *it seems more like a church service than a political gathering*, and noted that the meetings always ended with a prayer for himself and Shiwa. To the outrage of other whites, he even wrote a foreword to Kaunda's book *Black Government?* – saying, 'Those of us who know Mr Kaunda feel we can trust him.'

Apparently unaware of how deeply his friend was already involved, Welensky wrote that he had seen open letters in the *Northern News* and *African Mail*, urging Gore-Browne to return to politics. 'Well you could do a lot worse,' he advised. 'I look back on those days when you and I worked together in Northern Rhodesia as some of the most fruitful I have ever participated in . . . I feel more frustration today as a Prime Minister than I ever felt as leader of the Unofficial members . . .' He added bitterly that he had no time for his home, his beloved wife Lizzie, or 'Lady Liz' as she was known, the gardening he so enjoyed, or fishing with his son Michael, and that he had recently dreamt that he was lying in his coffin. 'I frankly don't give a damn about politics today,' he ended, revealing the pressure he was under and his sense that his days as Prime Minister were numbered. 'If I were to be kicked out tomorrow I should lose no sleep at all. The type of life I lead isn't the kind of thing I'd inflict on a dog.'

In fact, beyond his immediate family and the top UNIP leadership, few people realized how committed Gore-Browne had become to the nationalist cause. Kaunda had promised him a constituency when the British government finally agreed new democratic elections. But in the meantime they had decided that it would be more useful to start with if, rather than being the first prominent white (other than a couple of missionaries) to openly champion UNIP, he stayed in the background, acting as a channel between Kaunda and British government officials. Gore-Browne wrote to Sir Alec Douglas-Home, Iain Macleod, and Duncan Sandys, the Commonwealth Secretary, urging negotiations with Kaunda to avoid an extremist taking power, pointing out what had happened in the Congo and personally recommending Kaunda as a man they could deal with. Eventually they had promised constitutional talks. Later Kaunda was to credit Gore-Browne with enabling the Zambians to achieve independence without bloodshed, and to describe him as 'one of the most visionary people of Africa – I can't think of any settler who made a similar contribution to cutting across the racial boundary anywhere.'*

*Interview with the author, March 1997.

20

Shiwa Ngandu, Zambia, 15 July 1967

Even as a young man Gore-Browne had always hated cold weather, and though for most of the year he enjoyed Shiwa's clear plateau, he dreaded those few mornings in early July when the temperature plummeted and he woke to see a dusting of hoar frost stiffening the tips of the grass. As he got older and his joints ached in the night, he was finding it harder and harder to be up with the first drum. *6 o'clock on a bitter Monday morning makes me shew the least pleasant side of my character*, he wrote to Welensky, adding, *a beastly hacking cough keeps me awake at night which is quite contrary to my habits*.

He walked slowly these days, an eighty-four-year-old man with a face lined like chamois leather, and leaned on a carved wooden stick, his long legs stiff as marionettes as the frosty lawn crunched under his tread. He no longer ventured far. But he thought it important that the servants see him up and about, even if he often forgot their names and his failing eyesight and hearing meant he could no longer *spot a slacker a mile off* as he had in the days when he was the feared Chipembele. '*Mwasibukeni*,' or 'Morning, *bwana*,' the workers called with a quick salute as he passed, and he nodded, remembering how once they would have prostrated themselves on the ground. Sometimes children, out of sight of their parents, would gather round him, chanting, 'Coin, coin', and he would pull something from his pocket, only distinguishing a *tik* (threepence) from a shilling by the volume of their whoops of delight as they ran off to buy candy or condensed milk at the Indian store.

On those morning walks before breakfast, he noticed how the flower-beds were overgrown, his ex-wife's beloved rose bushes full of dead heads which no one had removed, and the brick wall crumbling into yellow dust *like that which seems to cover everything in this part of the world*, and he thought how sad Lorna would have been to see such neglect. But almost a quarter of a century had passed since the days when they had last walked together at Shiwa, strange and occasionally brilliant ideas tumbling out of her head in no particular order. Sometimes, when he thought about those times, he confused her with the first Lorna and their youthful rambles across the Dorset downs when his now weakly beating heart had pounded with what he only later – too late – realized was love.

Since his return to politics had been brought to an abrupt end by the creation of an independent Zambia and the election of a black government in which, to his distress, there was no place for a white man, even a long-time sympathizer, his daughter Lorna had urged him to get a dog to keep him company on his solitary excursions. But he had vowed never to replace Belle, his faithful Ridgeback, feeling that he couldn't face another loss in his life. Besides, John Harvey had eight dogs including an Afghan hound and *a shoal of small fox terriers*, which he thought was *quite enough dogs for the estate*. He often visited Belle's grave under the great big bamboo tree, by the clump which had caught fire in the 1960s when they all thought the Mau Mau had come.

Sometimes he walked past the sawmill, where men were hard at work cutting poles for a government contract, and on to the brick building which housed the distillery, pained to see it lying abandoned. Inside, the sky was visible through holes in the roof where tiles had fallen in the rains, and the once-gleaming copper vats and pipes were turning green and rusted, and he could see some parts had been pilfered. Apart from a few experiments with geranium oil, nothing had been distilled there for more than ten years, and it must have been terribly painful to see all his hard work towards creating a new industry for Northern Rhodesia going to waste. Some lime experts had been through earlier in the year, claiming to have a cure for the *tristezia* virus which had wiped out his trees. If he was younger he would have tried again, but he was too old to do it alone and his son-in-law was not interested, preferring to focus his energies on cattle.

When he was feeling strong enough, Gore-Browne would wander down to the lake, particularly enjoying this time of the year after the rains when the light was clear and pearly. Often a fish-eagle would be circling noisily above, though in recent years he had noticed each season brought fewer animals, the large herds of zebras and elands that used to congregate by the waterside, or even the few that he would often come across cavorting in a clearing, long gone, and he could not remember the last time he had seen an elephant on the estate. Even so, watching a few web-footed black sitatunga on the shore flit away like long-legged shadows as they sensed his presence, he thought it was more than fifty years since his first sight of his magical kingdom of Shiwa Ngandu, the Lake of the Royal Crocodiles, and yet each year it seemed to get more beautiful.

Returning to the house for breakfast, he would rest awhile in the loggia where his wife used to lie and where in the summer months he had taken to sleeping at night. A family of martins had constructed a nest in the corner of the rafters and he could sit for hours, fascinated by their skill in building it and the way they flew straight into the small hole, *without ever having to go round the airfield twice.*

He found it loneliest during term-time when his grandchildren Penelope, Charles and Mark were away at their public schools in England, a traumatic transition for children used to running wild and barefoot in Shiwa's vast open spaces, particularly Charlie, who to Gore-Browne's immense pride had killed his first crocodile at the age of six and tried his first glass of port, pulling a terrible face, and was now at Gordonstoun. Gore-Browne missed his daily meetings with his oldest grandson, when Charlie would list what birds and other creatures he had killed. Lorna Katharine had recently had a fourth child, David, but he was still a baby, too young to read to or talk to, and she was currently away with him in London, where the children were visiting their grandmother Lorna, or GL as they called his ex-wife, before returning to Shiwa for their summer vacation. The Bemba had a saying, 'When the children are away *nganda ya tailala*' – the house is cold – and he thought it very true. His greatest joy during these times was getting letters with news of their antics, his daughter writing of how Mark had taken his shoes off in Trafalgar Square, and how Charlie, on a visit to the Montagus at Beaulieu, had sat with lords and ladies after dinner watching a soprano singing Berlioz on television, and asked, 'What would happen if a fly flew into that open mouth?' Penelope, the eldest, was fourteen and growing more and more like Aunt Ethel, in looks and ways, as all visitors remarked on seeing her near the big picture of Ethel which dominated the sitting-room. The African servants who remembered Ethel from her trip to Shiwa said her *mupashi* or spirit had entered the girl, and as Penelope got taller, sometimes even Gore-Browne had to check himself.

A lot of his time was spent as always in replying to mail,

though his Christmas card list was getting shorter as many old friends died off, and he had to be helped by Henry because his eyesight was so poor. The post now came twice a week, Tuesdays and Fridays, and occasionally included postcards from his ex-wife in strange places like Albania, thanking him for her monthly allowance. Much of what he received were thank-you letters, scribbled on carefully ruled lines full of crossings-out and misspellings by people who had probably never written a letter before. Some were from political activists whose families he had helped when they were in jail in the difficult days of the early 1960s, but mostly they were from parents of children whose schooling he was funding, former workers whom he had helped set up a farm and occasionally wrote asking for money, or current staff with problems, such as Goodson Silwimba, who had come to ask for a loan of £10 which he had to pay his in-laws in compensation for the death of his wife in childbirth. He never really expected them to pay him back and was always delighted if they did.

Often people came asking for jobs, and sadly, under strict instructions from his daughter, he would turn them away, usually slipping them some food or money. Through drastic cuts, the family were just about living within their means, the previous year's current expenditure of £18,400 compared to an income of £15,682, the deficit being made up by income on his share portfolio. They had built the cattle herd up to 2,000, despite the best efforts of lions, leopards and crocodiles, and Welensky referred to him jokingly as *the cattle baron*. But the estate was still not making money and he called himself *a potato farmer*. Recently the new Zambian government had been forced to impose petrol rationing, after in neighbouring Rhodesia the fighter pilot turned Rhodesian Front leader Ian Smith had swept the 1965 elections and announced his unilateral declaration of independence (UDI). As a result

Zambia had been cut off from its export routes and fuel supply, and no one knew what the future held for Africa's youngest country and its 3.5 million people.

Unlike Welensky and most white settlers, who felt betrayed by the Conservative government back home of Harold Macmillan who had set independence in train, Gore-Browne was optimistic. He was the first white man to renounce his British citizenship to become a Zambian citizen. In pride of place on the wall of his study, next to his knighthood and framed invitations to the coronations of King George VI and Queen Elizabeth in 1937, and that of Queen Elizabeth II in 1952, hung a framed invitation to the celebrations for the Independence of Zambia on 24 October 1964, an event he described in his diary as *one of the greatest days of my life*, even though in the end he had been a guest and not a participant as he had once dreamed. Both he and Henry had been invited to the commemorations, though Henry's seat was not with his in the VIP stand, and the nearest Henry got to the Garden Party and State Ball was waiting at the wheel of the car outside.

Everyone present that night would always remember the silence in the Independence Stadium as if the whole nation were holding its breath, when just before midnight on Friday 23 October 1964 Sir Evelyn Hone, the last Governor of Northern Rhodesia, and Kenneth Kaunda, the first President-elect of Zambia, had risen from their places just along from Gore-Browne in the grandstand, and walked down into the arena. Stopping by the two flagpoles, the old white man in all his colonial regalia and the young black firebrand turned to face Princess Alice, the Princess Royal, sister of King George VI.

Ordering the slaughter of two bulls at Shiwa and a day's holiday in commemoration, Gore-Browne had no illusions that Zambia's new rulers would have an easy time. He recalled in an interview with *The Times of Zambia*, 'I once asked my old nurse in France why there were so many fleas in the old sea-side lodgings we used to go to and she replied "these things are sent to try us".' Zambia was almost entirely dependent on copper for its income, and thus at the mercy of world commodity prices. Being landlocked, it was reliant for its outlets to the sea on Angola and Rhodesia, both of which had hostile governments – the former, the Portuguese colonial administration, and the latter, that of Ian Smith who was determined to preserve a bastion of white supremacy in Africa. But perhaps Kaunda's biggest challenge was the lack of trained men to run the country – at Independence fewer than 1,000 Zambians had finished secondary school and only seventy were graduates. Though slightly concerned to see pictures of Kaunda popping up in every office as very much 'the Big Man', Gore-Browne wrote to Welensky, *I've always liked the fellow and he's got a big job before him.*

He was only sorry that he would not be a part of it. He had officially joined UNIP on 29 March 1961, after a meeting with Kaunda at party headquarters in Lusaka. *Decided to throw my lot in with his*, he wrote in his diary, a decision with which, as Northern Rhodesia's foremost elder statesman, he made headline news all over the Federation, stunning the white community, as well as raising many eyebrows back home in the British Colonial Office. From then on he was openly back in the thick of things, holding meetings with the Governor, Sir Evelyn Hone, urging the government to make haste towards a new Constitution allowing for a majority government, accompanying Kaunda for negotiations with Iain Macleod, the clever Secretary of State for Colonies, and attending the party conference in Mulungushi where he sat on the platform just behind Kaunda, despite the blazing sun and *tedium* of everything being interpreted into three or more languages, writing that he was *strangely moved* by the singing of 'God Bless Africa'.

For a while the situation had looked dangerous, and he feared the British government was going to offer too little too late. His two great friends Kaunda and Welensky were at daggers drawn. Welensky, whose huge bulk led the London *Observer* to describe him as 'a crumpled Roman Emperor', insisted, 'Federation is mine and I'm prepared to fight to keep it.' Throughout the sweltering summer of 1961, unrest swept across the country, Africans setting fire to buses, bridges and schools and placing roadblocks. Three blacks were killed after Sir Evelyn Hone authorized police action, prompting Kaunda to threaten, 'My patience is completely exhausted. I cannot sit and see my people shot down.' The arson attacks multiplied and this time even Shiwa was badly affected. Although the house was not touched, the Mansya and Mpandala bridges were burnt, cutting off the estate, and the Timba school razed to the ground, forcing Gore-Browne to cable for troops and sleep with a gun by his pillow, as helicopters whizzed in and out. Shortly afterwards, in March 1962, Kaunda spent a weekend at Shiwa accompanied by Mervyn Temple, a white missionary, who led prayers in Shiwa chapel and preached a sermon on Abraham leaving his house, not knowing where for.

With the whole country in a state of fear and waiting, in April 1962 Gore-Browne accompanied Kaunda and T. L. Desai, a prominent Indian member of UNIP, to the United Nations in New York to plead their case. They made a strange trio, all three taken aback by the size of the cars and the crenellated skyline of tall buildings as they crossed Brooklyn bridge into Manhattan. They were much fêted by the local African community, Kaunda, dressed in a violet toga and waving his trademark large white handkerchief, as emotional as ever, breaking down in tears as he described British police firing on his people. For his part, Gore-Browne addressed the UN Committees in his usual forthright manner, insisting, 'I am convinced that Northern Rhodesia must inevitably become a black country. The sooner this is resolved, the more peaceful will be the transition.'

On the way back Gore-Browne stopped off in London, staying at his club, the Army and Navy in Pall Mall, as Studley, the last remaining Locke King property, had been sold. An experienced traveller by now, Henry flew out from Northern Rhodesia to join him, staying at a hostel for Ghanaians. Together they enjoyed their usual round of shopping, being fitted out at Hoggs, Gore-Browne's tailors, as well as trips to the opera and the Curzon cinema, Henry particularly enjoying *West Side Story*. They dined on Gore-Browne's favourite oysters, and once lunched, at Henry's request, at what Gore-Browne described as *a queer Wimpy bar*. Sometimes Henry went to a dance with his African friends, and Gore-Browne dined with Lorna, his ex-wife, whom he found he got on with far better now that they had grandchildren in common. At Fords in Regent Street he bought the latest red Zephyr 4, and, with Henry at the wheel, drove down to Weybridge to visit Ethel's grave and Caenshill, where Gore-Browne was so depressed by the number of houses that had been built on the land (*at least 60*) that he was physically sick when he got back to his rooms at the club, and then lost his false teeth down the plughole of the bath. Gore-Browne stayed several days with his brother Robert and sister-in-law Margaret at their large house, Vineyards, in Beaulieu, and tried out some of the wine they were producing, while spending the evenings watching television, later commenting in his diary, *What a dreadful form of progress!*

Northern Rhodesia was never far from his thoughts. Much

of his time in London was spent at the publishing house Heinemann, producing a foreword for and helping edit Kaunda's autobiography *Zambia Shall be Free*, which had mostly been written while staying at Shiwa. He held talks with R. A. Butler, the new minister in charge of the Central African office, describing him as *civil but not very impressive . . . I got the idea he'd been warned against me . . .*, and dined with the Duke and Duchess of Devonshire at Petworth, where Henry amused the assembled dignitaries by saying that Cowdray Park 'would be a good place for buffalo'.

Promoting Kaunda's cause at meetings of the Fabians and the Anti-Slavery Society, Gore-Browne also met journalists, all of whom were intrigued by this feudal old man with his impeccable three-piece suit, bowler hat atop a bald head, large nose, monocle, and bristly moustache. The *Daily Express* described him as 'Kaunda's white shadow', quoting him as admitting he often gave the black nationalist leader advice 'and it is usually taken'. It went on to say he insisted on calling himself a traditionalist: 'It might seem a contradiction but as the old Duke of Cambridge once said to my grandfather, "I am not against progress. I am all for progress when it is inevitable."'

Finally, laden with eleven trunks and suitcases full of purchases for themselves and gifts for Gore-Browne's grandchildren and Henry's thirteen children, the pair set off in the red Zephyr on the long journey back to Shiwa. Driving across France, they laid flowers on Kerr's grave at Ypres and revisited Arras, *the river where we used to bathe under the horse-chestnuts and all the old well-remembered places*, and the battlefields, *when the moonlight came and there seemed no reason why one shouldn't see the dead alive again.* More happily, they crossed the French Alps where he photographed a grinning Henry, arms outstretched, holding a snowball in each hand – a picture which would grace that year's Christmas card – and recalled how touched Ethel had been when Henry had cried at Brooklands the first time he had ever seen snow. Eventually they reached the Italian port of Genoa, where they boarded the *Braemar Castle* bound for Africa. For the first time in all their travels together, Henry was invited to the captain's cocktail party, prompting Gore-Browne to note in his diary, *Times have indeed changed!*

Docking at Mombasa two weeks later, they were met by Angela, her two daughters, Karen and Mandy, and the new man in her life, John Sutton,* a big game hunter who had been brought up in Kenya, shooting his first rhino at the age of fourteen, and of whom Gore-Browne wrote *I heartily approve*, rare praise from a man who, even more than most fathers, thought nobody good enough for his daughters. Going on to spend a few days with Gerard Portsmouth at his beautiful coffee estate at Mount Elgon, they finally left Kenya for home, driving the 1,101 miles from Nairobi to Shiwa in two and a half days. They arrived back in August 1962, just in time for the UNIP conference at Magoye where the party voted to participate in the forthcoming elections, despite its reservations over the incredibly complicated system devised by the Colonial Office, and the literacy and income requirements which disenfranchised many Africans.

Shortly afterwards, Gore-Browne was summoned to UNIP headquarters in Lusaka, Kaunda turning up a record nine hours late for their appointment, to inform him that he had been chosen to contest Chambeshi, one of four completely bi-racial national seats. It was a large constituency, stretching

*Sutton went on to become director of top safari company Ker & Downey, and was consultant and in charge of logistics for Sidney Pollack's 1985 film *Out of Africa*. He died in 1997.

from Isoka and Chinsali in the north, encompassing Mpika, Shiwa, and Serenje, to Kitwe on the Copperbelt in the west. *It's a pretty tough job but I suppose it suits me*, read his diary entry for that day. Later he wrote to Welensky, *I have no delusions as to my chances of getting elected; I can't imagine many people, White or Black, wanting an old blighter like me for their member . . . You probably think I'm silly and should stick to potato farming . . .*

Basing himself at Kitwe's new Edinburgh Hotel, with Henry staying nearby with relatives, Gore-Browne launched himself into six weeks of campaigning with remarkable vigour for a seventy-nine-year-old. He finally seemed to have won back the Africans' trust, and was surprised by the number who appeared to know and welcome him. He was even more delighted when at a meeting in Nakonde the UNIP regional Secretary Chapoloko introduced him by saying, 'He helped us when we had nothing and he helps us still when we are powerful.'

But white voters were hostile, particularly the mineworkers, seeing him as betraying their race and fearing for their own futures under a black administration. Even supposedly liberal whites, hosting a mixed tea party, served tea in cups to the Europeans and gave bottled soft drinks to the Africans, causing the UNIP member to ask, 'What do they think would happen if we used the same cups? Would we leave our black skins in the cups?' One white man told Gore-Browne he thought Kaunda had horns, and he admitted in his diary, *Europeans are going to be my big difficulty*. He was right. Under the complicated election system, candidates had to poll at least 10 per cent of the vote in each racial group. On election day, 30 October 1962, he and Henry cast their votes at Shiwa, then drove around local polling stations, impressed by the long quiet queues of Africans voting for the first time. Two days later the wireless reported his defeat. Chambeshi was a 'frustrated constituency', which meant that none of the candidates – neither Gore-Browne from UNIP, nor those from Harry Nkumbula's ANC, or Welensky's United Federal Party, had got enough votes, both black and white, to win. Gore-Browne had polled 11,264 African votes – a staggering 93.4 per cent of the total, but only 55 European votes – or just 1.3 per cent, which meant that he lost his deposit of £25.

With UNIP largely victorious elsewhere, Kaunda insisted that Gore-Browne recontest the seat, and he and Henry returned to Kitwe, having first enjoyed a few days' break at Shiwa where they opened champagne to celebrate Harvey's killing of a large elephant, thought to be that which had trampled Gore-Browne's old hunter, Paraffin, to death earlier in the year. Back on the campaign trail the rains had started, water sheeting down from grey swollen skies, and Gore-Browne often found himself addressing rallies, stripped to the waist and shouting to compete with the bucketing heavens.

Election day, 10 December, also dawned rainy as Gore-Browne noted in his Lett's Desk Diary, under the printed words 'End of Grouse Shooting Season'. He was not surprised when once more the seat was 'frustrated'. Afterwards he placed an advert in the local *Northern News*, saying: 'May I thank the 101 Europeans and 10,567 Africans who voted for me but whose work was made useless by the peculiar rules of the Constitution under which we live and which was imposed on us by the British government.'

Despite failing to get elected, Gore-Browne continued to advise Kaunda on strategy, and when the British government announced new elections for January 1964 which would lead to self-government and independence, he asked him for a seat. Kaunda was sympathetic but pragmatic, and with some embarrassment wrote to him that the party Central Committee had refused his request because they had too many deserving black officials wanting seats. After the expected UNIP victory (winning 55 of 65 seats), Kaunda was sworn in as Prime Minister with an entirely African cabinet, and independence promised for later in the year. Shortly after the swearing in, Gore-Browne received a telegram informing him he had been rejected as a member of the Peace Commission. *From now on politics is well and truly an African prerogative*, he wrote in his diary.

Bitterly disappointed, he once more retreated to Shiwa. *I can understand their fear of neocolonialism but that doesn't make it easier*, he confided to Welensky, adding, *I won't pretend I'm not disappointed to be left out of the struggle.* From October 1964 Welensky was also out of things, having lost his Salisbury constituency to a candidate from Ian Smith's Rhodesian Front. Furious at Macleod's successor, R. A. Butler, and the British government for 'acting behind his back' in the negotiations to break up the Federation, and predicting dire consequences for Africa, Welensky bade farewell to Salisbury and Government House and retreated to a farm in Cape Town. There, with his beloved wife Lizzie, he planned to write his memoirs and finally find the time for fishing in the motor launch presented to him by his parliamentary colleagues, which he named *Elizabeth*. Gore-Browne sent him the skin and claws of a lion recently shot by Harvey, and on hearing that the Royal Society of the Blind proposed to produce a Braille version of Welensky's forthcoming book, he was inspired to recall a schoolboy limerick:

There was a young lady of Hale
Who Offered her body for sale
For the sake of the blind
She embossed her behind
With a list of her prices in Braille.

Shortly after Independence, a beaming Kaunda brought his entire family to Shiwa for the day – his wife Betty, their nine children and two nannies – to thank Gore-Browne personally for all his work on their behalf. Kaunda joked about all the police accompanying him, this time as guards rather than searching for him as in the past. After a splendid banquet, Gore-Browne, whose chequebook for the past few years was full of stubs for contributions to UNIP, made a last bid at somehow joining the government. Kaunda told him, 'Enjoy your much deserved retirement, you've done enough for this country,' and sadly, he saw his role was over. *I'd be a mug if I didn't realize I'm a backnumber*, he wrote to Welensky. *I've still got Henry and some more of his like to see to my personal needs and I'm very lucky that it is so.*

He continued to receive invitations for state events such as the opening of Parliament and the inauguration of Zambia's first university, to which he donated 750 books, and Kaunda sent him a telegram on 3 May every year for his birthday, telling him in the latest 'it is a great achievement to be 84 years young'. But his life increasingly shrank back around Shiwa. There were always disputes to resolve, usually over domestic matters such as Bufi, his clerk, accusing his second wife of poisoning the three children of his first wife. But mostly Gore-Browne felt himself not needed. To avoid death duties, he had made Shiwa into a trust and legally transferred the estate to the Harveys so that when he died Lorna and John would control everything, though they were legally bound to leave it to one of the grandchildren to ensure it stayed in the family. It was not an easy relationship. Harvey was frustrated at being known as Gore-Browne's son-in-law or Lorna Gore-Browne's husband, which he resented, while his father-in-law made little secret of disapproving of the way he did things, and made sure the door between their two parts of the house was kept firmly locked. For his part, Gore-Browne often felt himself to be in the way, stuck in the past, and wearied by the constant battle to keep the house and estate in order, bridges and roads repaired, roofs and foundations rebuilt because they had been eaten away by white ants or destroyed by rains, all of which whittled away at his little remaining capital, and with workers *who seem to have little interest in the enterprise*, not having been involved in the original building.

After a slight stroke and attack of pneumonia landed him in Kasama hospital, the doctor ordered that he stay indoors as much as possible, a terrible blow for a man who so loved the outdoors life. He spent much of his time in his study, reading through his papers, fearing he had left it too late to write the autobiography he had always dreamed of, and updating his burial instructions which he then locked in the safe. He had asked to be buried with Henry next to him, on Bareback Hill, where Livingstone had passed by in 1867 not long before he died. 'There indeed was a man,' he often said to Henry, wondering what the great explorer would have thought of the place now, and somehow thinking he would have approved. Witnessed by Henry and dated 24 February 1965, Gore-Browne's handwritten note read:

I wish to be buried wrapped in mats and not in a coffin at the summit of the hill known as NACHIPALA ('Bareback'). I attach two letters in which Senior Chief Nkula and Paramount Chief Chitimukulu give their permission, the hill being outside the boundaries of my estate. I wish a plain obelisk or cairn, consisting of rough stones to be erected over the site with a plain brass or copper plaque on it on which my name, the dates of my birth and death only, are to be inscribed. AND I DESIRE [his capitals] *that my servant the said Henry Mulenga when he comes to die to be buried in my grave as he wishes in accordance with the custom of the Bemba tribe . . .*

His will included £5,000 for Angela, the creation of a scholarship fund, and sums of money for various old retainers, as well as a generous annual pension for Henry, to whom he also bequeathed his car and £500 – the same amount as he left each of his six grandchildren. He worried about what would happen to Henry when he was gone – the last couple of years had been rough on his faithful manservant. Shortly after Independence, Henry's youngest daughter, little Mary – one of the twins whom he often used to bring to see Gore-Browne – had fallen into the fire and died. Henry and his younger wife Mary were heartbroken, as Bembas consider twins to be blessed. One night he told Gore-Browne that he had dreamt that the little girl had asked for a cup of cold water, and Gore-Browne gave him a china cup and saucer which he solemnly placed on her grave. The same year Henry's farm was burnt down, apparently by someone with a grudge over his favoured treatment by the *bwana*. Gore-Browne helped him build a new one, sending him workers to plant mealies and ordering him some orange trees, which Henry planted in the hope of selling fruit to passengers on the bus going up the Great North Road which stopped only five miles from the farm. Gore-Browne wrote to Welensky, *I want him to be provided for when I'm no more and besides a pension, I'm giving him a two-storied house, a gun and rifle (which he said 'made him feel like a man') and a motorbike. If anyone deserves to be made comfortable it's Henry.*

When all his paperwork was finished, Gore-Browne liked to be taken out in the car to Kapishya, his beloved hot springs. With a boy to help his aged limbs in and out of the warm water, and another to pass him a glass of port, he would float on his back, listening to the rustle of the palm trees and losing himself in past dreams. Other times, he wandered round the house, passing guest-rooms which were rarely used any more, so many that once asked at a dinner how many bathrooms the house had, he had to reply that he had no idea. The servants noticed that he never ventured up the steps to the tower-room where Lorna used to play the violin, and whispered to each other superstitiously that at night they could hear violin music and the hyenas howling in reply. A large black and white photograph of Lorna still hung in his study, taken when she had just arrived, sitting under an arch with those knowing eyes and faraway look far beyond her nineteen years. In the sitting-room was the huge painting of a dashing strawberry-haired Ethel, and opposite that now hung a portrait Gore-Browne had sat for, in a kind of 'laird of Shiwa' pose, with the estate behind him, done in pastels by Ian Mackinson, an ex-provincial officer. A film of red dust covered everything. The house-boys were getting slovenly, he complained in his diary, but there was nothing he could do. *When Henry is away* [at his farm] *I can ring and ring for service and no one comes.* Cobwebs hung from some of the ceilings, and several times, stumbling along the passage at dusk before the lamps came on, a bat had brushed his face.

His favourite room remained the library, made cosy on cold mornings and nights by the fire crackling in the grate, under the oil-painting of his grandmother, the redoubtable Harriet, and the carved letters on the mantelpiece reading 'Ille Terrarum Mihi Super Omnes Angulus Ridet'. The heavy bookshelves were completely full since the addition of almost another 1,000 volumes from Caenshill after Ethel's death, mostly philosophical works such as Locke's *Treatise*, the *Complete Works of Carlyle*, and biographies on people from Byron to Marie Curie, Florence Nightingale to Siegfried Sas-soon. On one shelf, by the glass case containing his medals and Ethel's DBE, were his photograph albums providing a yearly record of life at Shiwa, starting from shooting his first rhino by the lake in 1914. On another were logbooks of his old cars, going right back to *Bird*, the capricious Renault he had bought for his twenty-first birthday and toured France in with Ethel.

On the shiny surface of the circular mahogany table which stood near the terrace windows was a pile of leatherbound visitors' books, in many ways a testament to the life of the house, which had often seen more visitors in a month than days. Comments of guests were interspersed with photographs and details of major events at the house, written in Gore-Browne's neat black copperplate, such as his arrival with his wife Lorna, the building of the Mansya bridge, the christening of their two children, Lorna and Angela, the landing of the first plane, the distilling of the first limes, and the christening of Charles Stewart. The signatures of guests ranged from leading lights of *Burke's Peerage* to missionaries, local chiefs and political leaders, showing the breadth of Gore-Browne's acquaintances. Viscount and Viscountess Bledisloe; the Earl of Portsmouth; Viscountess Nancy Astor; Baron Felix Schimmelpeninck van der Cyr, who had kept them amused at dinner one night with his stories of hunting big game; the Marquis and Marchioness of Graham; the Duke and Duchess of Montrose; Paramount Chief Chitimukulu, chief of all Bemba; Monsignor Rugambwa, the first African to become a Cardinal; writers Elspeth Huxley and Nadine Gordimer; N. P. Imlach, an odd bearded gentleman who had turned up saying he was 'walking to London' yet had no gun, no tent, no companion, no bed and very little food; Kenneth and Betty Kaunda; Lord Egerton of Tatton Park; Lord and Lady (Belinda) Montagu of Beaulieu; Lord Llewellin, the Governor-General, who had told naughty tales about Churchill over port; Roy and Lizzie Welensky; Jomo Kenyatta, who had stopped by for coffee while fleeing to Tanganyika; the beautiful Lozi Princess Nakatindi, who had called in for tea with her husband then asked to borrow money; and Sir Stephen and Lady Virginia Courtauld. Some had sent thank-you letters which had been stuck in, such as that of Lord Hailey of Chartered Bank London, which stated, 'my gratitude indeed for your kindness and hospitality in your marvellous house . . . something very different indeed from the Biblical "lodge" in the garden of cucumbers.' Another, from the Archbishop of Central Africa, written in 1964 (one of 170 guests that year), read: 'I much enjoyed returning to Shiwa after an absence of four years and finding that in spite of all the difficulties that have arisen during that time, Shiwa remains an important influence for good.'

These days Gore-Browne entertained few visitors, though he always managed to hold his usual Waterloo Lunch every 18 June to commemorate the victory of 1815. There were occasional cinema shows in the library – borrowed newsreels on the doings of the Queen, and documentaries on wild animals, at which a few selected servants would be invited, usually Henry, Kasaka and George Mwanza, the African manager, before the films were shown to the public at the Welfare Hall the following night. Sometimes, if there were guests staying, he held a formal dinner, with seating plans and name cards, after which, as always, the house servants would be summoned and each given a glass of port which they stood solemnly drinking, then filed silently out. On the last occasion a surprised guest from England, a university professor, had asked him, 'Do they like port?'

'Do you know, I've never asked them,' he had replied, somewhat surprised himself.

He was happiest when Henry came over from his farm and

they lunched alone together, Gore-Browne managing just a boiled egg and some mango fool, writing in his diary afterwards, *Lunched with H. Just like old times*. On those days they would sit in his bedroom where on the wall besides his bed were Durer's two etchings, one representing *Death as an Enemy* and the other *Death as a Friend*. When he was feeling stronger they would sit in the library, remembering old times, reading out letters from Welensky who always sent his compliments to Henry and had recently written, 'I've struck few nicer men in my life . . . as long as I live I shall never forget the picture of seeing Henry transported from a vanette on the road between Lusaka and Salisbury to your club in London, all dressed up in an overcoat and bowler hat, and it is to his credit that he looked the part as well.' Sometimes, as the boy came in with afternoon tea and more logs for the fire, Gore-Browne asked Henry to put *La Bohème* on the gramophone, the new complete LP set the Harvey family had given him the previous Christmas. Recently the servants kept finding snakes in the library, which he had heard them call ngoshi or green mamba, the most deadly snake of all, and knew they thought they were spirits coming to take him.

All in all he thought there was a lot to be pleased about. He had recently written a paper entitled 'As I Look Back', about how Northern Rhodesia had changed in the fifty plus years he had known it, in which he admitted: 'Public School, Royal Military Academy, twenty years in the Artillery, four years of modern warfare, had taught me precious little that was calculated to show me how to make a success of life in Central Africa.' In an interview with the *Times of Zambia*, he said: 'unless one is a millionaire, able to order unlimited quantities of materials and to employ professional architects and artisans (in which case one could produce Chatsworth or any of the other great stately homes of England), one is really limited by the skill of the local people, local materials and climate.' Even so he had built the house of his dreams, which, if neither self-supporting nor quite as grand as he had envisaged, had survived against all odds and was a place of legend to most Zambians and one which struck awe in visitors passing through. He knew that across the country if Zambians said they came from Shiwa Ngandu, their fellow men would smile and say, 'Ah, Chipembele.' His grandchildren were growing fit and strong, and as for his own health, though he had suffered several small strokes and recurring attacks of pneumonia, and was getting vague, he was still mobile.

Although Gore-Browne had never got over being so completely left out of the post-independence set-up, he was pleased to feel he had played some role in the transition and enormously proud that Kaunda had just made him the first ever Grand Officer of the Companion of the Order of Freedom, the Zambian equivalent to a knighthood – the only white man to receive such an honour. Too weak to type any more, he wrote in shaky hand to tell the news to Welensky, as well as thanking him for the recent birthday greetings. *Yes, 84 years are plenty . . . I find my memory is quite childishly feeble now . . . However I've had a good life and lots to be thankful for.* Looking out from the library terrace as he liked to do, over the shining blue lake where everything had begun, he finished, *Henry sends his respectful regards.* It was his last letter.

Postscript

'Stewart Gore-Browne was one of the most visionary people in Africa – he was born an English gentleman and died a Zambian gentleman' – *Kenneth Kaunda**

Stewart Gore-Browne died aged eighty-four in Kasama hospital at 1.25 p.m. on 4 August 1967. He had been rushed there five days earlier after suffering a heart attack, and succumbed to pneumonia. His daughter and son-in-law Lorna and John Harvey were at his bedside when he died. Henry Mulenga was outside.

Among his possessions was a faded postcard by a little-known Italian artist of a girl and sheep.

The *Times of Zambia* of 5 August devoted its entire front and editorial pages to an account of Gore-Browne's life. Under the title 'The Man Who Was Called Chipembele', it described him as 'a monocled English aristocrat' who 'lived in semi-feudal splendour' with servants who 'wouldn't have disgraced London's Dorchester Hotel'. He was 'a man who judged his fellow men on their merits alone and not on the colour of their skin'.

His one-time protégé President Kenneth Kaunda ordered a state funeral and flew to Shiwa Ngandu on the morning of 6 August with a vast delegation including three cabinet ministers, the Chief Commissioner of Police and the Zambian Airforce Commander. Hundreds of workers and local people turned up, and had to stand outside during the service, which was held in the family chapel, presided over by the Anglican Archbishop of Central Africa, two Roman Catholic Arch-

*Interview with the author, Lusaka, 1997.

bishops, one white and one black, and Reverend Paul Mushindo, the local Presbyterian minister and included the hymn 'The Lord's My Shepherd'.

Pallbearers from the 2nd Battalion of the Zambian Regiment carried the coffin, draped in a Zambian flag, up to the top of Peacock Hill, not the higher Nachipala (Chitane's Mountain) as Gore-Browne had wanted, officially because the granite was too hard, but probably because it would have been too much of a trek for all the VIPs. Trees had been cut on the hilltop to give an uninterrupted view of the lake, shining blue far below. A trumpeter sounded the 'Last Post' and the coffin was lowered into a grave in the shade of an acacia tree and beneath a stone marked simply 'Chipembele'.

At the grave, Kaunda made a moving speech, tears flowing, saying, 'at a time when everything seemed bleak for us Sir Stewart Gore-Browne emerged as our inspiration . . . we mourn him because we loved him.' Bemba elders signalled the beating of royal drums, used only on special occasions, which echoed solemnly round the hills, and a war dance was performed usually reserved for the death of a Paramount Chief. The entire funeral was broadcast to the nation on state television and radio, and the Zambian flag was flown at half-mast from the library terrace.

More than thirty years on, Gore-Browne remains the only white man in Central Africa to have received both a state funeral and a chief's burial. His grave, with its privileged view over the lake, is overgrown and rarely visited, and outside of Shiwa few people remember his name. Visitors to the National Museum of Lusaka may see the white man's battered bowler hat, walking stick and ink-bottle in a glass case on the first floor, labelled simply 'Stewart Gore-Browne: A White Man who supported the Independence Movement', and wonder what they mean.

*

The passing away of Gore-Browne was not the final chapter in the story of the Africa House. After his death, the estate, which had only ever covered its costs in a handful of years in the 1940s, continued to be a financial black hole. His daughter Lorna and her husband, Major John Harvey, struggled valiantly with crumbling ceilings, servants who after independence had become increasingly recalcitrant, wild animals killing cows, and rains smashing tiles off the roof and damaging bridges. They kept up the tradition of raising the flag and a muster parade of workers after the morning drum. Despite being almost bankrupt, they carried on funding scholarships for local children, as well as entertaining in style, holding enormous house-parties at Easter and Christmas, John Harvey taking Gore-Browne's place at the head of the enormous dining-table, set with silver and crystal, and becoming known as an excellent host and raconteur.

Finding the sawmill and cattle not enough for the estate's upkeep, not to mention four children at public school, in the 1970s the couple began keeping chickens and battery hens to sell meat and eggs all over the Northern Province. For a while this venture made money, supplying the workers building the Chinese-funded Tazara railway which stopped at Mpika, sixty-five miles from Shiwa.

But the fortunes of the estate mirrored those of Zambia. The nation which at independence had the highest per capita income in black Africa was by 1991 the world's most indebted nation (on a per capita basis), with yearly inflation over 100 per cent. The railway workers went back to China, and few others had the money to buy poultry and eggs. By the late 1980s the project had come to an ignominious end.

Ever inventive, and seeing the rise of tourism in neighbouring countries, Harvey decided instead to set up a safari company. Shiwa Safaris was the first organization to take tourists into the stunning wilderness of North Luangwa. Harvey, the one-time hunter, became a leading force in trying to stop poaching and was made an honorary senior game ranger for his efforts. But he found himself up against powerful vested interests. Zambia was a major source of ivory, plundered by unscrupulous dealers, officers from the South African army coming over the border from Angola, where they were engaged in fighting, to shoot rhino and elephants, as did members of the African National Congress (ANC), which was headquartered in Zambia during its long banning in South Africa (lifted in 1990) and needed funds.

In the end this last battle may have been fatal. On Sunday 17 May 1992, the Harveys were sitting reading by candlelight after dinner when four gunmen burst in and brutally murdered them, shooting right through Lorna's book, then escaping in the couple's Toyota Landcruiser. The bodies of sixty-three-year-old Lorna and sixty-seven-year-old John were found by their youngest son, David, who immediately put out a reward for finding the killers over the radio, knowing this was the best way to spur the police into action.

The murders provoked nationwide outrage, and Kaunda (ousted from power the previous year) found himself sending another condolence telegram. The funeral was held at Lusaka's Anglican Cathedral, the choir singing 'Brother James' Air' just as had been sung at the Harveys' wedding, and the couple were buried on Peacock Hill, next to Gore-Browne.

Three of the gang were caught and appeared in Lusaka High Court charged with murder and aggravated robbery. Michael Monyatse (36), Jackson Motlatsi (30) and Joe Gugulethu Mashingo (36) were all South Africans, describing themselves as freedom-fighters and claiming to be members of the ANC. The local branch admitted that Monyatse and Mashingo were members, but disclaimed all responsibility for the crime, which it roundly condemned.

But suspicions were aroused. If it was simply a burglary, little had been stolen (the car, a radio, a ladies' watch and a double cassette-player). The family and others, including Kaunda, believe the Harveys were assassinated, though they have been unable to prove this. The pace of the Zambian justice system is so slow that it took four years for the men to be sentenced. Pleas for extradition were turned down and at the time of writing they are on Death Row at Mukabeko maximum security jail in Kabwe.

For some years afterward only David Harvey and his Canadian wife Carol lived on the estate, along with an orphaned baby elephant that had wandered into Shiwa and that they had adopted. They lived not in Shiwa House with all its rooms and ghosts and overgrown terraced gardens, but in Mpandala, the old house of the Macminns, the Scottish missionaries. With the nearest telephone over an hour's drive away and the only contact with the outside world the BBC World Service on a crackling radio powered from the car battery, it was a lonely but a rather extraordinary life, by the lake of the royal crocodiles, one in which cries of lions would punctuate the night.

For a while the couple tried to revive the memory of the man who was called Chipembele. Though so strapped for cash that they had to sell their herd of goats in order for Carol to fly home to visit her family, they began clearing tons of bat droppings and cobwebs from the house in the hope of opening it as a museum, a little piece of British history in what even today is remotest Africa.

Yet with every passing day the bush seemed to be encroaching more and more into the house and keeping it at bay became a Herculean struggle. Some of the corridors were unsafe because termites had eaten away the floorboards. There were gaping holes in the roof where the rain came in. An owl had made its home in Kakoma, the tower room. Gore-Browne's precious collection of first editions had to be removed from the library and taken over to Mpandala because they were going mouldy. Woodworm was devouring the paintings of ancestors that Lorna II had found so intimidating. Pathways had become so overgrown with gnarled tree roots like giant fingers blocking the way, that in some places it was difficult to walk. Most of the Bemba still living on the estate had reverted to living in mud huts, Gore-Browne's dream of future villagers making their own bricks, roof-tiles and chimneys long forgotten.

A year after the birth of their first child Sophie in 1999, the couple decided it was too remote and moved to Lusaka where David advises small farmers and Carol makes cheeses. 'It's a destructive place, the testament to one man's vanity,' said David of Shiwa House. 'I'll never live there again.'

His eldest brother Charles, Gore-Browne's great hope for the future, had no stake in the house, having fallen out with his father Major Harvey over the running of Shiwa and been cut out of his parents' will. 'John was jealous of him and very, very cruel because he was Gore-Browne's favourite,' explained Charlie's wife Jo. 'It was a bitter blow and he vowed one day to get Shiwa "back", no matter what.'

In the meantime he had overcome severe dyslexia to set up a successful business, running hunting parties for rich businessmen such as Microsoft founder Bill Gates and a thriving game farm in Chisamba, about an hour north of Lusaka. He described Shiwa Ngandu as 'a dream that went sour'.

Their sister Penelope lives in Oxford with her husband Mike and two children and says of Shiwa: 'it has never been a happy house.'

Mark is a leading safari guide, taking parties to Lake Bangwelu, North Luangwa and the hot springs of Kapishya, mixing up an excellent gin and tonic and regaling them with his stories of encounters with lions and elephants.

Lorna the Second lived on alone in north London until her death in December 2001 at the age of 93, shortly after being moved into an old peoples' home following a hip operation. She had never remarried, though attracted many admirers well into old age, and always went by the name of plain Mrs Browne.

The poky flat in Highgate in which she spent her final years was reached by a rickety iron fire escape behind a shop on a hill. With its scatter cushions on the floor and travel posters of Eastern Europe on the wall, it looked like a student digs and one would never have guessed she had once been chatelaine of a grand estate in Africa.

Eccentric to the last, she spent her days learning new languages such as Greek and Serbo-Croat and composing music on strange instruments she had picked up on her travels. Although as a mother she had been a shadowy and absent figure, in later life she seemed to attract young people, her direct manner making her a confidante to other people's children.

Only on rare occasions after a few vodkas could she ever be persuaded to talk of Africa. But she refused to talk of her own African years even with her own grandchildren, saying one should live for the future not the past. After her death, her family found an old brown envelope containing a sheaf of typewritten sheets recounting her difficult childhood during her mother's long illness in Africa then being passed between unwilling relatives. In her only known reference to her husband's love for her mother, she ended by writing: *I think she was very lonely and communicated this somehow. It was sad to think that just before she died Stewart was coming to see her and they might have married.*

Angela Sutton is living in Nairobi in a beautiful house complete with Shiwa-inspired arches. Her eldest daughter Karen lives in Jersey where her husband manages the zoo and her other daughter Mandy lives in Los Angeles.

Henry Mulenga died in 1979 and was not buried in Gore-Browne's grave. The Ford Zephyr which he had inherited had been sold long before by his son James, who drove off with it. The Caenshill farm at Chisoso village is overgrown. All that remains of Henry's time with Chipembele is a fading exercise book of photographs kept by his brother Kalaka, Gore-Browne's old hunter, and the man famous locally for killing nine buffaloes with one axe. 'I don't like to go back to the house because it's very sad,' he said, as he thumbed through the yellowing pages.

Afterword

More than 80 years after Gore-Browne led a line of porters to Shiwa to set up home in the place he described as 'my own personal paradise', another trek to north-eastern Zambia took place.

One sunny morning in October 2001 his eldest grandson Charlie set off from Lusaka with his wife Jo, two children Tom and Emma, and 800 cattle on a three-day train journey followed by a ten day walk leading the cows through the bush. Incredibly only one calf was lost, trampled by the others, while one was born en route. They then repeated the same journey several times by truck, heading up the Great North Road with 600 sheep in double-decker trucks, 500 assorted oryx, zebra, sable, hartebeest, wildebeest and impala on trailers, eight horses, 34 African staff and their families (averaging six a head), various possessions including Gore-Brown's canopied four poster bed, and a menagerie of pets – five cats and five dogs, a parrot and a wood-owl.

They had sold everything they owned to buy out Charlie's brothers and sister and make the journey to restore his grandfather's dream. Unlike Gore-Browne, they would have to make the estate pay. 'We were determined to settle and breathe life back into Shiwa again', wrote Jo.

Charlie had always insisted, 'I don't want strangers sleeping in my bed', but had reluctantly accepted that opening up the house for *wageni* or paying guests was the only way for it to make money.

The most immediate task was patching up the roof to stop the rain coming in, an almost impossible feat for as quickly as one leak had been repaired another would develop elsewhere. Solar panels were then set up to power hot water and radio communications as there was no electricity supply or phone lines. For the first time television came to Shiwa but the terrible events of 9/11 and the war on terrorism in the outside world seemed only to reinforce Gore-Browne's sense of haven.

The next step was renovating rooms and modernizing the bathrooms with their great thunderbox toilets, as well as installing a river turbine as another source of power in order to restart the sawmill for timber.

During the years of neglect, the Bemba had got used to doing what they liked on the estate and the lake had been so over-fished that Charlie decided the only answer was a full-time motorboat patrol. The boats of any poachers caught were converted into cattle troughs and their nets used at the hospital to prevent bats from flying in.

The couple reopened Charlie's parents' old butcher's shop in Mpika, about 90 minutes drive away, to which they send meat, milk and wood and bring back cement and fertiliser.

At Christmas 2002, after 14 months of incredibly hard work, Jo was able to write: 'Shiwa is thumping and thriving with life. The farm has taken on new dimensions, cattle and sheep yards renovated and shiny as a new pin, camps and handling facilities built to perfection and turning the farm income to a plus, perhaps for the first time in many, years.'

They had resolved from the start that any money made from the farm would be ploughed back into the house, enabling Jo to work on redoing the gardens, the highlight of the first year being the rejuvenation of the Brooklands hydrangeas which were soon once again flourishing in a large bed outside the chapel. The lower terrace, home to a pile of rubble that was once the swimming pool, now has large beds of Jacobean lilies and a new lawn, and beds of iris in yellow and white brighten up the lower end of the garden. New gate pillars have replaced the old crumbling ones and a rockery set into the hillside beyond, full of wild plants, aloes, succulents and flame lilies.

She also set about restoring the frames of all the old drawings and watercolours, and tackling the books in the library. This was a mammoth task, involving opening and feather-dusting every page, then placing each book in a 'bomb box' with a fumigant, something she described as 'definitely a job for the insane.'

Charlie's own dream was to see wild animals grazing on the lakeshore again and this has started to become a reality. In their first year in residence, the family witnessed a host of new calves including 11 wildebeest, 7 hartebeest, 3 zebra, 7 lechwe, 3 impish little puku, and an impossible to count number of impala as they are always jumping away.

'I doubt the old-time poachers who plagued Shiwa for so many, many years on the ground and on the lake had any idea just what they would be up against', wrote Jo. 'One wants to be apologetic but the results have been so rewarding with resident game now breeding well and the lake taking on a new dimension in bird and wildlife, with catches of bream up to 1.5kg and two resident troops of clawless otters to boot!'

With its intriguing history and renovation underway, Shiwa found itself back on the map, attracting 140 visitors a month from as far away as Scotland and Dubai, New Zealand and the United States and, in February 2003, hosting 70 Classic Car enthusiasts for an overnight stop on the Cape Town to Mombasa rally.

Jo had warned the organisers that it rained all February and that Shiwa could not accommodate more than 12 people so it would have to be a tented camp. Her e-mail describing the preparations had echoes of Gore-Browne:

Camp would be fine they replied, but February it remained. The sample tent arrived. Once up, Isaac, our grounds man, observed 'Madam, is this tent for children or chickens?' Out went the tent and in panic our imaginations lurched into motion. How about building 20 log cabins? In six weeks? Easy! Well, sort of . . . We began the task of building 20 little rooms on Shiwa lawn while we managed to find room for 20 in the house (cupboards excluded). 500 poles cut for an uncollected order were hastily commandeered. A specialized heavy-duty plastic used for capturing game forms the sides and roof of what now looks like a barracks from Asterix. *Wooden beds, reed partitions and chitenge doors (local printed fabric) make up the rest of the little 3'×3' rooms. All we need is sunshine because the boss said 'I'm not sure if it's waterproof'!*

With two days to go before the event she wrote:

By midday today, the gardener had not managed to locate ten of the chickens scheduled for the celery and chicken breast salad. They must have overheard a conversation in the kitchen last evening and by 6 o'clock this morning were seen heading for the lake. The lawnmower ran away and ate its own cable after Isaac forgot to take it out of gear while scratching for a few red ants that had found their way up his trouser leg. A bird of now unknown species flew into the wind generator and it is now not turning so well, and a collection of water frogs gummed up the water pump pipes so the last scrub down has been delayed. We spent a sleepless night with a sick horse and Basil the chef fell off his bicycle and is now at the hospital having stitches in his leg. To add insult to injury, it is now pouring with rain and we had to drag 30-odd mattresses inside because the capture plastic is indeed not waterproof.

Despite all this, the event passed off successfully and the farm continues to expand. A grant from the British High Commission has enabled one ward of the hospital to be renovated and work is underway on a maternity ward and solar power and water tanks have been installed. Four new classrooms are being built for the school as well as four houses for teachers. A women's group has been set up and provided with hand-operated sewing machines with which they have made the hospital sheets and are now producing school uniforms.

The lake's famous crocodiles continued to make their presence felt. One in particular, which claimed four cows and some game, was finally shot after he attempted to dine on a small child. The strange calls every night that guests were told was a singing python, turned out not to be a snake at all, but a buff-spotted fluff-tail, an elusive and rather beautiful bird that flits about the forest floor every night.

Last Christmas was like old times for the house as the family hosted 26 for a turkey dinner complete with Christmas pudding, brandy butter and all the trimmings. Among the guests was Charlie's aunt, Gore-Browne's daughter Angela Sutton. Staying in the house for the first time in more than 30 years, she wrote: 'the hot water still comes out brown, just as it used to when I was a child'. As had always happened during her father's dominion, estate children were invited up to the house for Christmas gifts. She wrote: 'on Christmas Day we helped hand out little packets (we'd packaged them on Christmas Eve) to 300 estate children and Aids orphans. Rained while we were doing this, and we had to huddle on the verandah of the school during the storm! Some little kids were terrified at being handed to large white girls by their proud mothers . . . and foster mothers. They had a happy feast afterwards.'

Back home in Kenya, she wrote to her daughter Mandy describing the house's 'faded grandeur' and adding, 'as far as I'm concerned the ghosts have scuttled away, never to return'.

But perhaps not all the ghosts. There in Shiwa Ngandu, far from the traffic hum and terrorist alerts of modern-day living, walking amid dusky shadows in the green light of the gardens, the frogs croaking softly on the lake down below, it is not hard to imagine a stiff-backed Englishman with a monocle in his right eye, looking out from the terrace across his lands, while up above a violin is playing in the tower room.

New Year, 2004

Bibliography

Books

C. Kate Bertram and Janet Trant, *Letters from the Swamps*, privately published, 1991.
Eileen Bigland, *The Lake of the Royal Crocodiles*, Hodder & Stoughton, 1939.
John Buchan, *A Lodge in the Wilderness*, William Blackwood & Sons, Edinburgh, 1906.
Alexander Campbell, *The Heart of Africa*, Longmans, 1954.
Sacha Carnegie, *Red Dust of Africa*, Peter Davies, 1959.
Monica Fisher, *Nswana, the Heir*, Mission Press, Ndola, 1991.
Roy Genders, *A History of Scent*, Hamish Hamilton, 1972.
Robert Gore-Browne, *An Imperfect Lover*, Collins, 1929.
John Gunther, *Inside Africa*, Harper, New York, 1953.
Thomas Hardy, *Winter Words*, Macmillan, 1928.
John Heminway, *The Imminent Rains, A Visit Among the Last Pioneers of Africa*, Little, Brown, Boston, 1968.
Dick Hobson, *Tales of Zambia*, Zambia Society Trust, 1996.
Lawrence James, *The Rise and Fall of the British Empire*, Abacus, 1994.
David Livingstone, *Missionary Travels and Researches in South Africa*, John Murray, 1857.
—— *The Last Journals*, Harper, New York, 1875.
Lyn Macdonald, *1914, The Day of Hope*, Penguin, 1987.
—— *Somme*, Penguin, 1983.

Martin Middlebrook, *The First Day on the Somme*, Penguin, 1971.
Nina Nelson, *The Mena House Hotel*, privately published, 4th edn 1997.
Thomas Pakenham, *The Scramble for Africa*, Random House, 1991.
Lord Portsmouth, *A Knot of Roots, An Autobiography by the Earl of Portsmouth*, Geoffrey Bles, 1965.
Hortense Powdermaker, *Copper Town, The Human Situation on the Rhodesian Copperbelt*, Harper & Row, New York, 1965.
J. S. L. Pulford, *The Locke Kings of Brooklands*, Walton and Weybridge Local History Society and Brooklands Museum, 1996.
Andrew Roberts, *History of the Bemba*, Longmans, 1973.
Robert I. Rotberg, *Black Heart, Gore Browne and the Politics of Multi Racial Zambia*, University of California Press, 1977.
—— *The Rise of Nationalism in Central Africa*, Cambridge University Press, 1965.
J. B. Stabler, *Northern Rhodesian African Opposition to Closer Union with Southern Rhodesia: The Role of Sir Stewart Gore-Browne*, unpublished thesis, Indiana State University, 1978.
Don Taylor, *The Rhodesian: The Life of Sir Roy Welensky*, Museum Press, 1955.
Roy Welensky, *Welensky's 4000 Days*, Collins, 1964.

Archives and periodicals

British Commonwealth & Empire Museum, oral history archive
Bulawayo Chronicle

Imperial War Museum
Journal of the Royal African Society
LegCo Debates, Library of the Zambian Parliament
London Missionary Society archive, School of Oriental and African Studies, London University
National Archive of Zambia
Northern Rhodesia Journal
Public Record Office, London
Rhodes House, Oxford: The Welensky Collection
Rhodesian Agricultural Journal
Royal Military Academy, Woolwich
The Times, London
The Times of Zambia

Primary sources

Letters and papers of Stewart Gore-Browne (1899–1967)
Diaries of Stewart Gore-Browne (1899–1967)
Letters of Ethel Locke King
Letters of Kenneth Kaunda to Stewart Gore-Browne
Correspondence of Roy Welensky and Stewart Gore-Browne (1940–67), from the Welensky Papers, Rhodes House, Oxford
Audrey Richards letters to family 1931–4
Letters of Lorna Gore-Browne to Stella Monck
Sapphire Hanford (*née* Gore-Browne) Memoirs of growing up, unpublished
'As I Look Back' – unpublished article by Stewart Gore-Browne on his fifty years in Northern Rhodesia
'The Central African Problem: Reasons for Partition' – leaflet circulated by Stewart Gore-Browne, 1950
Unpublished memoir of Lorna Gore-Browne